Narrative Landscapes of Female Sexuality in Africa

Samantha van Schalkwyk

Narrative Landscapes of Female Sexuality in Africa

Collective Stories of Trauma and Transition

palgrave
macmillan

Samantha van Schalkwyk
Stellenbosch University
Stellenbosch, Western Cape, South Africa

ISBN 978-3-030-07411-1 ISBN 978-3-319-97825-3 (eBook)
https://doi.org/10.1007/978-3-319-97825-3

Softcover re-print of the Hardcover 1st edition 2018

This Palgrave Macmillan imprint is published by the registered company Springer Nature Switzerland AG
The registered company address is: Gewerbestrasse 11, 6330 Cham, Switzerland

Preface

I began researching women's experiences of gender abuse several years ago. The very first setting I worked in was a small impoverished community called Garden Village in Cape Town, South Africa. The women from this community worked at the same factory shop, sewing garments day in and day out. They had to travel long hours on public transport to get to work. The women arrived home from work to unsafe and deeply stressful situations. They lived in fear of the violence happening in the streets of their community, the threat lurking around every corner. Often the harshest violence awaited these women when they returned to their homes after work. I still remember one interview vividly. It was late in the afternoon. The warehouse was cold and unwelcoming. I sat at an unused sewing table scattered with bits of material as I listened to the worker's story. Her fragile body trembled when she told me about coming home from work late one night to find her boyfriend on the floor of her make-shift house strangling and raping her three-year-old daughter. The image still lives with me.

Yet, the women still have hope. I witnessed what women in these communities do to get through life every day. They found the energy to smile, to laugh, to give, and to care for others. Stories like these are the delicate threads through which my consciousness about the gendered world has been weaved. These stories have helped me understand the complexities of being human more than any feminist theory has.

These encounters with women ignited my awe of human strength. I love listening to women's stories because I am always amazed at the way in which women can renew their sense of self after facing dehumanising violence. The vigour of the human spirit continues to amaze me again and again as I listen. This appreciation led to my journey of studying women's experience with a focus on agency created in the face of persistent violence. I have worked in many communities since. This book is a product of my work with a support group for abused women in an area not so far from the community where I began my work.

I am not satisfied with ways in which women are represented—in all spheres but particularly in research. *Narrative Landscapes of Female Sexuality in Africa* is about finding new ways of exploring women's experiences and their response to the world. In a sense, the book also captures the evolution of my research and my grappling with the complexities of what it means to document others' experience. This book stands as my contribution to challenging harmful patriarchal scripts and carving alternative ways of making sense of our capacity as human beings. I hope that this text will inspire and educate others for their work in chipping away at this thing we call patriarchy.

Stellenbosch University, Stellenbosch, Western Cape, South Africa

Samantha van Schalkwyk

Acknowledgements

I would like to thank the women who opened their hearts and minds so bravely and passionately. I will never forget your stories. You are sources of inspiration in a chaotic world. I express deep gratitude and thanks to Professor Pumla Gobodo-Madikizela for her amazing spirit and inspirational life's work. Her unfailing support and guidance has made this endeavour possible. Great thanks also go to Professor Jennifer N. Fish for encouraging me to explore more of my own subjectivity in my work and providing me with rich feedback on earlier versions of my writing. Professor Fish encouraged me to turn my writing into a book. I would also like to thank my husband, Melvin Hayes, for his love and constant support.

Contents

CHAPTER 1

Narrative Landscapes of Female Sexuality: Introduction

Introduction

In countries, like South Africa, where violence is an ever-present part of life, where babies and old women are raped on a daily basis, where young girls' maimed bodies are found dumped on empty fields, women have to face these images and try to deal with them in their own way. Women have to make sense of such violence and what it suggests for their own body and sense of value in the world. Living within such violence, whether one has experienced direct physical force on the body or not, shapes women's subjectivities in powerful ways. It is of critical importance to examine what it means psychically to inhabit a female body in such contexts.

Sexual violence is a core strategy to control women and maintain patriarchal order. The underlying function of such violence is to communicate to all women that they are worthless, to strip them of their subjectivity and render them inferior (Hydèn 1994). Many women internalise misogynistic messages that shape the meanings that they attach to their sexualised bodies (Bakare-Yusuf 2011). This is exactly how patriarchal oppression of female sexuality works. How then can women break free from such negative internalisations and claim a positive sense of self in the world? What are the potentials for studying women's agency within contexts where social resources are scarce and poverty a harsh reality of life? What alternative understandings about the self can women create, and claim, in the face of harmful oppressive discourse, and what would such strategies look like?

S. van Schalkwyk, *Narrative Landscapes of Female Sexuality in Africa*, https://doi.org/10.1007/978-3-319-97825-3_1

This book addresses these complex questions by focusing on the sexual dimension of women's collective responses to the oppression of female sexuality in Africa.

Postcolonial feminist scholars have highlighted the importance of moving away from Westernised lenses of African women's powerlessness, towards a focus on women's culturally specific sexual agency (see Bakare-Yusuf 2013; Mohanty 1991). However, few studies explore women's psychological experiences of sexual oppression/agency in any real depth. This book contributes knowledge about the ways in which women from Africa experience patriarchal oppression of female sexuality and how they may resist this oppression in multiple and creative ways. This book is about the experience of patriarchal oppression of female sexuality as a very particular kind of 'everyday' continuous form of trauma that women face. This trauma is often 'invisible' and is textured around ongoing and persistent fear and degradation of the self. In many African contexts, the expression of female sexuality is silenced and rendered taboo (Kambarami 2006). In South Africa, there exists a deep silencing and shaming around female sexuality. Women who do not keep 'in line' with patriarchal prescriptions of 'good' sexuality are blamed and shamed. Often women are subject to severe violence on their bodies (Gqola 2015). Sexual violence in a country that has been dubbed the 'rape capital' of the world is a mode for controlling female sexuality and maintaining patriarchal order. The effects of living in constant threat of violence and control are devastating and constitute a form of trauma in itself.

Westernised language of trauma, in turn, does not 'speak' to the textured and often 'invisible' everyday life experiences of women (Rajiva 2014). Limited and decontextualised meanings around 'victim' and 'trauma' silence women because they do not offer a language through which to express the complexity of experience (Lamb 1999). Much of women's experience related to gender, race, class, and citizenship constitute 'everyday' traumas which have been naturalised to such an extent that it is necessary to 'excavate' them in order to see them as social traumas (Forter 2007). However, such experience works subtly and pervasively to erode the human spirit (Root 1992). There is no language through which women can express the complexity of their experiences. The narratives presented in this book 'speak' to a much broader conceptualisation of trauma than what is currently imagined. This book is about the 'invisible' violence that accompanies the oppression of female sexuality—the violence to the self and soul which mutates/silences women's knowledge about their sexual subjectivities and bodies (McFadden 2003). It is also about how women may collectively disrupt patriarchal power in creative ways and find a language through which to preserve a sense of humanness and worth.

Colonial imagination has consistently constructed African sexuality as dangerous, exotic, and morally lacking (see Arnfred 2004). Such discursive elements linger on in current postcolonial settings. Meanings around female sexuality are fuelled by deep-seated patriarchy, racism, and xenophobia, which construct certain people as different and inferior in relation to Westernised models. Such meanings shape the manifestations and textures of patriarchal oppression of female sexuality—the ways in which violence is enacted onto women's bodies and minds and the ways in which women experience such violence. It is important to add here that I do not aim to generalise about 'Africa' or 'African experience' acknowledging that Africa is a continent that encompasses a vast array of cultures and people with different personal histories (de Vos 2015; Mohanty 1991). Rather, I base my analysis on one specific group of women, a micro-context which serves as a rich case study.

I draw on a three-year project with a support group for abused women based in South Africa. All the women had travelled from their home countries in Africa to South Africa in search of a better life with more employment opportunities. The support group consisted of a varied group of heterosexual women from many different countries—Zimbabwe, Kenya, Rwanda, Congo (DRC), and local South African women. As the book title suggests, I examine the textures of the women's narrative landscapes of female sexuality. The plural attests to the multiple geographical and psychological landscapes the women have travelled through. The focus is on three central motifs identified in the women's collective narratives traced through their stories of their memories of 'back home' in Africa; travelling through border posts, or physical entry points between African countries; and their current experience living in post-apartheid South Africa. The book is structured around these central motifs in Chaps. 4, 5, and 6 respectively.

I trace and unpack the narrative landscapes which were generated collectively within the research setting, focusing on the creative design, the substance, the linguistic and discursive elements and the silences of these women's talk. Through a feminist poststructuralist and social remembering lens (Weedon 1987; Davies 1991; Haaken 1999), I explore these women's narratives and what they tell us about their experiences of patriarchal oppression of female sexuality. A crucial element is a focus on the narrative strategies used by these women to manage and psychologically resist harmful discourses surrounding female sexuality and women's bodies. This focus on women's collective agency provides a fresh approach for the study of women's experience that moves away from standard Westernised scripts of women's static powerlessness.

A core contribution of this book is the unique collective methodology through which I utilised creative means (drama, visual memory work, ongoing dialogue) in ways that opened space for the expression of previously 'unspeakable' aspects of experience and for the women to tell their stories in their own ways drawing strength from their shared narratives. The book offers rich insights into these women's experiences living as foreigners in South Africa and the intersections of gender and sexuality, class, race and citizenship, situating the narratives within the wider context of poverty and migration in sub-Saharan Africa. As such, it contributes to the rich body of work which draws on the concept of intersectionality (see Crenshaw 1991). Throughout the text, I illuminate these vectors of oppression through integrating threads of my own positionality as a white woman researcher and feminist, adding another layer of analysis which enriches knowledge about gender violence research in Africa.

In what follows I set the scene for the research project. I discuss the research setting and my motivations for engaging in the work. I then outline the unique collective and longitudinal methodology used to explore women's experience of patriarchal oppression of female sexuality. This is accompanied by an overview of the theories of the self utilised for making sense of women's voices—the language of agency which has informed my interpretation of their narratives. I end with a brief summary of the chapters to follow.

Exploring Collective Narratives of Female Sexuality

My motivation to engage in such a book project emerged from my years of work with women who have experienced gender violence in many communities in South Africa. Throughout my work, I have been struck by the challenges which women face and the disastrous lack of support for these women from government sources. I realised that so many women 'fall through the cracks' and do not have their stories heard. They do not have any support systems through which to give voice to their experiences.

This book is based on extensive volunteer work and research with a support group for abused women based in Cape Town, South Africa. For this book, I draw on selected focus group discussions from phase 2 of the broader research project. These are discussions which best illuminated women's experiences of, and resistance to, patriarchal oppression of female sexuality. These discussions consisted of only migrant women from Zimbabwe, Congo (DRC), and Kenya who were and still are living in South Africa. Scholarly research on gender and oppression globally and in Africa has not focused sufficiently on the experiences of migrant/refugee women living in Africa—a stance perhaps reflective of wider discourses about social worth and whose experiences are worth documenting. Migrant women living in South Africa have not been given much voice in mainstream psychological research and their voices stand as what Macleod (2006, p. 368) calls the 'absent trace' in relation to Westernised hegemonic discourse of experience.

The research discussions drawn on for this book did not include South African women support group members. As researcher, I was the only South African woman present. I realise now that the absence of South African women created a unique space within which these migrant women told their stories. All these women had experienced a multitude of forms of gendered abuse across their lifetime, including sexual violence in childhood and adulthood, rape, battering and ongoing violation of their bodies in public spaces such as train and bus stations. They had all travelled from their home countries in Africa to South Africa in search of a better life to provide for their families. Scholars have shown that it is exactly because of experiences of marginalisation and stigmatisation that women develop a unique vigilance about life. This vigilance acts as a powerful lens through which women can reflect on the temporality of their life journeys—both real and metaphorical (Munt 2011). In other words, journeys through space, place, and temporal moment are remembered textually, viscerally and imaginatively through a deep observation of the world (Munt 2011). The women's accounts of their travel were coloured by the dangers of transit—a journey which they described as chaotic, confusing, and dangerous. These stories of their travels are documented in Chap. 5 of this book along with an analysis of the landscapes of their narratives.

In addition to the women's experiences of gendered abuse and displacement, these women face the position of 'other' in a country which is hostile and violent towards 'foreign' Africans. Current post-apartheid South Africa has seen a relatively new kind of violence, xenophobia, which manifests in violent attacks on African foreigners who are seen to be a threat 'stealing' valuable jobs and housing. Such violence reached critical stages in May 2008 and then again in 2011; however, xenophobic attitudes are still pervasive today. The result is that African foreigners are often rendered 'other' status pushed outside the boundaries of humanity by being denied a social-valued existence (Strauss 2011). Psychologically and socially the experience of being rendered 'other' means being marginalised and excluded from hegemonic discourse (Macleod 2006) to exist outside of what is considered 'normal' and desirable. It means inhabiting a space that is denied full humanity. Such a position and the accompanying troubles in terms of a sense of belonging in the world, of course, powerfully affect women's experience of patriarchal oppression of female sexuality. Themes of difference and social belonging were pervasive throughout the collective narratives. I explore the psychological implications as well as the women's collective narrative strategies for working against such oppression in Chap. 6 of this book, which focuses on foreigner women's imaginative constructions of the sexual world of black South African women.

My first visit with the women's group took place in a small library in an impoverished area in Cape Town. I had been invited to attend one of their storytelling sessions organised by the founder of the group, a woman from Kenya. The public library offered the women space to work free of charge. As I entered, about eight women were seated in a circle on plastic chairs in a quiet section of the library. The group leader immediately asked if I would facilitate the storytelling session (Unbeknown to me previously!). I felt anxious and hesitant at the arrangement, having been given no prior notice. I did not know any of the women and I did not know their background history or anything about the way these sessions usually take place. I felt like a foreigner in this space. However, the session flowed beautifully. It felt just right.

In retrospect, the group leader perhaps chose to place me immediately in a position of power because of my affiliations with a university and psychology department. This is a sign of very particular power dynamics that were at play initially. However, over the years, the power dynamics shifted when I grew to know the women and they grew to know me. During my years of work with the women, I was very aware of the constant shifting back and forth of my position as an insider (woman/friend) and outsider (researcher). This is a thread that I comment on throughout the book.

A few weeks after the initial meeting, the librarian contacted the group to say that they could no longer hold the sessions at the library as it was under new management. I remember picking up the group leader in my car and driving from library to library, and church to church, knocking on doors to ask if they would be willing to let the women use a room on their premises for the workshops. I remember that after some time and multiple rejections, I felt a sense of disillusionment. How could churches turn a group for abused women away, a group that was doing so much good for the community?

Eventually, we stopped on the doorstep of a pastor who lived on the church premises. I will never forget the warm way he took us in and listened to the founder's story about the women's group. Initially, he let the women use the space in the church. During some of the sessions the women were seated on the pews their voices echoing in the huge space of the church. This had a calming, almost sacred feel to it. Later, after the church had done renovations to other buildings on the premises, they gave the women's group space to use a large hall which was perfect for the workshop activities and drama sessions. The pastor also provided the women with a small wendy house[1] to conduct beadwork. I went there to visit after my research and was privileged to see the colourful jewellery items for sale, fruits of the women's creativity and hard labour.

From then on, we established regular workshops which I led and participated in. These sessions were structured around storytelling and other creative activities through which rich stories of the women's gendered lives emerged. We engaged in role-plays about violence, we read stories about violence and reflected on the stories of others, we explored images through deep memory work and we connected our imaginings to our own lives. It was a powerful space charged with emotion and pain, although the positive spirit of the group and the strength of the created connections were always there, giving us a sense hope. The visit to this small library led to a long journey with many learnings on both academic and personal levels.

During the storytelling sessions that took place over the years, the women spoke about their lives as women, opening their hearts to each other and to me. The work taught me much about life, pain, and human relationships. It also fuelled my deep respect for the women. They had been through so much trauma to their bodies and minds, yet there was

[1] The term 'wendy house' is used in South Africa to refer to a small house structure made out of wood.

also so much strength and determination to do what needs to be done every day to ensure the survival of their children. I saw the amazing power ignited through this collective space and realised that such spaces are exactly what is missing for women in the South African context. I wanted to document the stories and the unique journeys I could see developing throughout these group dialogues. This is how the research was born. This book reflects my main discoveries.

A Collective Methodology for Studying Oppression and Agency

In the face of Westernised hegemonic knowledge, Macleod (2006) argues for a radical plural feminism as a form of intellectual activism for the post-apartheid South African context. Such a plural feminism should, according to Macleod (2006), deconstruct the 'centre' while foregrounding marginalised voices; focus on social and historical conditions to understand discursive power and social transformation; and link micro-level and macro-level analysis within what she calls the 'patchworks' of global patriarchies (Macleod 2006, p. 348). Such an approach necessarily requires methods that pay detailed attention to the social texture of oppression in specific contexts and women's unique individual life experiences—place/space, temporal moment and individuality are important features of such an analysis. I needed a methodology that would help me achieve such a textured view of these women's experience.

For this research I adopted a collective biography approach with two distinct phases (see Davies and Gannon 2006a, b). The first phase involved conducting workshops with the women during which I drew on creative methods such as drama, role-plays, and visual memory-work methods (see Kuhn 2000). These creative methods allowed the women to engage with their memories and intuitions in ways that were appropriate for them, allowing identity work that is unrestricted by pre-set questions and carving a space for 'new' meaning to emerge. The powerful element of such creative strategies is that it allows women to engage with images of the past in active ways—past experience is re-processed through one's current perspective (Davies and Gannon 2006a; Kuhn 2000). Rich data emerged about their gendered experiences. I engaged in a preliminary analysis of this data and took the themes back to the women in phase 2 of the research—the focus group discussions. During these discussions in phase 2, we engaged in a collective analysis of the data moving into deeper engagement about gender and trauma.

Collective biography work is deeply tied in with feminist poststructuralist theory which views identity as multiple, fluid, and constructed in relation to others (see Weedon 1987). Such an approach provided me with theoretical means to study the individual and collective dimensions of the women's experience. Individual experience/memories were interwoven with the collective providing insights into the construction of relational selves. Collective biography focuses on understanding the *process* of constructing a self (Davies and Gannon 2006a). Participants' stories no longer signify individual identities but are interpreted through the lens of a collective process, making visible the ways in which lived experience is discursively constituted (Davies and Gannon 2006a). Selves are constructed in concert with others through the taking up and resisting of discourses (Davies et al. 2006). The rich narrative landscapes documented in this book are a result of this deep collective engagement. I outline the methodological processes and practices of this work in Chap. 3.

Theories of the Self: The Language of Agency

This research is located within a social constructivist perspective. I draw specifically on feminist poststructuralism and social remembering approaches to make sense of these women's voices. A feminist poststructuralist view departs from traditional psychological notions of an inherent 'self' that exists within a person (Weedon 1987). Through this lens, I view identities as multiple and as constructed through language. Language is not understood as a transparent tool reflecting experience. Rather, the social meanings embedded in participants' language are interrogated to find deeper meanings. Such an approach offers the possibility for exploring a new kind of agency—analysed through participants' shifting location in relation to social discourses (Davies 2000).

A social remembering approach looks at the creative strategies around the act of remembering—how one remembers and what they remember. Such an approach acknowledges that ways of remembering are intricately linked to what kind of self the narrator is creating in a particular space. A narrators' relationship to the past is never immediately settled, rather identity and agency are continually managed in powerful and strategic ways (Haaken and Reavey 2012). According to such a view, memories are, in fact, social landscapes that are creatively designed by the narrator who chooses what to tell and how they will tell it. It is through such ways of remembering that narrators create themselves. Importantly, ways of remembering are also shaped by broader systems of oppression and meaning—what can be said and how it can be said in any specific context. Such ways of remembering are intricately linked to careful negotiations 'within' patriarchal discourses and meanings around morality. Narrating experience which is silenced by the broader culture often involves creative work with multiple webs of meaning and imagination. As Culbertson (1995, p. 179) eloquently states,

> What we normally call memory is not the remembered at all of course, but a socially accepted fabrication, a weaving together of the thin, sometimes delicate and intertwined threads of true memory, the remembered, so that these might be told. Memory is always in the end subjected to those conventions which define the believable.

These theoretical lenses informed the ways that I made sense of the women's narratives. I did not try to discover any 'truth' of the women's narratives. Rather I viewed their narratives as a collective act through which particular 'selves' were created within the specific moments of the collective biography research. I discuss these approaches in more detail in Chap. 2.

Researcher Positionality

This research was also a personal journey for me. In such collective work one can never separate oneself; presence always matters (Melucci 1995). In this book, I write about what I have witnessed in the world and the emotions that have moved me listening to women's stories of pain and healing. A crucial part of this work was revisiting the data for the purposes of writing this book. Distance and detachment from the research process can often help us think about the data in different, more meaningful ways (Mauthner and Doucet 2003). My first analysis of these women's voices was intricately shaped by my life experiences and emotional geography at the time. During my initial writing, the women—their personalities, their pain and happiness—were sitting close to me. I felt that my writing was blocked somehow. I now realise that this was because I was concerned about the ways in which I was representing these women. Over time the process of 'looking back' helped me unpack a whole other layer of meaning evident in the women's stories. This was the story about female sexuality which emerged persistently throughout the data—a thread which was demanding to be heard. During my first engagements with the women's voices, I did not pick up on this thread in any meaningful way. Perhaps this was due to patriarchal constructions which fuel uncomfortable feelings about the topic of sexuality. Perhaps I was worried about portraying the women in a way that could be received in a negative light. My interpretation of the data has necessarily shifted over time from my first 'sit down' to my more recent re-reading for the purposes of this book. Time and distance have given me the ability to reflect and re-examine, ultimately allowing me to engage with the women's voices on a deeper level.

During my work, I have tried to engage in a more meaningful reflexivity that provides insight into my own interiority, as researcher, and how this shaped the processes and practices of my research. I pay close attention to my subjectivity and the conditions through which my data and writing were produced. Tamale (2011) says that in gender research on sensitive topics it is crucial to examine the process through which we, as researchers, mobilise painful memories—our methods, gaining rapport, and emotions of the participants and researcher during data gathering. How can participants express what is meaningful for them? Is there a language to do this? (see Tamale 2011). Relatedly, Sjoberg and Nett (1968) argue that the researcher is an important variable in the research design and we need to make our subjectivity visible. This is not only about being transparent about the research design and participant inclusions/exclusions. It is also about stating our assumptions about human beings and society and the ways in which these assumptions have shaped all areas of our research, including how we interpret the data (Sjoberg and Nett 1968).

I weave these two threads throughout the rest of the book. I engage in a subjective 'turning back' and comment on the ways in which my presence may have affected the women's narratives and what they chose to tell. I also reflexively explore the impact that the women's voices had on me. By writing in my own subjectivity, I believe I give you, the reader, greater insight into the processes and production of the text. I weave throughout the text reflections on my own narrative landscapes, providing commentary on the emotional repercussions of engaging in such work in the current intellectual moment in post-apartheid South Africa. At moments I write in more visibility of myself, so that you, the reader, can gain better understanding of the processes of sense making that took place during the writing of this book. At the same time, I hope that these methods offer insight into alternative methods for those who seek to engage in a fuller, more meaningful, reflexivity in their work. I outline the assumptions behind such a process in Chap. 3.

Chapter Summaries

The analytic threads provided in this book are of utmost importance for understanding how African migrant women living in South Africa experience patriarchal oppression of female sexuality in a country which degrades women's sexuality and worth and which is often unkind and cruel to African foreign nationals. I provide an in-depth micro-analysis of key participants' voices, while at the same time situating these individual life narratives within the larger political and cultural context, commenting on the social forces that play a part in shaping their subjectivities. It is through this textured examination that I trace and track the political complexities of women's agency. This book is divided into seven chapters.

Chapter 2, 'Patriarchal Oppression of Female Sexuality in Africa: Textures of Violence and Theorising Agency', sets the context for making sense of the identified narrative landscapes to follow in the rest of the book. I outline the textures of patriarchal oppression of female sexuality with a specific focus on the post-apartheid South African context of violent control, shaming, and silencing of female sexuality. I provide an overview of African-based research that focuses on women's culturally specific strategies for agency in the face of patriarchal oppression. I then critically theorise the concept of agency drawing on a much-needed distinction between what has been identified as 'resilience' on the one hand and 'resistance on the other'. I end the chapter with a description of the theoretical lenses framing my study—feminist poststructuralism and the social remembering approach.

In Chap. 3, 'Collective Biography: A New Chapter for Exploring Agency in the South African Context', I situate the research within wider postcolonial feminist concerns which framed my choice of methodology. The first is the goal of re-writing master narratives and working with fresh previously 'hidden' frames of meaning—the 'retrieval' of subjugated knowledge which forms a new knowledge of resistance and struggle (Macleod and Durrheim 2002). The second is the aim of empowering people who take part in research, engaging in new knowledge production which actually produces change in participants' lives. I outline powerful intellectual debates and critiques of Western feminism to frame new goals which move towards an African-gender perspective—seriously acknowledging the deep intersections of race, class, and location which shape women's experiences of patriarchal oppression of female sexuality. I then provide a detailed picture of the processes and practices of my research and the ways in which

I adapted the unique collective methodology to suit the women who took part in the study. I highlight the possibilities of such a methodology for advancing theory and for facilitating practical transformation in women's lives.

Chapter 4, 'Mubobobo: Memories of the Past, Metaphors for the Current Self', is an exploration into the world of mubobobo, a central motif of the women's collective narratives. I draw on voices of Shona women from Zimbabwe who spoke about mubobobo drawing on their memories of 'back home'. The women described mubobobo as an act whereby men obtain a magical muti[2] which enables them to rape women from a distance, without any physical contact. I begin the chapter with rich description of the post-apartheid South African context within which these women narrate their stories—the 'everyday' invisible forms of violence which function through what Gqola (2015) terms 'the female fear factory'. Situated within Root's (1992) concept of insidious trauma (unrelenting trauma that persist because of one's social position), I argue that there is no language with which to express these everyday traumas so integral to the experience of being a woman in South Africa. Using a feminist poststructuralist lens and Davies et al. (2006) reworking of Barthes' concept of decomposition, I argue that mubobobo is a culturally acceptable tool through which the women resist patriarchal oppression of female sexuality by voicing the complex often 'unnaratable' aspects of their sexual subjectivities and re-creating themselves through a new language of gendered trauma.

Chapter 5, 'Crossing Borders in Africa: Collectively Narrating the "Foreigner" Within', moves to the women's stories of crossing border posts and illegal physical entry points (such as forests and rivers) during their journey from their home country to South Africa. These stories are about crossing borders—both geographical and psychological. The women crossed physical border posts, entry points between different countries. They also crossed psychological borders, evident through their narratives of borders of morality and sexuality that they had to cross in order to survive in the space of transit. The stories are about sex at the border posts and specifically having sex with men in exchange for money to survive. The narratives convey rich meaning about their actual and symbolic consideration of these border posts—what these spaces mean for

[2] 'Muti' is a term for traditional medicine in Southern Africa. It usually consists of herbs and other natural products such as parts of trees or plants and is prescribed by African traditional healers.

them now. Evident was a strong 'cultural pull' towards the position of 'good' female subject and on the other hand the reality of poverty and desperation which 'push' women into engaging in sexual acts regarded as shameful/deviant. I explore the next central motif of the women's collective narratives—the 'foreigner self' in transit—through which the women narrated themselves as desperate and damaged and constructed a temporary self in transit that had no agency or morality. I argue that the 'foreigner' self was a narrative strategy through which the women could voice their complex experiences in transit in a socially acceptable way and, by doing so, they were able to manage the shame that is so intricately linked to female sexuality. They could express their experiences in transit while at the same time constructing positive morally correct selves in their tellings.

Chapter 6, 'Psycho-Social Borders and Imagining the South African Female "Other"', reaches the final stage of the women's geographical journeys. In this chapter, I explore the women's stories of life in South Africa with a specific focus on their narrative imaginings of the sexual world of black South African women. Their constructions of these symbolic female 'others' shed important insight into the ways in which these migrant women experience patriarchal oppression of female sexuality in post-apartheid South Africa rife with xenophobia, racism and deep-seated poverty. I open the chapter with discussion of the context of xenophobic violence in South Africa and the psychological implications the position of 'other' may have for African foreign nationals living in the country. I then argue that the third central motif of the women's collective narratives—South African women as faulty feminine subjects—served as a linguistic resource whereby the women narratively projected negative aspects of their female sexuality onto the image of black South African women. In doing so, they constructed positive selves related to worth and belonging in their social world.

The final Chap. 7, 'Narrative Landscapes of Female Sexuality in Africa: Concluding Thoughts', brings together important themes and findings from the book linking them to the broader picture of social change and gender research for the African continent.

This chapter has outlined the core content of the book. It sets the scene for the chapters which follow by providing background into the research context and process. It provides detail about the epistemological and ontological lenses which frame my interpretation of the women's voices. The concept of agency that I draw on throughout this book is about voice and resisting patriarchal discourses that maintain unequal relations between men and women. It is about resisting harmful subject positions outlined by patriarchy. It is about challenging the discourses that work to silence women and (re)-creating a positive sense of self amidst the chaos (Davies 1991). True agency, then, is the capacity to tell one's story in one's own way according to one's own purpose (see Davies 1991; Davies and Gannon 2006a).

In this book I present African migrant women's stories and the ways in which they give powerful voice to previously 'unspeakable' aspects of their existence. Through their shared narratives, the women claimed a common humanity in the South African context which is textured by deep oppression. My documentation of this work highlights theoretical insights about transformation *and* insights into practical processes for healing in this context. The importance of such work in the face of silencing and pervasive violence cannot be overstated. This book stands as testament to women's psychological strength in an abusive world, a world that is racist, misogynistic and unkind to people considered 'foreign'. After reading this book you will have a very different perspective about what 'agency' means and you may want to use this enriched understanding as a tool to work towards a more just world—what a crucial task for feminist scholars and activists. This is the core contribution of the text.

References

Arnfred, S. (2004). Re-thinking sexualities in Africa: Introduction. In S. Arnfred (Ed.), *Re-thinking sexualities in Africa* (pp. 7–17). Sweden: Almqvist & Wiksell Tryckeri AB.

Bakare-Yusuf, B. (2011). Nudity and morality: Legislating women's bodies and dress in Nigeria. In S. Tamale (Ed.), *African sexualities* (pp. 116–129). Cape Town: Fahamu.

Bakare-Yusuf, B. (2013). Thinking with pleasure: Gender, sexuality and agency. In S. Jolly, A. Cornwall, & K. Hawkins (Eds.), *Women, sexuality and the political power of pleasure* (pp. 28–41). London: Zed Books.

Crenshaw, K. (1991). Mapping the Margins: Intersectionality, identity politics, and violence against women of color. *Stanford law review, 43*(*6*), 1241–1299.

Culbertson, R. (1995). Embodied memory, transcendence, and telling: Recounting trauma, re-establishing the self. *New Literary History, 26*(1), 169–195.

Davies, B. (1991). The concept of agency. *Social analysis, 30, Postmodern critical theorising*, 42–53.

Davies, B. (2000). *A body of writing 1990–1999*. Walnut Creek: AltaMira Press.

Davies, B., & Gannon, S. (2006a). The practices of collective biography. In B. Davies & S. Gannon (Eds.), *Doing collective biography* (pp. 1–15). New York: Open University Press.
Davies, B., & Gannon, S. (2006b). A conversation about the struggles of collaborative writing. In B. Davies & S. Gannon (Eds.), *Doing collective biography* (pp. 114–144). New York: Open University Press.
Davies, B., Browne, S., Gannon, S., Hopkins, L., McCann, H., & Wihlborg, M. (2006). Constituting the 'feminist subject' in post-structuralist discourse. In B. Davies & S. Gannon (Eds.), *Doing collective biography* (pp. 167–181). New York: Open University Press.
Forter, G. (2007). Freud, Faulkner, Caruth: Trauma and the politics of literary form. *Narrative, 15*(3), 259–285.
Gqola, P. (2015). *Rape: A South African nightmare*. Johannesburg, South Africa: Jacana Media.
Haaken, J. (1999). Heretical texts. In S. Lamb (Ed.), *New versions of victims: Feminists struggle with the concept* (pp. 13–31). New York: New York University Press.
Haaken, J., & Reavey, P. (2012). Why memory matters: Disturbing recollections. In J. Haaken & R. Reavey (Eds.), *Memory Matters: Contexts for understanding sexual abuse recollections* (pp. 1–13). New York: Routledge.
Hydèn, M. (1994). *Women battering as marital act: The construction of a violent marriage*. Sweden: Scandinavian University Press.
Kambarami, M. (2006). *Femininity, sexuality and culture: Patriarchy and female subordination in Zimbabwe*. Africa regional sexuality resource centre, understanding human sexuality seminar series (1–10).
Kuhn, A. (2000). A journey through memory. In S. Radstone (Ed.), *Memory and methodology* (pp. 179–196). Oxford: Berg Publishers.
Lamb, S. (1999). Constructing the victim: Popular images and lasting labels. In S. Lamb (Ed.), *New versions of victims: Feminists struggle with the concept* (pp. 108–138). New York: New York University Press.
Macleod, C. (2006). Radical plural feminisms and emancipatory practice in post-apartheid South Africa. *Theory & Psychology, 16*, 367–389.
Macleod, C., & Durrheim, K. (2002). Foucauldian feminism: The implications of governmentality. *Journal for the Theory of Social Behaviour, 32*, 41–60.
Mauthner, N. S., & Doucet, A. (2003). Reflexive accounts and accounts of reflexivity in qualitative data analysis. *Sociology, 37*, 413–431.
McFadden, P. (2003). Sexual pleasure as a feminist choice. In *Feminist Africa 2: Changing cultures* (pp. 50–60). Rondebosch: African Gender Institute.
Melucci, A. (1995). The process of collective identity. In H. Johnston & B. Klandermans (Eds.), *Social movements and culture* (pp. 41–63). Minneapolis: University of Minnesota Press.

Mohanty, C. T. (1991). Under western eyes: Feminist scholarship and colonial discourses. In C. T. Mohanty, A. Russo, & L. Torres (Eds.), *Third world women and the politics of feminism* (pp. 51–80). Indianapolis: Indiana University Press.

Munt, S. R. (2011). Journeys of resilience: The emotional geographies of refugee women. *Gender, Place & Culture: A Journal of Feminist Geography, 19*, 555–577.

Rajiva, M. (2014). Trauma and the girl. In M. Gonick & S. Gannon (Eds.), *Becoming girl: Collective biography and the production of girlhood* (pp. 137–158). Toronto: Canadian Scholars' Press.

Root, M. P. P. (1992). Reconstructing the impact of trauma on personality. In L. S. Browne & M. Ballou (Eds.), *Personality and psychopathology* (pp. 229–265). New York: Guilford Press.

Sjoberg, G., & Nett, R. (1968). *A methodology for social research.* New York: Harper & Row.

Strauss, H. (2011). Cinema of social recuperation: Xenophobic violence and migrant subjectivity in contemporary South Africa. *Subjectivity: International Journal of Critical Psychology, 4*(2), 103–120.

Tamale, S. (2011). Introduction. In S. Tamale (Ed.), *African sexualities. A reader* (pp. 1–7). Cape Town: Fahamu Press.

de Vos, P. (2015). The Limit(s) of the law. Human rights and the emancipation of sexual minorities on the African continent. In D. Higginbotham & V. Collis-Buthelezi (Eds.), *Contested intimacies: Sexuality, gender, and the law in Africa* (pp. 1–16). Cape Town, South Africa: SiberInk.

Weedon, C. (1987). *Feminist practice and poststructuralist theory.* New York: Basil Blackwell Ltd.

CHAPTER 2

Patriarchal Oppression of Female Sexuality in Africa: Textures of Violence and Theorising Agency

In a lecture at our university early this year, Professor Melissa Steyn conveyed the powerful intellectual observation: the control of women's sexuality lies at the heart of patriarchal oppression. I believe that this is not stated enough. Any oppressor needs to control what he fears the most, and men fear women's sexuality precisely because when women challenge and move beyond patriarchal borders of 'good female sexuality', they threaten the very core of manhood—as sexually dominant and active. In patriarchal contexts, there exist deep social anxieties about women's sexual freedom and sexual choices (McFadden 2003, 2007).

> The desiring woman becomes transgressive; her sexual agency makes her a potentially disruptive threat to the containment of women, and to family structures built on meeting the desires of men. (Jolly, Cornwall, and Hawkins 2013, p. 6)

Such fears about the destabilisation of the patriarchal power system manifest in various forms of control of women's sexuality. Social discourses function to degrade female sexuality and render it inferior. There is deep silencing of positive aspects of female sexuality, which denies women the right to engage with their sexualities and desires for their own pleasure and joy (McFadden 2003).

Such oppression is evident across the globe. In the wake of transformations in Western representations of rape in psychology and the media, harmful undercurrents still exist. The recent global #metoo campaign has

S. van Schalkwyk, *Narrative Landscapes of Female Sexuality in Africa*, https://doi.org/10.1007/978-3-319-97825-3_2

shed light on the pervasive undercurrents of patriarchal violence and oppression which have been previously silenced. In her book *Just Sex: The Cultural Scaffolding of Rape*, Nicola Gavey (2005) traces social discourses and practices which maintain a rigid patriarchal heterosexual system that values men's sexual power and degrades women's. Discourses drive meanings around women's sexual insufficiency or disturbing sexual excess—'slut', 'whore', 'slag'. Such a discursive system serves to convey meaning that any sexual behaviours or desire that fall outside of this heterosexual system is deviant or pathological. Gavey says, 'The image of a woman actively seeking sex is still, perhaps, regarded as something almost desperate and dangerous' (2005, p. 12). Women are considered shameful and guilty if they do not adhere to the positions prescribed by these patriarchal policing discourses. Such meaning systems constitute ways of understanding the world that are based on patriarchal assumptions about female sexual subjects. These are not 'truths', but rather socially constructed knowledge to serve a particular agenda—the control of women.

Although the core aspects of fear and control underlie patriarchal oppression in many contexts across the world, the textures of oppression play out in unique ways in different contexts. In African contexts, specific histories and contemporary politics shape violence and the manifestations of patriarchal oppression of female sexuality (Pereira 2002). Gendered dynamics and textures of violence in South Africa, for example, are shaped by continued effects of colonialism, apartheid, and poverty. Patriarchal power and control function with increased urgency in those African countries which are experiencing rapid social transformation and increased rights for women (Reid and Walker 2005).

Throughout the period of colonialism in Africa, African women's bodies were constructed as hypersexual, barbaric and in need of being civilised—seen through the often-cited example that during this time it was not considered possible to rape an African woman (Tamale 2011). Constructions of African sexuality were set up in opposition to the notion of Western, white sexuality as pure and moral. This constituted part of the wider strategy to take control over and colonise the black race in Africa (Tamale 2011). Colonial legacies still linger on today through meanings surrounding sexuality on the African continent. These can be seen through particular research agendas. Research that medicalises sexuality and equates sexuality with reproductive health focuses on curbing reproduction rates and confine women's sexuality to the heterosexual family and women's mothering roles. Within the era of HIV/AIDS panic, research promotes meanings about the dangers of female sexuality with regards to the spread of the HIV virus and the hope that cultural change (i.e. a change in sexual behaviours) will curb the spread of the virus (Nyanzi 2011). Such work perpetuates the notion of African women as perpetual victims, unable to claim positive aspects of their sexuality.

In this chapter, I unpack core social meanings surrounding patriarchal oppression of female sexuality in Africa. I focus specifically on the South African context of violent control and degradation—echoes of the country's brutal and dehumanising past. I provide an overview of the textures of oppression—the violence, silencing, and degradation which shapes women's experience as female sexual subjects. This chapter sets the context for the women's stories which follow in the rest of the book. This is the context within which the migrant women are telling their stories about trauma and transition. It is therefore of critical significance for understanding the meaning that they make about themselves in the world.

I then discuss research on women's agency drawing on African-based feminist work that urges us to move beyond Westernised frameworks of women's powerlessness. I engage with this work highlighting important findings about creative and culturally centred strategies which women use to subtly, yet powerfully, express aspects of their sexuality in contexts within which such expression is taboo. In the last section of this chapter, I critically interrogate the concept of agency and provide an outline of my chosen theoretical approach. I argue that a feminist poststructuralist and social remembering lens serves as a powerful tool through which to explore subjectivities of African foreigner women living within a South African context coloured by deep-seated intersecting oppressions. This chapter provides rich insights about the study of women's agency, providing a model for shifting understanding of women's experiences of, and resistance to, patriarchal oppression of female sexuality in Africa.

Patriarchal Oppression of Female Sexuality in Africa

> African women know the threat of sexualized terror almost instinctively. This is one of the first forms of coercion they encounter when they enter the public sphere and quickly realise that cultural boundaries are vigilantly policed by both men and women. They know that while their societies have learnt during the decades since independence to "bend" a little to the demands and claims that women are making, there are cultural zones within their living, working and thinking spaces where the penalties for any transgression on their part are dire and swift. (McFadden 2003, p. 3)

Far from being a private act, sexuality, like gender, race and class, is a system of power through which dominant socio-political structures define what is acceptable behaviour for women and men in our societies (Tamale 2011). In his editorial to the *Sexuality in Africa magazine and monographs*, Oloruntoba-Oju (2010, p. 3) succinctly says, 'Cultural mores and observances socialize us into believing what may or may not be desired, what even if desired may not be pursued, how our desires may or may not be expressed.' It is important to note that the issue of sexuality in Africa is complex and the textures of psychic and social experiences surrounding sexuality are deeply tied in with lingering oppressions of colonialism, racism, and poverty (Mama 1995; Mohanty 1991). In many African contexts, there exists a dangerous tension between the realities of private desire and social perceptions of what it means to be an appropriate human being (Oloruntoba-Oju 2010). Female expression of sexuality and desire, especially the expression of sex for the enjoyment of sex, is rendered taboo and often deeply stigmatised (Kambarami 2006).

With few exceptions, throughout the African context, male promiscuity and (hyper)active sexuality is valorised as part of successful masculinity and the social repertoire of 'powerful African man' (Spronk 2007; Tamale 2011). On the other hand, most women in African contexts are expected to be passive sexual objects who do not readily express desire or act on their sexual impulses. Women's bodies are constructed as subordinate to men, and thus as sexual beings they are under the control of men and considered always available to men sexually (Dosekun 2007). Women are taught that to be 'good' feminine subjects, they need to take the backseat and function to sexually please men without active desire on their part. A 'proper' and respectable woman should control her sexual lust and should not approach men (Haram 2001). Such meanings have taken on a more powerful texture within the context of concern about the spread of the HIV virus. The moral discourses surrounding HIV/AIDS have codified the boundaries between 'good sex'—sex that adheres to normative cultural rules—and immoral 'bad' sex, sharply dividing people into these either/or categories based on their sexual behaviour (Spronk 2005, 2007).

The women whose voices I draw on in this book described what it is like for them as feminine subjects in their cultures. Akeyo speaks specifically about the Shona culture from Zimbabwe, from her current position living in South Africa.

> **Akeyo:** In my culture they used to say we need to get some medication for you to tone you down because your feelings are too high. It's not normal, you know. It was like taboo. It will be shocking like 'You started with a man, what! [you initiated sex with a man]. So, it was a big deal. If you are with a man you expect him to start.
>
> (Focus group discussion 1)

And,

> **Akeyo:** Like for example in our culture in the whole country (Zimbabwe), not basically my culture, we were never open to express our feelings even to say you want a man you love a man like to approach or to accept that you have feelings for a man. You know to tell a man you are interested or even to show a man that you are interested, then you will be regarded as a whore.
>
> **Women's group:** Yes!
>
> (Focus group discussion 1)

Such narratives serve as a backdrop for women's narrations in the chapters which follow in this book. Speaking from their position living in South Africa, the women were constantly negotiating discourses of sexual restraint with what seemed like a deep urgency to engage differently with their sexuality. Cultural discourses which the women 'brought' with them from 'back home' were central to their stories but were powerfully intersected with threads of meaning about female sexuality in South Africa. I unpack these intersections later in the book.

Patriarchal oppression of female sexuality functions inherently around notions of pure versus impure female bodies tied in with shame, blame, and stigma. Social discourses convey meaning that the black female body is 'dirty', disgusting, shameful and inferior. In her article 'Sexual Pleasure as Feminist Choice', Patricia McFadden (2003, p. 5) says the following:

> In all patriarchal societies, women and girls are taught, consistently and often violently, that their bodies are dirty, nasty, smelly, disgusting, corrupting, imperfect, ugly and volatile harbingers of disease and immorality.

Another powerful element is cultural meanings surrounding 'good' and 'bad' sexuality which are linked to places/spaces. Women who are married and keep within the personal space of the home are considered clean, pure, and safe. On the other hand, single women who venture into public spaces by themselves are doubted and subject to discursive assaults on their sexuality (Haram 2004). It is particularly important for women to practise self-surveillance and 'proper' conduct when they are in public spaces (Kambarami 2006). Dosekun (2007), for example, has shown that in South Africa women feel that they have to restrain their sexuality or dress less sexy in public so as not to encourage rape. The meanings around this are clear: If women do not restrain their sexuality and monitor their dress in public, they are to blame if they experience violence and rape.

The suppression of female sexuality is maintained through vigilant cultural surveillance (McFadden 2003). Men are at the core of this. The so-called redemption of the pathologised black female body is constructed as happening through fathers and husbands who 'protect' female sexuality in various ways and keep it in line and strangers who control women's bodies through violence or the threat of violence (McFadden 2003). As McFadden (2003, p. 5) states,

> A denied right, misinformation, a frown, a disapproving scowl, a raised voice, and angry reprimand, a verbal insult, a shaken fist, a shove, a slap, a punch, rape, a slit throat—these are all part of the routine processes of socialization and gendered identity construction through which girls and women are persistently reminded that they are chattels of men in our societies.

There are negative consequences for women who do not adhere to patriarchal rules—women who engage with their sexuality, who overstep the boundaries of expression, and who openly challenge oppressive definitions of the feminine sexual subject. Such women are often 'pushed' into the discursive terrain of 'bad' female subject—a position at which their interiority and humanness is targeted (McFadden 2007). Social mechanisms set up various forms of shame and blame of women that is a pervasive and ever-present part of women's lives (Gqola 2015). In some contexts, this may translate as labels of 'whore'/'slut' or online shaming and harassment. In others, shame may manifest through stigma and social exclusion. At the most extreme, social anxieties about female sexuality translate into a visceral fear inciting rage and violence enacted upon women's bodies. Such violence often results in extreme trauma or even death. South African feminist scholar, Lillian Artz (2009, p. 174), provides a rich description of the social hierarchies that function to maintain social order through the control of women.

> The projection of a patriarchal image onto women—constructions of good or bad mothers, wives, daughters, sexual behaviours and so on—is maintained through violence and silencing women who seek to go beyond these constructions through the threat of punishment: sexualized women provoke rape; undisciplined or inadequate wives and partners will be beaten; "unfit" mothers will lose their children. Terror is used as a means of setting patriarchal boundaries.

Contemporary South Africa has some of the highest rates of violence against women in the world. Recently South Africa has been dubbed the 'rape capital of the world' where women are more likely to be raped than educated. The country also has devastating rates of femicide documented in 1999 as 8.8 per 100,000 women over the age of 14 years old. It has been suggested that the country has an entrenched *culture of violence* stemming from the country's violent and dehumanising system of apartheid (Hamber and Lewis 1997). Embedded is an implicit acceptance of violence as a means of social control—deep undercurrents inherited from the apartheid system (Harris 2002; Vogelman and Lewis 1993). Some have argued that in post-apartheid South Africa, sexual violence has become a socially endorsed punitive strategy for maintaining patriarchal order (see Moffett 2006). Rape is a strategy used to keep women in line. Men use rape to inscribe subordinate status onto women. Sexual violence is often explained through justification strategies, deeply embedded in patriarchal ideas about men's entitlement to control women's bodies and linked to legitimisation of violence as a means of control (Moffett 2006).

One just needs to think of the practice of 'corrective rape', well documented as a pervasive part of life for women living in black townships in South Africa. 'Corrective rape' refers to men raping lesbian women in an effort to remind these women that they are women and they should be having sex with men. Men's motivations surrounding this rape are to 'correct' women's sexuality, to push them back in line with the heterosexual ideals which fit so neatly in line with passive female sexuality and powerful male sexuality. These actions signify men's deep-seated need to control women's sexuality (Brown 2012).

Rape is also a pervasive part of life for heterosexual women. In her article '"These Women, They Force Us to Rape Them": Rape as Narrative of Social Control in Post-Apartheid South Africa', Helen Moffett (2006) discusses a television interview during which a South African taxi driver discussed how he and his friends would cruise around on the weekends looking for women to grab and 'gang bang' (the group of friends would all forcefully have sex with the chosen woman). Importantly, Moffett comments on the fact that this man showed no awareness of the fact that he was talking about rape. He explained that they chose women who 'asked for it'—who walked around with confidence in certain places. The justificatory element of his narrative and sense of male entitlement to control women's sexuality is powerfully evident through his statement: 'But these women, they force us to rape them!' (Moffett 2006, p. 138). This example clearly shows the social accepted-ness of rape as a means of social control for women who do not fit in line with patriarchal ideals of 'good' femininity.

Violence against women is a way of maintaining social control over women's sexualities (Artz 2009). It is through the threat of violence that women learn that it is safer to conceal aspects of their sexual desire, almost like a process of detaching from embodied sexualised memories and experience (McFadden 2003; Tamale 2011). Many women have learnt that it is safer to remain silent about feelings and emotions associated with their sexuality, with some even suppressing these things for themselves. Women have come to exist in a precarious relationship to their bodies and their desires (Bakare-Yusuf 2013). McFadden calls this policing and silencing the 'muting' of female sexual desire and memory. The result, says McFadden (2003, p. 1) is akin to

> A sexual and political cul-de-sac of violation and repression: all too often women find themselves in a dark, dreadful place, windowless and airless, with seemingly no way out.

Many women do not have the space or socially accepted language to express aspects of their sexuality and embrace their full sexual subjectivity. The socially constructed fear of sexuality is often so insidious that it shapes women's conscious memories—what they remember and how they remember it. This in turn has powerful effects on women's sexual subjectivities. A complex tension may result between women's feelings as a sexual being and the 'strong pull' of culture which silences and suppresses these feelings. This may result in anxiety, shame and ambivalence about knowing oneself in the world (Herman 1992; Profitt 2000). Cultural scripts may not offer women much space within which to express the sexual nature of their bodies, but at the same time within the context of cultural taboos women *do* have knowledge about their bodies as sexualised vehicles. They are able to express these elements of their sexuality and desire in creative ways (Tamale 2005). McFadden's metaphor of muting, referred to above, suggests such possibilities. 'Muting' provides us with a sense of muffling or softening the intensity of women's expression of their sexuality. It underscores the disconnection of women's vibrancy, energy, or sound, but at the same time suggests that the sexual 'vibration' is still active. Despite patriarchal restrictions and cultural taboos, women engage with their sexuality in a multitude of different ways which challenge and resist harmful discourses.

Researching Women's Agency

Research on women's sexuality both globally and in the African context has largely focused on negative aspects of sexuality, linking sexuality to women's health, reproduction and the spread of HIV/AIDS. Health-related research, for example, uses the term 'sexuality' in an instrumental manner ignoring the complexity of women's sexual subjectivities (Spronk 2005, 2007). Such a focus closes down examination of the complexity and varieties of female sexuality in African contexts (Reid and Walker 2005).

This absence of positive aspects of female sexuality is reflective of broader patriarchal scripts and, while some scholars might have the best intensions, reinforces these ideas of female sexuality as intrinsically dangerous, passive and in need of monitoring and control (Nyanzi 2011). In other words, such research supports and maintains the policing of women's bodies through implicit generation of negative representations (Bakare-Yusuf 2013). A cohort of 'curious outsiders' from North American and Europe have generated much research with the aim of 'acting on the black female body' (McFadden 2007, p. 5). Ironically, the focus from the West has largely reinforced the two-pronged patriarchal construction of women's sexuality as ***dangerous*** and in need of intervention.

As a result of absorbing, on various levels, this dominant view of sexual agency as dangerous, many researchers and activists (globally and in the South African context) have tended to steer away from exploring women's sexual agency. Tamale (2011) suggests that researchers and activists have long had a negative visceral reaction to the topic of female sexuality. This idea deeply resonates with my own experience as researcher. For the broader project on which this book is based, I aimed to explore women's experiences of gender-based violence and the way they collectively made meaning of this violence in terms of their victimhood and their agency. In my first written work engaging with the women's voices, I almost completely overlooked the central theme that was shouting to be heard—women's narratives of sex and sexuality. I skirted around their language of sexuality. A core undertone of these women's narratives was their experiences as sexualised subjects. Often these stories were not about overt sexual experience, but rather included images and phrases that had a sexual tone. These meanings emerged persistently throughout the work, but I did not engage with them in an in-depth way. I knew that there was some level of depth missing from my work but could not put my finger on it until later when I returned to the data.

Patriarchal ideology conditions us to be silent about female sexuality. I realise now that my initial reading of the data was shaped by a deep fear that these narratives were somehow dangerous—for the women narrators and for me. Deeply aware of the negative connotations associated with female sexuality, I did not feel that it was safe to foreground these narratives and explore the deeper meaning. I was anxious about how such representations would be interpreted by the reader. I was worried that such narratives would convey a view that these women were hypersexual subjects or 'bad sexual subjects'—positions that are powerfully assumed and constructed in patriarchal culture. Perhaps I was also protecting myself from the powerful emotions that emerge when we engage with the topic of sexuality in a serious way. In my second reading of the data, I engaged more meaningfully with the narratives, finding deeper meaning about what these foreigner women were subtly communicating about their sexual subjectivities. I realised that these stories about women's experience in the world were not all about their powerless position. The act of communicating aspects of their sexual subjectivities in this space was profoundly agentic. It was a thread of their experience that demanded to be told.

Much feminist academic work has focused on a Westernised hypotheses which dictates universal female subordination, without acknowledging the nuances of culture or the many ways in which women in Africa may creatively work to resist their oppression (Reid and Walker 2005). Such Western discourses about women's powerlessness are often imposed on other cultures and used as a normative lens with which to theorise people's lives and meaning-making processes (Mohanty 1991). In this narrative, to inhabit a female African body is to be defined as fearful, psychically suffering object (Bakare-Yusuf 2013). Such constructions have powerful political and material implications for women. Any analysis that focuses purely on women as passive and powerless results in a 'reification of suffering and victimhood' (Gready 2008, p. 141). That is, suffering becomes associated with the very material essence of womanhood/femininity. The focus on women's powerlessness means that sexual terror becomes the foundation of women's sexual subjectivity rather than one aspect which shapes it (Bakare-Yusuf 2013). What this does is set artificial limits on how we can engage with the topic of women's sexuality. As Bakare-Yusuf (2013, pp. 30–31) states,

> It thereby circumscribes the production of meaning and the development of alternative narratives that attempt to portray and articulate female lived experiences—today and in years to come. But most debilitating of all, we lose our capacity to resist and change our situation, and to imagine new horizons of possibilities around sexual safety, choice, autonomy and pleasure.

Of course, we cannot deny the psychic and bodily effects of living as a feminine subject in a harmful patriarchal world. While it is important to continue to interrogate patriarchal domination of women, we also need to produce counter-narratives which speak to the complexity of women's lives (including women's agency in the face of oppression). It is important to generate alternative narratives to the dominant discourse on sexual terrorism. This sheds light on the complexity of women's subjectivities and opens a way for exploring avenues for disrupting hetero-patriarchal control (Bakare-Yusuf 2013). The role of contemporary research in Africa is to challenge the dualities and dichotomies of the colonial gaze that has been so influential in shaping and understanding women's experiences (Reid and Walker 2005).

So, what kinds of research are needed? Spronk (2007, p. 3) says that researchers should acknowledge the multifaceted power tied to sexual being and knowledge.

> 'Sexuality' refers to the quality of 'being sexual', it is a concept depicting the social arena where power relations and moral discourses are played out, and it also refers to sexual desire. These different aspects of sexuality highlight

the need to define the term 'sexuality' in concepts such as sexual practices, categories, desire, identity, etc., in order to clarify what is being studied.

Sexuality research should, according to Spronk, aim to understand the ways in which societal factors and relations between people organise sexualities and how these processes shape the experiences of women. When we aim to understand women's experiences of the oppression of female sexuality, we need to acknowledge that the sexual dimension is deeply personal and shaped by individual life histories and values (Spronk 2007). The personal needs to be taken into account in the generation of knowledge about sexualised experience. Arnfred (2015) argues that the study of female sexuality in Africa is in need of a conceptual reframing that moves away from dominant Western taken-for-granted assumptions. Such a view, according to Arnfred (2015), must look at the contextual nuances of gender relations and explore shifting (cultural) positions, beyond understandings of men as sexual subjects and women as static sexual objects.

Only within the last 20 years has there been generation of work that looks at the complexity of women's experience and the ways in which they may work with cultural scripts in nuanced ways, negotiating agency through various routes. This work has paid increasing attention to the misrepresentation of women as sexual subjects and the silencing of important aspects of women's sexual subjectivities (Adomako-Ampofo, Beoku-Betts, and Ngaruiya-Njambi 2004). Recent work that seriously addresses the complexity of female sexualities within particular social, historical and geographical sites of Africa have contributed important insights and stimulated new questions.

The book *Re-thinking African Sexualities* (2004), edited by Signe Arnfred, highlights voices of research participants from diverse parts of Africa. Collectively, the contributors interrogate existing lines of thought about sexuality in Africa (women as passive and statically oppressed) and create space for the study of women's agency using feminist and postcolonial theory as lenses to explore new questions. *African Sexualities: A Reader* (2011), edited by Sylvia Tamale, provides an African perspective examining different sexual cultures in diverse areas of Africa. The contributors amplify the voices of African people on the topic of sexualities, informing readers about the complexity of sexuality in Africa—including desire, presentations of sexuality, identities and transgressions from patriarchal norms. The text challenges Westernised assumptions of women's lack of sexual agency and forefronts important aspects of sexual subjectivities which have previously been silenced. Another important volume is *Women, Sexuality and the Political Power of Pleasure* (2013), edited by Susie Jolly, Andrea Cornwall, and Kate Hawkins. The authors explore aspects of women's sexual agency in different ways, from re-conceptualising meanings around prostitution, transformative all-women groups, creative bodily representations of sexuality, and the sexual desire of disabled women. The book sheds light on a much more complex picture than the one provided by scripts of women's static powerlessness in relation to oppressive patriarchal discourses. Other examples of work that has taken a critical approach to the study of sexualities/female sexual oppression is the *Culture, Health and Sexuality Journal* (2005) special issue on African sexualities and the *African Sexuality Magazine* through which scholars aim to critique the emphasis on disease and pathology inherent in studies of female sexuality and make a call to focus on women's sexual agency. Such research has begun to break the rigid silence about women's capacity to actively engage their sexuality in a multitude of creative ways.

In her work with the Baganda tribe in Uganda, Tamale (2013) explored the sexual initiation institution, Ssenga, within a social context within which women's sexuality is suppressed and silenced. This was initially a practice whereby older women educate younger women how to be good wives and how to pleasure their husbands. The Ssenga's role was to prepare the girls for marriage and to socialise them into 'proper' conduct. Tamale found that over the years the practice has changed. Although the Ssenga practices are still based on traditional patriarchal scripts which privilege men's sexual pleasure over women's, there exist some elements of subversion. Core findings suggested that the Ssenga now teach women to leave their husbands and go back to their parents if the men do not satisfy them sexually. Women are taught about their right to sexual satisfaction. Tamale found that the modern Ssenga tutorials focus on sexuality, eroticism and aphrodisiacs (erotic beads, oils, scents). Importantly, within Ssenga the women were exempt from certain taboos about talk about sex. Within these initiations, talk about sex and knowledge about sex were transmitted from the older women to the younger women in a masked form—with the use of metaphors and symbols which conveyed meaning about sexual desire and sexual power (Tamale 2013, p. 272). Tamale says,

> Metaphors and symbols play a central role in the Ssenga discourse. Referred to as okwambaza ebigambo (dressing words), metaphors and symbols

> provide an acceptable medium of accessing the secret world of unverbalised sexuality, shifting it from the private to the public realm.

Beneath the surface of political repression of women's sexuality were the Ssenga women's subversive and counter-hegemonic 'silent struggles', which Tamale refers to as the realm of 'women's secrets' (p. 271). Tamale argues that the Ssenga practice has evolved in such a way that the practice promotes a re-interpretation of entrenched norms concerning femininity, masculinity and subjectivity.

In her work with Afro-Surinamese women in Suriname, Wekker (1997) explored the practice of mati—all women's groups within which women explore their sexuality and express important aspects of their desire. Such expressions, says Wekker, are in deep opposition to hegemonic middle-class sexual values in this context. Wekker found that the women spoke about their sexuality using clipped talk such as jokes, innuendos, and body language. They therefore transmitted knowledge about their sexuality in a disguised form which was understood by women who took part in the practice. In their mati relationships, the women defined themselves as active, full sexual subjects. Wekker argues that through the mati work the women succeeded in regaining control over their sexualities—providing an example of how an oppressed group works against dominant gender ideologies.

Thompson (2011) explored women's linguistic strategies in Zanzibar, a context within which religious and cultural mores prevent women from expressing aspects of their sexuality. She examined women's talk about supernatural sex—the narrative of popobawa, described by participants as a form of witchcraft embodied by a mystical bat-like creature which is believed to attack and sexually violate women in certain areas of Zanzibar. The women's narratives focus around graphic details of the sexual encounter with popobawa. Thompson (2011) interprets these as resistance narratives. The women used the shared and culturally accepted narrative of popobawa to talk about sex and position themselves as sexual agents in a context within which the expression of female sexuality is taboo (Thompson 2011).

In another context—north India, Sharma documented processes of sexuality workshops with women living in rural areas. She discovered that while there was a hesitancy to speak overtly about sexuality, the women used metaphors related to food to discuss sex. The rural women in this study described a need for sex as *shareer ki bhook*—'hunger of the body'

(Sharma 2013, p. 45). They described their lack of sexual satisfaction through the language of their hunger not being satisfied—wanting five rotis but only being given two. Their discussion also centred around taste for food and change in tastes. They discussed similarities between sex and food and the social constructedness of likes and dislikes and the ways in which gender, class, and religion influence these tastes. Sharma (2013) interprets this 'food discourse' as a code for women to talk about their sexual desire. This language allowed the women to discuss sexuality in less moralistic ways that would not be judged by others (Sharma 2013).

In her research on female sexuality in Nairobi, Kenya, Spronk (2005) found that young professional women are challenging conventional gender roles by actively pursuing sexual pleasure. The young women in her study were exploring new types of heterosexual interactions. Their professional status allowed the women more leeway for exploring different sexual behaviours with less social control placed on them. Importantly, to avoid criticism about being 'inappropriate' women they adopted aloof, 'hard to get' attitudes towards men, and sometimes feigned sexual innocence. Spronk (2005) argues that it is through such behaviours that the women managed to maintain respectable sexual reputations. In the pursuit of sexual pleasure, the women had to constantly work through moral conflicts about 'good' versus 'bad' sexuality (Spronk 2005).

Haram (2004) studied the experiences of Meru women in northern Tanzania where women are increasingly moving from rural to urban areas in search of better economic opportunities. Haram found that many of the women engage in sexual relationships with a number of men in exchange for money to improve their lives (to start business, build houses, etc.). According to Haram (2004), these women are 'ploughing new paths' to a more successful way of living, transcending the oppressed and dependent way of life of their mothers. Often disillusioned by the search for a faithful and respectful husband, these women instead chose to have fleeting relationships with men who would support them financially. Haram interprets these acts as women's way of coping with controlling husbands. She says,

> Women can only solve or reduce the bad influence of an oppressive and authoritarian 'husband' by shuttling in and out of such loose and temporary unions with men, frequently changing partners and mothering children by two or more men. (Haram 2004, p. 226)

Importantly, in the face of these practices the women had to deal with stigmas surrounding the status 'unmarried woman' who travels the towns—insults and shaming such as Malaya (whore) were a common part of these women's lives (Haram 2004).

So, what important insights have been gleaned about women's agency in relation to the oppression of female sexuality? A central theme is the acknowledgement of the ways in which cultural norms, behaviours, and practices are slowly changing in a modern world. Globalisation, capitalism, rights discourse, and the media/internet are all factors which promote change in power relations and a shift in the ways that people relate to their culture. The above work highlights the subtle, yet powerful, ways in which women can, and do, engage their sexuality in the face of patriarchal oppression which silences and suppresses. Women create their own subversive language to engage with their sexuality in the face of oppressive discourses. In this work, agency is conceptualised as women's capacity for action within the nexus of power relations that foster oppression. We see that often these acts of agency are disguised from view. Women adopt strategies which camouflage their expressions. Such strategies are understood by the women involved but not by outsiders or men in their culture who may hold patriarchal views about female sexuality. The women express their sexuality in ways that are safe from stigma, blame, shame or physical violence. Such work conveys the complexity of women's agency, the work that women do to carefully negotiate a tightrope between 'acceptable' and 'shamed' femininity. Agency is always negotiated within power systems of patriarchy, capitalism and racism. The important point is that at times when it appears that women are powerless in relation to patriarchal structures, there are actually deep undercurrents of agency at work 'behind the scenes'.

But, at other times what appears to be examples of women's agency could, in fact, be interpreted as survival strategies. Haram's (2004) interpretation of Meru women's experiences is a case in point. Women's strategies of utilising their sexuality for material gain seem more like a response to desperation—survival strategies in a deeply oppressive capitalist system. Women may be forced into such situations to survive. Ecological approaches in the field of community psychology have shown that people find creative ways of coping every day in the face of harsh, often life-shattering circumstances (Mendelsohn, Zachary and Harney 2007; Pinnewala 2009). The word that should be emphasised here is *coping*. Often in the literature 'resilience' is equated with 'resistance'. This is incorrect, and it complicates any clear analytical picture of what we are observing. Ways of coping, or what has been termed 'resilience', should not be used interchangeably with the word 'resistance'.

In my earlier work, I struggled to define women's actions and experiences through these lenses. I did not have the terminology for what I meant when I was talking about agency—because any analysis of acts of agency can so often also be interpreted as desperation or survival strategies. One powerful story comes to mind. A woman who I interviewed several years ago was living in a small impoverished community in the western Cape called Garden Village. She had been experiencing ongoing and severe abuse at the hands of her husband. She told me the story of her turning point. One day after a particularly severe episode of physical abuse, her husband grabbed a knife and chased her out their small 'wendy house'.[1] She described 'running for her life' through the narrow streets with her husband right behind her brandishing the knife. That is when she suddenly 'snapped'. She turned and grabbed the knife from him and stabbed him repeatedly. Her face was neutral when she told me the story. She seemed disconnected from it. Initially, I interpreted her act of stabbing her husband as an example of resistance. However, after many critical discussions among my network, I realised that this was in fact an act of desperation to preserve her own life. It was a survival strategy in the face of no other option. She knew that the man would have killed her, had she not acted.

The important point here is that we need to be clear about what it is we are talking about when we use the word 'agency'. 'Resilience' has been defined as women's capacity for 'physical and mental *survival*', their adaptability and potential to reconstruct their lives in the face of oppression and trauma (Schrijvers 1999, p. 323). 'Resistance', on the other hand, is often conceptualised as a process through which women become conscious of their less powerful position in relation to men. 'Resistance' is about challenging the givenness of situational power relations (Ewick and Silbey 2003, p. 1331). It is about working to change the meaning one makes about oneself in the world. In this sense 'resistance' entails women's processes of challenging dominant discourses and working to position themselves outside the borders of patriarchal thinking. Resistance is about

[1] The term 'wendy house' is used in South Africa to refer to a small house structure made out of wood. It is a form of accommodation for low-income people, usually erected in someone's back yard.

engaging in strategies that contribute to imagining new ways of being and creating new stories about the world and women's place in it. I would argue that both resilience and resistance are important aspects of women's agency that are indeed interlinked. Real life cannot be neatly fragmented by concepts. However, if we aim to enrich our understandings of the social world, we need to be clear about what specific definitions we are utilising. Promoting resilience among women would entail engaging in community interventions that offer social and material support for women's healing. Working towards resistance, on the other hand, is fundamentally linked to the aim of developing a critical consciousness about patriarchal power structures.

To strengthen research on women's experiences of, and resistance to, patriarchal oppression of female sexuality, what is needed is a strong theoretical foundation, an appropriate lens through which to explore what women's experiences mean for them. How do women make sense of their experiences and how may they redefine themselves in the face of oppression? Women's identity work needs to be explicit in such an exploration. What would such a theory of agency look like? I turn to this question next.

Theorising Women's Agency: Identity, Multiplicity And Creative Discursive Work

Agency and victimisation are not mutually exclusive categories. Perspectives that focus on women's agency should do so in a way that incorporates an analysis of the complex co-existence of power and powerlessness—the continual shifting between positions of victim and agent. Women constantly negotiate a sense of self made up of threads of power and powerlessness. These threads manifest in different ways according to a particular woman's geographic, economic and cultural location and the social resources that she has at her disposal (Sokoloff and Dupont 2005). Culture provides vocabularies of understanding through which individuals make meaning of personal experience. Dominant cultural discourses, for example, shape meanings around the acceptability of violence and women's place in the world. Thus, any exploration of women's subjectivities in relation to violence cannot ignore the significance of the socio-cultural environment within which women are located.

In her much-cited article, 'Mapping the Margins: Intersectionality, Identity Politics, and Violence Against Women of Color', Kimberlè

Crenshaw (1991) coined the term 'intersectionality' to explain the unique texture of oppression experienced by African American women. The term is much used today to understand subjects' experience of interlocking systems of power. It has been well argued across disciplines that an intersectional approach is most useful for capturing the complexity of identity (Prins 2006). Social categories of gender, ethnicity, class and race co-construct each other in a myriad of ways. So, women's experiences of patriarchal oppression of female sexuality are shaped by multiple intersecting oppressions related to class divisions in society, race/ethnic discrimination, and sexual terrorism. Some theorists such as Mama (1995) have referred to this as 'triple oppression'. Then, when considering the women whose voices are documented throughout the rest of this book, one must acknowledge a crucial additional level. Within the context of xenophobia, African migrant women living in South Africa have little opportunities to experience a full socially valued existence (Strauss 2011). The status of 'foreigner' is another layer of oppression. Work in the broader field of violence against women provides useful insights about women's agency in the face of patriarchal violence. Below I discuss some of the central debates, before outlining the approach that I utilise in this book.

Multiple Meanings of Women's Agency

In an attempt to move away from conceptualisations of women as static powerless victims, many feminist scholars have worked to identify and describe ways in which women exhibit agency in their lives. In the context of intimate partner violence, Lempert (1996) and Hage interpret rationalising violence, minimising violence and self-blame as agentic strategies. They argue that these strategies are ways of containing men's violence and preserving positive identities in the face of abuse. However, such strategies of 'saving face' and coping with the abuse do not directly challenge one's situation as powerless in relation to abusive men. Such actions do not seem to represent any 'choice' at all but rather seem to be survival mechanisms in an oppressive world.

Scholars have identified the act of leaving abusive relationships as an act of agency. This has been described as processes of 'moving on' or 'shedding' the identities of victim (see Wuest and Merritt-Gray 2001). The understanding is that women who have experienced violence eventually reach a stage after much healing when they no longer identify with the position of victim or survivor, as if the emotional remnants magically disappear. Others such as Taylor (2002) and Mills (1985) have identified various chronological stages that women move through during the process of 'leaving' abuse—stages vary from managing the abuse and a positive sense of self; physically moving away; maintaining barriers; and working to restructure self in positive ways.

Such theorising is problematic for a number of reasons. Such categorisations and strict definitions are not useful for exploring women's lived experiences in a world which is 'messy' and shaped by deep intersecting oppressions and violence. Healing for poor women in impoverished contexts might entail two steps forward with multiple steps backwards as they have limited resources to deal with the ever-present and continual forms of violence against their bodies and spirits. When one form of violence 'ends', others are still pervasively present. The transition from 'victim' to 'survivor', or perhaps more aptly stated, the position of moving from a place of relative powerlessness to a position of increased power in relation to the abuser/the patriarchal system is not a smooth one. This is particularly true for poor women living in third world countries, such as South Africa. The very act of 'leaving' abuse may disempower women economically and render them further vulnerable to abuse at the hands of other men.

Secondly, we can never assume a clear distinction between 'victim' and 'survivor'. We need to examine contextual meanings surrounding such positions. How do women identify with such positions? What are the meanings ascribed to 'victim'/'survivor' in different contexts? How do women work with these meanings? These are important questions which need to be considered before 'forcing' labels on women's experiences. Swedish gender scholar Margareta Hydèn (2005) discusses that the category of 'victim' is not fixed, but rather is a product of culture and language. The very position of 'victim' has different meanings in different spaces/places. In some contexts, there may even be discursive limits on who will be considered a 'victim'/'survivor' status. Foreigner women living in South Africa, for example, may find it difficult to take on the position of survivor—because their lives are textured by ongoing challenges related to poverty, racism, and hatred of foreigners in their current setting.

What is needed is a theoretical approach that allows examination of how women may resist hegemonic patriarchal discourse and move away from harmful understandings of the self. This necessarily demands in-depth analysis of the complex and context-dependent nature of subjectivity.

We also need to explore the different ways in which women identify, and work with, categories of 'victim' and 'survivor'. I have found feminist poststructuralist theory a useful tool for exploring these complex dimensions of subjectivity.

Feminist Poststructuralism: Multiplicities of Identity and Power

Postmodern and postcolonial thought has led to the emergence of critical feminist approaches to research. Although varied in focus and premise, such approaches have in common a view that patriarchy is an organising system in most societies; an acknowledgement that the personal is political—individual experience is deeply intertwined with and shaped by broader social forces of power—and the idea that knowledge is multiple, shifting and contextually situated. The premise is that we can never access one 'truth' of experience.

According to traditional (Westernised) psychological perspectives, identity has been conceptualised as an essential, individual, and coherent self. In this sense individuals 'have' pathology, rather than being affected by multiple factors in a pathological and oppressive society. Feminist poststructuralist thought moves us away from such understandings. It provides an understanding of identities as inherently socially embedded. According to feminist poststructuralist scholar, Chris Weedon (1987, p. 32), subjectivity is 'the conscious and unconscious thoughts and emotions of an individual, her sense of self and her ways of understanding her relation to the world'. Rather than conceptualising a stable and unified self, feminist poststructuralist work recognises subjectivity as constructed through positioning vis-à-vis social discourses (Davies and Gannon 2006; Gavey 1989). Language is not seen as a transparent tool that reflects experience, rather the social meanings surrounding words and concepts are interrogated to find deeper meaning about the construction of identity. Several scholars both internationally and from the African continent have discussed the benefits of such a theoretical approach. Amina Mama (1995, p. 112), for example, says,

> If we start with the premise that people are not rigidly fixed by a single identity, then we can study the ways in which they are able to change, to resist and oppose dominant discourses, either by taking up positions outside these discourses, or by developing alternative one's, or both.

In her book *A Body of Writing*, Davies (2000) argues that feminist poststructuralism creates the possibility for understanding and exploring a new kind of agency—the acknowledgement of an individual's (shifting) location in relation to social discourses

> through recognizing the constitutive force of discourse, rather than seeing it merely as a tool for describing the real world, we can see ourselves as being spoken into existence. We can also see both the potency of speaking in new ways and the possibility of refusing the old, undesirable ones. This is not an individual but rather a collective task, though the possibilities it opens up may be experienced as profound liberation. (Davies 2000, p. 41)

A feminist poststructuralist approach provides a means for exploring the ways in which women work with socially defined identity positions and how, through this struggle, they may discover alternative ways of defining their reality. Davies' notion of relational selves is central—people make meaning with others in a 'complex web of intimate and larger social relations' (Mauthner and Doucet 2003, p. 422). Importantly, such linguistic positionings are not merely theoretical observations. One's self-narrations have very real material implications, shaping the very ways in which individuals experience themselves in the world (Gavey 2005). When one works through deeply embedded conflicts posed by the co-existence of dominant and alternative discourses, when one names violation/oppression, an energetic and psychic liberation happens (Profitt 2000). This theoretical approach helped me to explore the meanings around women's narrations within the group spaces of the research. It helped me to conceptualise the power of interconnected stories and shared meaning and the role in which such collective spaces may play in the process of healing/transformation.

Social Remembering Approaches: Landscapes of Memory

Another theoretical lens which is integral to my analysis of women's narratives in this book is that of social remembering, similar to what Janice Haaken (1999) calls transformative remembering. Such a view does not assume the 'truth' of memory or the facts underlying the story being told. Rather, the 'truth' of memory lies in its narrative structure and the particular subject positions that are constructed through talk. The ways in which a person remembers, the ways in which they narrate their memory has everything to do with the construction of the self and what kind of self they want to present to those listening. A victim/survivor's relationship to their past is never immediately settled; rather identity and agency are managed in the present moment of telling (Haaken and Reavey 2012; Reavey and Brown 2007). As Eisikovits and Winstock (2002, p. 79) state,

> Memories become tactics for manipulating occurrences in everyday life to achieve personal, interpersonal and social aims.

An integral part of this narrative function is presenting the self in ways that shape (or limit) the moral judgments that listeners can make. It is through telling our stories again and again that we engage in a self-in-progress which is continually changing, morphing in relation to new meanings and possibilities—here, we see the link with Haaken's use of the work *transformative*. Haaken (1999) refers to the past as 'another country' through which women make meaning about their experiences by seeking linguistic landmarks. Such landmarks, or culturally accepted scripts, provide narrators with a means for orientating the self—amidst the chaos, confusion and conflict of multiple and contradicting social discourses. Narrators make meaning about themselves in the world through utilising the cultural landmarks that are at their disposal at any given time. Women remember in certain ways to achieve certain social aims within the moment of telling. Telling is agency and the ways in which we choose to tell has significant implications for our sense of self in the world (Culbertson 1995; Gobodo-Madikizela, Fish and Shefer 2014).

The Concept of Agency Utilised in This Book

Throughout this book, I utilise Davies' concept of agency, based strongly on feminist poststructuralist theories of identity. This theoretical lens is also intricately tied in with the social remembering perspective described above. Both focus on the multiple, shifting nature of narrative and the active production of identities through language (Davies and Gannon 2006). Davies (1991) outlines three core points related to agency, which I draw on in the rest of this book:

(1) The discursive constitution of a person having presence; a right to speak and be heard

(2) A person as author of their own meanings and desires; one who can speak with authority
(3) The act of going beyond the given meanings in any one discourse, and forging something new; re-creating words and concepts through a combination of previously unrelated discourses

Davies (1991) says that linguistic work along these three dimensions captures a shift in consciousness that is beginning to occur, through the individual imagining what is not, but what might be. Irigaray (1985, p. 29) provides a rich descriptive thread of how we may approach such work.

> One would listen with another ear, as if hearing an "other meaning" always in the process of weaving itself, of embracing itself with words, but also getting rid of words in order not to become fixed, congealed in them.

This chapter sets the context for making sense of the three central motifs identified in the women's collective narratives in the chapters to follow. I have outlined the textures of patriarchal oppression of female sexuality, with a specific focus on the violent control, shaming and silencing of sexuality prevalent in current post-apartheid South Africa. I highlight important debates about sexuality research and the absence of positive aspects of sexuality—research trends which reinforce dominant ideas about female sexuality as dangerous and in need of control. I then discuss African-centred research which sheds useful insights about how women engage with aspects of their sexual subjectivity in subtle, yet powerful, ways in the face of patriarchal oppression. In the last section, I critically theorise the concept of agency and present the concept of agency used in this book. I provide a powerful theoretical model for better exploring women's experiences of, and resistance to, patriarchal oppression of female sexuality in contexts within which dehumanising violence is part of everyday life. In the next chapter, I address the unique collective methodology which I used to explore narrative landscapes of female sexuality in Africa.

References

Adomako-Ampofo, A., Beoku-Betts, J., & Ngaruiya-Njambi, W. (2004). Women's and gender studies in English-speaking Sub-Saharan Africa: A review of research in the social sciences. *Gender & Society, 18*, 685–712.

Arnfred, S. (2015). Female sexuality as capacity and power? Rethinking sexualities in Africa. *African Studies Review. ASR Forum on Women and Gender in Africa: Part, 1*, 149–170.

Artz, L. (2009). The Weather watchers: Gender, violence and social control. In M. Steyn & M. van Zyl (Eds.), *The Prize and the price: Shaping sexualities in South Africa* (pp. 169–191). Cape Town, South Africa: Human Sciences Research Council.

Bakare-Yusuf, B. (2013). Thinking with pleasure: Gender, sexuality and agency. In S. Jolly, A. Cornwall, & K. Hawkins (Eds.), *Women, sexuality and the political power of pleasure* (pp. 28–41). London: Zed Books.

Brown, R. (2012). Corrective rape in South Africa: A continuing plight despite an international human rights response. *Annual Survey of International & Comparative Law, 18*(*1*), 45–66.

Crenshaw, K. (1991). Mapping the Margins: Intersectionality, identity politics, and violence against women of color. *Stanford Law Review, 43*(*6*), 1241–1299.

Culbertson, R. (1995). Embodied memory, transcendence, and telling: Recounting trauma, re-establishing the self. *New Literary History, 26*(*1*), 169–195.

Davies, B. (1991). The concept of agency. *Social analysis, 30, Postmodern critical theorising*, 42–53.

Davies, B. (2000). *A body of writing 1990–1999*. Walnut Creek: AltaMira Press.

Davies, B., & Gannon, S. (2006). The practices of collective biography. In B. Davies & S. Gannon (Eds.), *Doing collective biography* (pp. 1–15). New York: Open University Press.

Dosekun, S. (2007). Don't be sexy, don't be there. Discourses of space, danger, and women's sexuality in South Africa. In *Sexuality in Africa magazine* (pp. 7–9). Lagos, Nigeria: Africa Regional Sexuality Resource Centre.

Eisikovits, Z., & Winstok, Z. (2002). Reconstructing intimate violence: The structure and content of recollections of violent events. *Qualitative Health Research, 12*, 685–699.

Ewick, P., & Silbey, S. (2003). Narrating social structure: Stories of resistance to legal authority. *American Journal of Sociology, 108*, 1328–1372.

Gavey, N. (1989). Feminist poststructuralism and discourse analysis. Contributions to feminist psychology. *Psychology of Women Quarterly, 13*, 459–475.

Gavey, N. (2005). *Just sex? The cultural scaffolding of rape*. New York: Routledge.

Gobodo-Madikizela, P., Fish, J., & Shefer, T. (2014). Gendered violence: Continuities and transformation in the aftermath of conflict in Africa. *Signs: Journal of Women and Culture in Society, 40*(1), 81–99.

Gqola, P. (2015). *Rape: A South African nightmare*. Johannesburg, South Africa: Jacana Media.

Gready, P. (2008). The public life of narratives: Ethics, politics, methods. In M. Andrews, C. Squire, & M. Tamboukou (Eds.), *Doing narrative research* (pp. 137–150). London: Sage.

Haaken, J. (1999). Heretical texts. In S. Lamb (Ed.), *New versions of victims: Feminists struggle with the concept* (pp. 13–31). New York: New York University Press.
Haaken, J., & Reavey, P. (2012). Why memory matters: Disturbing recollections. In J. Haaken & R. Reavey (Eds.), *Memory Matters: Contexts for understanding sexual abuse recollections* (pp. 1–13). New York: Routledge.
Hamber, B., & Lewis, S. (1997, June). An overview of the consequences of violence and trauma in South Africa. *Research report written for the Centre for the Study of Violence and Reconciliation.*
Haram, L. (2001). 'In sexual life women are hunters': AIDS and women who drain men's bodies. The case of the Meru of northern Tanzania. *Society in Transition, 31*(1), 47–55.
Haram, L. (2004). 'Prostitutes' or modern women? Negotiating respectability in Northern Tanzania. In S. Arnfred (Ed.), *Re-thinking sexualities in Africa* (pp. 211–229). Uppsala, Sweden: The Nordic Africa Institute.
Harris, B. (2002). Xenophobia: A new pathology for a new South Africa. In D. Hook & G. Eagle (Eds.), *Psychopathology and social prejudice* (pp. 169–184). Cape Town, South Africa: Cape Town University Press.
Herman, J. (1992). *Trauma and recovery: From domestic abuse to political terror.* New York: Basic Books.
Hydén, M. (2005). "I must have been an idiot to let it go on": Agency and positioning in battered women's narratives of leaving. *Feminism and Psychology, 15*, 169–188.
Irigaray, L. (1985). *The sex which is not one.* Ithaca: Cornell University Press.
Jolly, S., Cornwall, A., & Hawkins, K. (2013). Introduction: Women, sexuality and the political power of pleasure. In S. Jolly, A. Cornwall, & K. Hawkins (Eds.), *Women, sexuality and the political power of pleasure* (pp. 1–27). London: Zed Books.
Kambarami, M. (2006). Femininity, sexuality and culture: Patriarchy and female subordination in Zimbabwe. *Africa regional sexuality resource centre, understanding human sexuality seminar series*, 1–10.
Lempert, L. B. (1996). Language obstacles in the narratives of abused women. *Mid-American Review of Sociology, XIX*(1&2), 15–32.
Mama, A. (1995). *Beyond the masks. Race, gender and subjectivity.* London: Routledge.
Mauthner, N. S., & Doucet, A. (2003). Reflexive accounts and accounts of reflexivity in qualitative data analysis. *Sociology, 37*, 413–431.
McFadden, P. (2003). Sexual pleasure as a feminist choice. *Feminist Africa 2: Changing cultures*, 50–60.
McFadden, P. (2007). Contesting sexualities in the re-making of African female bodies as sites of power. In *Sexuality in Africa magazine* (pp. 4–6). Lagos, Nigeria: Africa Regional Sexuality Resource Centre.

Mendelsohn, M., Zachary, R. S., & Harney, P. A. (2007). Group therapy as an ecological bridge to new community for trauma survivors. *Journal of Aggression, Maltreatment, and Trauma, 14*, 227–243.

Mills, T. (1985). The assault on the self: Stages in coping with battering husbands. *Qualitative Sociology, 8*, 103–123.

Moffett, H. (2006). 'These women, they force us to rape them': Rape as narrative of social control in post-apartheid South Africa. *Journal of Southern African Studies, 32*(*1*), 129–144.

Mohanty, C. T. (1991). Under western eyes: Feminist scholarship and colonial discourses. In C. T. Mohanty, A. Russo, & L. Torres (Eds.), *Third world women and the politics of feminism* (pp. 51–80). Indianapolis: Indiana University Press.

Nyanzi, S. (2011). From miniscule biomedical models to sexuality's depths. In S. Tamale (Ed.), *African sexualities: A reader* (pp. 47–49). Cape Town, South Africa: Pambazuka Press.

Oloruntoba-Oju, T. (2010). Editorial: The social and cultural construction of desire and pleasure. *Sexuality in Africa Magazine and Monologues, 6*, 3.

Pereira, C. (2002). *Between knowing and imagining: What space for feminism in scholarship on Africa? Feminist Africa intellectual politics.* Cape Town, South Africa: African Gender Institute.

Pinnewala, P. (2009). Good women, martyrs, and survivors: A theoretical framework for South Asian women's responses to partner violence. *Violence and Victims, 15*, 81–105.

Prins, B. (2006). Narrative accounts of origins: A blind spot in the intersectional approach? *European Journal of Women's Studies, 13*(*3*), 277–290.

Profitt, N. J. (2000). Survivors of woman abuse. *Journal of Progressive Human Services, 11*(*2*), 77–102.

Reavey, P., & Brown, D. (2007). Rethinking agency in memory: Space and embodiment in memories of child sexual abuse. *Journal of Social Work Practice, 21*(*1*), 5–21.

Reid, G., & Walker, L. (2005). African sexualities: Editorial introduction. *Culture, Health and Sexuality Journal, 7*(*3*), 185–194.

Schrijvers, J. (1999). Fighters, victims, and survivors: Constructions of ethnicity, gender and refugeeness among Tamils in Sri Lanka. *Journal of Refugee Studies, 12*, 307–333.

Sharma, J. (2013). Challenging the pleasure versus danger binary: Reflections on sexuality workshops with rural women's rights activists in North India. In S. Jolly, A. Cornwall, & K. Hawkins (Eds.), *Women, sexuality and the political power of pleasure* (pp. 42–57). London: Zed Books.

Sokoloff, N. J., & Dupont, I. (2005). Domestic violence at the intersections of race, class, and gender: Challenges and contributions to understanding violence against marginalised women in diverse communities. *Violence Against Women, 11*, 38–64.

Spronk, R. (2005). Female sexuality in Nairobi: Flawed or favoured? *Culture, Health & Sexuality, 7*(3), 267–277.
Spronk, R. (2007). Beyond pain, towards pleasure in the study of sexuality in Africa. In *Sexuality in Africa magazine* (pp. 3–6). Lagos, Nigeria: Africa Regional Sexuality Resource Centre.
Strauss, H. (2011). Cinema of social recuperation: Xenophobic violence and migrant subjectivity in contemporary South Africa. *Subjectivity: International Journal of Critical Psychology, 4*(2), 103–120.
Tamale, S. (2005). Eroticism, sensuality and "women's secrets" among the Baganda: A critical analysis. *Feminist Africa, 5*, 9–36.
Tamale, S. (2011). Introduction. In S. Tamale (Ed.), *African sexualities: A reader* (pp. 1–7). Cape Town: Fahamu Press.
Tamale, S. (2013). Eroticism, sensuality and 'Women's secrets' among the Baganda. In S. Jolly, A. Cornwall, & K. Hawkins (Eds.), *Women, sexuality and the political power of pleasure* (pp. 265–285). London: Zed Books.
Taylor, J. (2002). "The straw that broke the camel's back": African American women's strategies for disengaging from abusive relationships. *Women and Therapy, 25*, 79–94.
Thompson, K. D. (2011). Zanbari women's discursive and sexual agency: Violating gendered speech prohibitions through talk about supernatural sex. *Discourse & Society, 22*, 3–20.
Vogelman, L., & Lewis, S. (1993). Gang rape and the culture of violence in South Africa. Published in German under the title. *Illusion der Stärke: Jugenbanden, vergewaltigung und kultuur der gewalt in Südafrika, in Der Überblick*, No. 2.
Weedon, C. (1987). *Feminist practice and poststructuralist theory.* New York: Basil Blackwell Ltd.
Wekker, G. (1997). One finger does not drink Okra soup: Afro-Surinamese women and critical agency. In M. J. Alexander & C. T. Mohanty (Eds.), *Feminist genealogies, colonial legacies, democratic futures* (pp. 330–352). London: Routledge.
Wuest, J., & Merritt-Gray, M. (2001). Beyond survival: Reclaiming self after leaving an abusive partner. *Canadian Journal of Nursing, 32*(4), 79–94.

CHAPTER 3

Collective Biography: A New Chapter for Exploring Agency in the South African Context

For this research project, I explore women's processes of transforming their past, collectively, within the spaces of a year-long series of research dialogues. I focus on the co-construction of subjectivities among a sample of the women from the support group—how they make meaning together and what their dialogues mean for their collective and personal sense of self in the world. In other words, what potential for change can be seen through these dialogues and why does it matter with regards to the broader South African capitalist, patriarchal, and xenophobic system within which the women are situated? My focus here is placed on how participants constructed meaning in terms of both their victimhood and agency within the broader framework of the oppression of female sexuality, and how the women may gain strength through these shared narratives.

To achieve these aims I needed a research paradigm that is compatible with my understandings of identity as socially and interactively constructed. I required a research paradigm that would allow me to examine how identities are constructed within micro-social interactions as well as in relation to broader social discourses of gender in South Africa. My chosen epistemology is a qualitative one, which allowed me to focus on the socially constructed, multiple, and relational nature of identities (see Parker 2005).

Women from poor, third world countries have not been given voice in mainstream psychological research. Their experiences remain on the margins as the 'absent trace' in relation to hegemonic discourse of experience

S. van Schalkwyk, *Narrative Landscapes of Female Sexuality in Africa*, https://doi.org/10.1007/978-3-319-97825-3_3

(white, male, middle-class, North American) (Macleod 2006, p. 368). When women are given the space to speak in qualitative research projects, the methodology of the project often stands in the way by structuring the content of women's stories in highly restrictive and oppressive ways (see Hofisi et al. 2014). Pre-set questions of research interviews capture exactly that—pre-existing views of researchers or other theorists—instead of participants' own unique perspectives and ideas. In addition, traditional qualitative methods such as individual interviews conducted with someone one has just met fall short in terms of their capacity to really capture the essence and complexity of participants' emotional and experiential worlds. Such brief interactions lack context in the sense that the researcher misses important detail about participants' lives. Researchers do not have time to develop rapport with participants and thus the conversations may be closed off, lacking the full texture and depth of continued discussions over time in a safe environment conducive to continued reflection. Such brief research encounters do not provide for the development of meaning over time or the interviewer and interviewee's emerging reflections about the narratives.

In my work with the women's group I was driven to address the limitations of mainstream research. I wanted to achieve something more than what I had previously gleaned from using traditional qualitative research methods to explore women's experience of gendered abuse. For this project, I adopted a research approach that provided space for women to express their intuitions, imagination, and the concerns central to their existence. In this chapter, I provide details about the research context and the workshops that I conducted with the women. I utilised creative and interactive techniques such as storytelling, role-plays, visual methods, and vignettes depicting scenarios of gender violence. Moving away from traditional methods of psychological research, I drew on a very different kind of methodology called collective biography, which is fitting with feminist poststructuralist approaches to agency and identity.

My work is adapted from the core principles of such collective work outlined by Bronwyn Davies and Susan Gannon, most recently documented in their book *Doing Collective Biography* (2006). The collective biography method was initially conducted by feminist scholars who utilised interactive workshops (phase one) and a collaborative analysis through collective writing processes (phase two). It is through such an approach that the researchers utilised feminist poststructuralist theory to examine their own gendered subjectivities. They were simultaneously researchers and participants. My approach was different. Throughout this chapter, I sketch my novel adaption of the collective biography approach describing how I adapted the methods to be fitting to the group of women who were participating in my research. None of the women had been officially versed in feminist theory and most did not have tertiary level education due to their socio-economic disadvantage and pervasive poverty in their African countries of origin. The chapter provides useful insights into the ways in which the collective biography research approach can be adapted to be more fitting for women who live in impoverished settings and who are not versed in feminist academic discourse.

I begin this chapter by outlining the qualitative epistemological approach of my research along with a description of the African-centred feminist theory that has shaped this project and my choice of methodology. I discuss the processes and practices of my research commenting on the process of revisiting the data and issues around representation and researcher positionality. I then unpack this distinct methodology, which is longitudinal in its approach, collectively based, and which foregrounds my partnership and connections with the women. Such a methodology served the purpose of both practically facilitating spaces for women to negotiate new kinds of agency in their lives as well as providing rich research data through which I could access the women's stories and generate theory about the agentic processes that emerged. As I argue, the processes and interactional spaces of this research provided a powerful context within which the women could express certain 'unspeakable' aspects of their gendered experience. Such expressions provide valuable insight into the women's experience of the oppression of female sexuality and their resistance to harmful patriarchal discourses which underpin such violence. They drew on African-situated narratives to make sense of their experiences and co-narrate their identities. I conclude the chapter with discussion about how I made sense of the women's stories—both theoretically and analytically.

In what follows, I write about the specific lenses that I used to make sense of the women's stories and the methods which I utilised to access their voices. During this project, it was my aim to allow the women to create their own self-representations through creative and open-ended methods. My focus is on their voices and imaginings. An important part of this process was being aware of my presence in the research space and reflecting on the ways in which my presence may have influenced the women's stories. Below, and throughout the rest of the book I also comment on how the women's stories affected me. Through the tracing of the practices and processes of this work I put forward ideas about a 'new chapter' for gender research for the African continent.

Conceptualisations of Knowing: How Do We Know and Through What Means Can We Know?

My research which forms the substance of this book is based within a qualitative epistemological orientation which acknowledges that identities are multiple and shaped by different contexts (Parker 2005). Such an interpretive paradigm pays attention to the cultural and political contexts within which interaction is embedded and is focused on producing an account of the depth and complexity of experience as well as thick description of participants' worlds. Qualitative research has been found to be particularly useful for generating data that challenges static patriarchal stereotypes related to violence (Fox et al. 2007; Gill 2004; Harned 2005). So, for example, the methods allow for participants' expression of their own ideas and frameworks, and what often emerges is data that challenges patriarchal scripts of women as all-powerless victims and men as all-powerful perpetrators. Qualitative methods allow for the emergence of accounts of life and experience in its full complexity. Such an approach allows participants to engage in their own narratives in an uncensored way, providing new information and insights about relatively understudied groups of women (Bacchus et al. 2006). This approach allowed me to explore the different ways in which the women's subjectivities were narrated within the micro-context of the group sessions through a collaborative weaving, each thread of story connected to and connecting the last. A cornerstone of qualitative work is a focus on how meaning is generated through social interaction. Here researcher-participant subjectivities are acknowledged as being part of an intersubjective process that is central to the production of narrative. Certain kinds of narratives are produced and reproduced during research encounters with the researcher and the people who take part in the research. Attention to power as it manifests through the process of research and attention to the researcher's subjectivity in relation to the researched is therefore paramount. Below, I outline my feminist assumptions about power and research which has served as intellectual scaffolding for conceptualising my method and process. Further on in this chapter, I address the issue of researcher subjectivity and my own ways of knowing.

Feminist Methodologies: Power, Plurality, and Context

Many feminist scholars proclaim that they were born feminist, or have been following feminist philosophy from their childhood, years before they were officially educated about the language and principles of feminism. In her recent book *Reflecting Rogue: Inside the Mind of a Feminist*, Pumla Gqola (2017, p. 134) writes about discovering the word 'feminism' as a teenager

> I had been feminist/womanist since I could remember. But I had just discovered the word "feminist" and was in love with the knowledge that I and others could use it, and in its use we would be able to recognise shared worldviews and ways of living without saying another word. My chancing upon the *word* made me embrace it as a signal of a community of women who questioned.

I only properly engaged with the word 'feminism' when I encountered it during my undergraduate studies at university in my early twenties. Feminist theories gave voice to my experiences and intuitions about the world. Today, I am acutely aware of how the word 'feminism' is so often given negative connotations to serve patriarchal agendas and how too the word 'feminism' is so often simply ('innocently') misinterpreted due to a lack of knowledge. Many strands of feminism exist and feminism means different things to different people. Witnessing the misuse of the word, I have become serious in my work about providing detailed and context-specific definitions of the specific feminist theories that I draw on for my work.

The word 'feminism' has come to represent a vast array of politically conscious ways of thinking and doing, ways that strive to uncover unequal power imbalances and disrupt dominant patriarchal discourses which foster oppression and violence. Common of all strands of feminism is the emancipatory project seen through various forms of academic critique and political practice (Macleod and Durrheim 2002). Feminist work is important for challenging and destabilising hegemonic power structures, particularly when scholarly work is combined with activism as a political practice (Derickson and Routledge 2015). De Lauretis (1987) provides substance to the understanding of feminism that I draw on for this book. She defines feminism as, 'A critical reading of culture, a political interpretation of the social text and of the social subject, and a re-writing of our culture's master narratives' (De Lauretis 1987, p. 113).

How do we begin re-writing master narratives? One way is to work with 'fresh', previously hidden frames of meaning to build up new knowledge. Macleod and Durrheim (2002) state that 'Through the retrieval of subjugated knowledge one establishes a knowledge of resistance and struggle' (p. 54). One of the aims of this book is to document women's voices in such a way that provides material to contribute to the feminist aim of re-writing harmful and oppressive narratives. I wanted to document the women's voices in new ways that counteract the powerfully circulating discourses about abused foreigner women (e.g. as weak, passive, desperate). I believe that one of the core components of feminist research is that it should provide spaces for women to express their stories through their own frames of meaning in a context with which they are familiar and comfortable. For this project, I conducted research workshops in venues which the women's group were already using during their regular meetings. The women were thus used to sharing their intimate experiences in these spaces.

A second important aim of feminist research is to empower the individuals and groups that take part in the research. Doing research in the past, I have interviewed women that I have not met before, and most often never saw again. This left me with an unsettling feeling. I began to question what significance my research had for the lives of the storytellers. I wanted to engage with new avenues of knowledge production that promote actual change in participants' lives. The roots of an African-decolonised psychology are about opening space for individuals to construct their own self-representations using their own words, intuitions, and frames of reference. In other words, participants' views, ideas, and imaginings should not be stifled or shaped by dominant (Western) agendas and frameworks. To promote change through research, one needs to carve space for an African-gender perspective which takes the lived experiences of people on the African continent seriously without blurring these experiences through comparison or critique. Westernised scholarship often falls short in this regard.

Dominant European and North American feminist scholarship has been critiqued for providing interpretations of third world women's experiences that are shaped by Western discourses and knowledge systems, with an in-built bias towards privileging Western perspectives as the standard, or benchmark of 'reality' (see Mohanty 1991). International feminist literature has long been dominated by North American standpoints—points of view which theorise the common oppression of all women. South African feminist scholar Catriona Macleod calls this process of producing normativity 'exclusion through inclusion' (2006, p. 348) in that the use of the generic term 'woman' brushes over the complexities of other vectors of oppression and places the experience of some women (white; middle-class; North American-situated women) as the reality of all women. Such theorisation misses the mark in that it neglects a focus on other pertinent dimensions of women's lives which significantly shape the experience of inequality (Fish 2006; Pereira 2000).

It has been well argued that African women living in parts of Africa face oppressions that differ in texture to the oppressions faced by white women from first world countries. African feminism(s) needs to take seriously the ways in which women's inequality is tied in with nationalism, political struggles, and deep-rooted class oppressions (Pereira 2002). Gender oppression and violence for black women living in post-conflict countries is deeply intertwined with other problems such as joblessness, hopelessness, conflict, racism, and displacement. 'Gender oppression cannot be the single leg on which feminism rests', says Johnson-Odim (1991) in her contribution to the book *Third World Women and the Politics of Feminism*. In other words, the parameters of feminism need to be broadened. Further, the agenda and goals of women living in impoverished postcolonial societies are very different from women living in affluent societies in the West. As Johnson-Odim (1991, p. 320) states of the goals of feminists living in the third world,

> In "underdeveloped" societies it is not just a question of internal redistribution of resources, but of their generation and control; not just equal opportunity between women and men, but the creation of opportunity itself; not only the position of women in society, but the position of the societies in which third world women find themselves.

So, it should be clear that discourses from the West can never be well suited for understanding and responding to the complex challenges that women in post-conflict settings like South Africa face on a daily basis (see Macleod 2008).

In her critique of Jean Baker Miller's book *Towards a New Psychology of Women*, Macleod (2008) asks important questions about the book's relevance for understanding the experiences of women at different locations in the world outside of North American 'white' borders. She points to the fact that when race, class, and location are left untheorised, the result is nothing more than imperialism, representing the experiences of white middle-class North American women as the experiences of all women. Similarly, in her seminal work, *Under Western Eyes: Feminist Scholarship and Colonial Discourses*, Chandra Talpade Mohanty (1991) argues that when white women from the West write about third world women they often privilege their stance as the standard/educated/correct way of being. By doing so, they construct third world women as politically immature beings who need to be versed in Western feminism (Mohanty 1991). One of the most severe dangers of this is that the realities of many, many women are denied and, therefore, gender-liberatory work cannot progress. In response to critiques about the inadequacy of Western frameworks, some feminist scholars have shifted away from theorising the commonality of women's experiences of oppression and have attempted to incorporate theories which are based on women's diversity. However, 'diversity' is often taken to mean culture and women of the same culture are repeatedly 'lumped together' as if they are homogenous (Bohler-Muller 2002; Narayan 2000). This constitutes a kind of cultural essentialism, which is theoretically problematic.

It is inaccurate to depict Africa as a monolithic entity—people of Africa do not share the same attributes, culture, experiences, or ideas, and their different locations and social positions mean that African people experience varied restrictions on their lives (de Vos 2015). There is not one African culture, but rather a range of African cultures seen within different social landscapes in the North, East, West, and South of Africa. Women also differ with regards to their exposure to their culture of origin. For example, the experiences of refugees from Rwanda who have been living in South Africa for many years but may not be assimilated into the country's culture are very different from Xhosa South African women who are still in contact with their culture and family ties. Education level and socio-economic status are important factors which shape women's engagement with culture. Culture essentialism often results in discourses of the West being compared to the 'Other' culture, often situating African cultures as inferior or less civilised (Okin 2000; Sokoloff and Dupont 2005) or positioning Western governments as 'saviour' of African victims (de Vos 2015). The effect is that African women are situated as politically immature objects who are unable to negotiate agency on their own terms (Yuval-Davis 1997). These representations echo the effects of patriarchal discourses of abused women—women are stripped of their subjectivity and denied value. As I argued in Chap. 2, this is evident in academic (and other) discourses about women's position within the nexus of power related to patriarchal oppression of female sexuality.

Furthermore, patriarchy manifests in different ways in different contexts and we need to acknowledge that dominant definitions of patriarchy may be insufficient to understand the manifestations of patriarchy in poor settings in South Africa. Many black men in South Africa face severe poverty and unemployment combined with the continued effects of racism and degradation. We cannot theorise in any simple way about these men's patriarchal power in relation to women. Often abused women are the ones working and supporting their families while the abusive men are unemployed. This complicates the picture and these intersecting power dynamics create very particular manifestations of violence and control (van Schalkwyk et al. 2014). To understand gendered dynamics in this country, we need to take into consideration the relentless effects of colonialism and apartheid, xenophobia, and the trauma of poverty.

Macleod (2006) rightly argues for the need for a radical plural feminism that can function as productive intellectual activism in current post-apartheid South Africa. Such a plural feminism should, according to Macleod (2006), deconstruct the 'centre' while foregrounding marginalised voices; focus on social and historical conditions to understand discursive power and social transformation; and link micro-level and macro-level analysis. Such a plural feminism must serve the function of analysing gender within the 'patchwork of global patriarchies' (Macleod 2008, p. 348), and it must take seriously transversal relations of commonality around oppression and oppressive practices, rather than focusing on categories of people, or a unitary notion of gender identity. Such an approach necessarily requires detailed attention to the texture of women's experiences of oppression and the context within which the women under study live and have travelled through. Place (space), temporal moment, and individuality are important features of such an analysis.

Another central point developed in the literature is related to the notion of agency—how do women respond to gender-based violence and oppression in different contexts and how does this differ from the responses of women in first world countries? Macleod (2008) argues that Western technologies such as individual psychological self-improvement (therapy, self-help, individualised psychological approaches) are not suitable frameworks for understanding the ways in which many African women may cope with violence. Internal struggles may not always be the central priority for women living in African contexts.

Taking South Africa as a case in point, scholars have argued that many women adhere to cultural philosophies which are collective rather than individualistic, and which place value on social and community connections (see Mkhize 2004). Family is often a point of solidarity and during turbulent political times during and post-apartheid, women and men were and still are often united in their struggles for freedom (Macleod 2008). Many African women may respond to gender violence by drawing on their connections with others in their family and community spheres. The women whose stories are documented in this book are a powerful example; they formed a community group to come together and share stories of abuse and support each other through the challenges of daily life in South Africa. In the chapters that follow, I argue that this collective contributed powerfully shaping the agentic strategies which the women could make use of in their tellings. Any analysis of agency in this context needs to take collective processes and worldviews into consideration. In developing methodologies which aim to elicit insights into the lived experience and psychological realities of women in Africa, we need to seriously consider intersubjective meaning making within the research space and beyond it.

Representation

South African feminist Pumla Gqola says that we need to 'constantly puncture the farce of patriarchal narrative's lies that women are free in South Africa' (2017, p. 39). To do this we as feminists need to begin to focus on promoting powerful ways of truth-telling, allowing women's experiences to be heard. Women's anger, rage, and pain need to be heard without trying to modify these emotions. One way of doing this is through feminist research that attends to foregrounding women's voices and ideas and which integrates the academic project with activism—research with a social justice agenda. This is about walking a tightrope of challenging patriarchal power in all its forms and facets, while constantly being aware of the ways that we, as researchers and activists may inadvertently reinforce such imbalances of power through representations labelled objective science. Representations are always subjective and biased, if we ignore this we ignore the power dynamics which are infused in research. We need to be sensitive and in tune with these power dynamics and the role that we, as researchers, may implicitly play in reinforcing harmful narratives. The goal of African-centred feminist work needs to be about generating representations which stand as alternatives to those entrenched socially and culturally by the colonialist patriarchal system.

Representation does not imply a search for an absolute 'truth' about the experiences of the women we write about. Rather, as Macleod (2006) contends, we should recognise representation as a process 'in which the discourses invoked by the intellectual and those invoked by the women in question meet, challenge, dovetail, diverge, and generally construct new, hybrid understandings' (p. 383). The story that we are telling through the analysis is but one of many possible interpretations (Fraser 2004).

Importantly, the stories that we tell as researchers, our analytical insights and conclusions, reflect our story as a person. Sometimes our interest in a given topic shifts and changes over time. So, as researchers, instead of trying to represent 'truth' we must acknowledge that there are multiple possibilities of representing data and our subjectivities as researchers influence how we will go about making sense of participants' worlds. What is important here is that researchers must examine the ways in which their personal history and biases influence the ways in which they represent others. Context needs to be given about how the project and the data originated. We must provide the reader with an understanding of our perspectives and how they have framed the sense that we make of participants' voices (Sjoberg and Nett 1968).

When engaging with the women's voices and writing up my findings for the first time I experienced resistance. I struggled to write about these stories. My mentor shed light on what was happening. I was fearful about writing about these women because I was constantly aware of how I was representing them, and I did not want to do so in a way that is damaging or harmful. I wanted to represent them in the 'right' way, as 'good' people. Due to my close involvement with the members, I had begun to know them as friends and confidantes and I was hyper-sensitive of all the many roads of betrayal that I could inadvertently travel through the very way that I wrote about the women. A feminist agenda demands that women's raw feelings and insights are given priority—sometimes even leading into taboo topics. In retrospect, my sensitivities became more pronounced when the topics of sex and sexuality were emerging as central themes of the women's stories. Was my representation of their stories of sexuality fair? What perspective of these women is cultivated in readers' minds when I represent them as sexually desiring subjects? What agenda could my interpretation drive on the part of readers? Had I overestimated the ways in which women are confined by culture, or had I underestimated this? My worry about how I was representing the women (although not conscious at the time) stemmed from my awareness that my experience as white, middle-class, South African woman whose privilege and difference stand as blinkers to understanding other worldviews, may have shaped my interpretation of the women's narratives in unproductive ways. My resistance to engage with the stories in an in-depth way was shaped by dominant Western discourses which connote the dangers of female sexuality—I automatically interpreted this as dangerous territory. My writing process became easier when I acknowledged my own perspectives and shortcomings as sources of data which can be engaged in meaningful ways.

Knowing Through Reflexive Self-Examination

Reflexivity has long been recognised as a key feature of qualitative research (Mauthner et al. 1998). This is true across different social science disciplines. The practice of reflexivity begins with an acknowledgement of the ways in which different positions of power shape research. Researchers need to reflect on how their subjectivity may have shaped the processes of the research, the production of narratives as well as their representation of this knowledge. Wright and Nelson (1995, p. 48) provide a useful definition of reflexivity as the following:

> A process of continuously moving from the intensely personal experiences of one's own social interactions in the field, to the more distanced analysis of that experience for an understanding of how identities are negotiated, and how social categories, boundaries, hierarchies and processes of domination are experienced and maintained.

As a budding student of qualitative research, one often draws on the concept of reflexivity without really knowing what it means. We insert the term into our essays or dissertations just because it must be there, and we 'throw in' the concepts of race, class, and gender while making weak comments about our privilege in relation to the people that we study. Sometimes sameness is overemphasised. At other times, difference is treated apologetically or cautiously. Often such reflections turn into guilt-ridden confessions about the intellectual's positioning vis-à-vis research subjects (Macleod 2006).

Mauthner and Doucet (2003) highlight the importance of extending one's definition of reflexivity, towards a fuller conceptualisation which moves beyond examining one's social position. We need to do more than merely reflect on sameness and difference in relation to participants based on social positions such as race, class, gender, and sexuality. We need to document the processes of the research and our accompanying emotions. Mauthner and Doucet (2003) argue for the importance of documenting the process through which we transform people's narratives into social science theory. In other words, they argue that we should pay more attention to reflexivity during the actual process of interpreting the data and the final write up of the resulting text—how do we read the narratives and in what ways do we write the narratives? This is about acknowledging our own subjectivity in how we analyse data and write up the final product. Within social science research there is general consensus that data analysis is a reflexive exercise through which meaning is not found, but made by the researcher, and this process of interpretation is shaped by our personal history and the analytical blinkers that we bring into these processes. Interpersonal and institutional contexts as well as ontological and epistemological assumptions embedded in data analysis methods all deeply influence how research is conducted and what sense the researcher makes of the data (Mauthner and Doucet 2003). Reflexivity should be something that one feels deeply; it should unsettle, disturb and astound, sometimes all at the same time. Reflexivity practised with effort produces knowledge. Researchers' experiences during the process of conducting the research and analysing the data are essential elements of the research (Mauthner et al. 1998). The experience of practising a reflexive gaze, or 'turning inwards' towards an analysis of one's own emotional and social landscapes (both during and after the research) is something entirely different to what most qualitative research textbooks offer, or at least the ones that I studied.

Researchers and participants are intricately connected emotionally. These connections shape the results of the project in many ways. Melucci (1995) says that we should not assume that narrative adequately reveals the meaning of an action beyond the relationship with the researcher in the context within which the research is produced. He says that if attention is not paid to the conditions of the production of a text, and to the ways in which researchers receive and interpret others' narratives, then we are merely practising a new kind of objectivity under the guise of 'subjective sources'. In collective work such as the research on which this book is based, researchers immerse themselves in the field inevitably becoming part of the community and are present at each stage of the 'discursive constitution work' of research (Davies et al. 2006c, p. 89). From such an approach, studying collective identity necessarily means redefining the relationship between researcher and researched because, 'we are not dealing with a thing, but with a process continually activated by social actors' (Melucci 1995, p. 62). Here Melucci implies that we cannot assume that we are studying a distinctive 'reality' of a given community, rather we are studying reality as it is constructed via circular interaction between us (the researchers) and the research participants. The conditions of the research and researcher subjectivity need to be made explicit during the write up of the research (Mauthner and Doucet 2003). Most researchers do not take up this task in any serious way.

Many questions remain about the appropriateness of white/Western/educated women conducting research on other women's complex emotional journeys when they do not share the same cultural experiences and knowledge with the women they study. Is it ever justified for women to explore cultures that they hardly know anything about? I believe it is when the qualitative researcher makes a commitment to document their stance and meaning-making processes. In other words, research on the 'other' is of value if the researcher confronts their subjectivity and the role they played in the production of data—albeit with the acknowledgement that we may never really know what it is we are seeking. Research is about more than trust and power—psychoanalytically we bring to the research fictions and fantasies which play out in different ways in our relations with others (Walshaw 2010). Such reflections constitute new knowledge in itself.

When reviewing previous drafts of my work, a colleague commented that they wanted to know more about my experience as researcher. She encouraged me to more deeply consider moments at which my own presence and identity impacted on the data itself. She made a call for me to process more concretely how my identities and relative privilege in relation to the participants may have influenced the ways in which participants narrated their intimate memories and what they were willing to disclose. She also made a call for me to include how the data impacted me. These two points significantly changed my thinking about my work and I felt called to enrich my work in this way. Throughout this book, I have tried to go further, to engage in meaningful reflexivity, in deeper self-reflection that will provide better insight into my own interiority, as researcher, and the way that it relates to the processes and practices of my research. I pay close attention to my subjectivity and the conditions through which the data and writing were produced.

I am a white, middle-class, heterosexual woman who at the time of the research was in a monogamous heterosexual partnership with no children. I was also at least five years younger than many of the women participants and I had lived my whole life in South Africa and had never visited or travelled through other African countries. I noticed that my education level (PhD) was one of the main markers which stood out for the women, as they often commented on my education and my affiliations with the university system. In this respect, I was in a position of power in relation to the women. I was more knowledgeable about research, psychology, and feminist theory, but in many respects the participants were the most knowledgeable—about Africa, travelling through Africa, and the unique experience of living as a foreigner in South Africa. They were truly the experts. In many respects I was the unknowing 'other'—a position which came through at various moments during our engagements, when the women participants did not position me as an outsider or insider, but rather positioned me as neutral observer, perhaps somewhere in between. Throughout the three empirical chapters that follow, I comment on three dominant threads which encompass this positioning to shed light on my subjectivity as researcher. I comment very briefly on this intersubjective reflection here before unpacking it in the following chapters of the book.

At the beginning of my research with the women I disclosed that I had been a victim of childhood sexual abuse and I narrated how this influenced my sexual subjectivity later in life. My narration did not, however, result in the women engaging with me as an insider with shared experiences of abuse (as I had expected). Rather, I felt that the women continued to explain their experiences to me, as to an observer. I felt that I took on more of a questioning role during the narratives of mubobobo when the women disclosed aspects of their sexual subjectivities and experiences. I was not situated 'within' the conversation as participant. During the women's narrations of their travel through African countries and border posts my privilege became more pronounced—I had never had to travel in this way and I knew nothing of the experiences of desperation while in transit. My race and socio-economic status came to the fore—this actually allowed the women to use strategic silences and to tell their stories in the way that they chose (because I knew nothing about transit). Thirdly, during the foreigner women's narratives of South African women as lazy and sexually promiscuous/immoral, I was not included in the descriptions, even though I am South African. This is another example of how the women participants positioned me in another space, not as insider or outsider. It seemed as if the women did not imagine me as a South African female 'other', perhaps due to my whiteness and my socio-economic status. In reflecting back on my initial writing, I realise that the women's constructions of South African women triggered certain emotions for me, my South African identity came to the fore, and I subtly engaged in defending black South African women in my writing. I reflect further on this in Chap. 6.

In a way, my reflection on my subjectivity signals my agency to respond in ways that can enhance the impact of my research. How does it enhance the impact?—by providing a new layer of reciprocal analysis to the work, and by providing information which connects the researcher and the researched and provides the reader with crucial insights into the production of the data. Such a layer provides fresh perspectives to the field of feminist research methods. Throughout the book I enhance these two threads above. Where relevant and at important analytical moments, I stop and reflect on the ways in which my presence could have influenced the ways the women told their stories. At other moments I write about some of my feelings throughout the process—my emotional states both during the data gathering and my engagements with the women's stories in the 'here and now' of my writing up. These two threads—how my presence influenced the data and how the data impacted on me—are offered as an additional layer to the women's stories and my interpretation of these voices.

Personally, I do not find such introspection an easy task. I strove to engage in this practice because of deep respect for the academic who made the comments and because of my own intuition that something was missing in my writing up. Living as a white South African who grew up in a relatively privileged middle-class family I feel deep shame for my privilege that afforded me comfort and education. I also experience my difference from the women in a visceral way. I have lived in South Africa my whole life. I did not have to travel through Africa in desperation facing danger and violation. I do not have children to support. All these factors coalesce to form my deep-rooted sense of responsibility to the women who took part in my research. I felt this from the moment I entered the first intimate truth-telling spaces of the research. Perhaps my discomfort in voicing more of my interior during my first phase of writing is the feeling that the more of my own subjectivity I divulge, the more human I will appear, and the more human I appear, the less I feel myself to be a capable researcher. Perhaps this is the intellectual hangover from always being taught through undergraduate school that quantitative work with strict objectivity is the only 'proper' research. Perhaps these lingering ideas about what constitutes intellectual work have affected many a researcher's capacity to engage in meaningful reflexivity?

Or, perhaps the difficulty with engaging in introspection arises because being open and honest about one's subjectivity as researcher may highlight scenarios or sites at which the research did not go smoothly or as planned. This can be unsettling as it 'speaks' to the reality of the messiness and complexity of research (that we do not want to acknowledge during funding or ethics applications or even in the final write up). One especially vivid memory for me of such a case was when I was confronted by the group leader, Lynn, in a scheduled meeting with other women present. I had been doing work with the women for a few months and had established good relationships and a sense of identity as affiliated with the group. It seemed as if the women had accepted me as a member of the group. Lynn had read a published paper that I had written on women's experience of gendered abuse and leaving abusive men. She was under the impression that the paper was based on the work that I had done with the women's group (as it was based on a similar topic) and confronted me about why I had not acknowledged the group in the written work. I had to explain that this was work that I had done with different women and that the paper was written before I had begun working with the group. The experience left me feeling unsettled. I felt like I was being unnecessarily attacked—what I now realise was my own fear related to the difficulties of establishing a trusting research relationship. I also realised that the women had their own fears about researchers coming in and using their narratives for their own gain. Such experiences fuelled my sensitivities about the research relationship and resulted in my initial phases of writing being careful and cautious. During the process of re-writing this book, I revisited the data to gain a less inhibited, more in-depth perspective.

Revisiting the Data

Qualitative researchers have long put forward the claim that interpretations are provisional and that different researchers will provide very different readings of the same data-set. This is also true for a researcher who revisits the same data-set at different moments of their lives. Researchers are prepared to know some things and not others at the moment of analysis, and this preparedness to know, or understand, changes over time. This means that analyses are always incomplete and partial (Rosaldo 1989, p. 8, as cited in Andrews 2008, p. 86). We all bring with us our own personal experiences which serve as a framework that influences the way in which we make sense of participants' narratives. Life is ever-changing and our frameworks for our sense-making change as our experience evolves (Andrews 2008). As Andrews (2008, p. 86) asserts,

> New experiences, and new understandings of old experiences, bring with them a new perspective not only on our own lives—our present as well as our pasts—but on the way in which we make sense of the lives of others.

Mauthner et al. (1998) highlight that looking back at one's original data analysis after a period of time provides one with important perspectives about areas one may have emphasised and other areas one may have neglected—this is evident when we realise that we could 'flesh out' a particular theme, but also when we realise that we have almost completely neglected a theme while prioritising something else. For the writing of this book, I returned to the research transcripts three years after my initial reading of the women's voices. I immersed myself in the written and spoken versions of the women's voices. This process of revisiting the data after some time provided me with other layers of meaning and a rich, complex multi-dimensional analysis.

Time has eased the way for me with these narratives. During the writing of this book, distance provided me the ability to revisit the voices and to write from a level of increased depth and intensity. Indeed, scholars have argued that revisiting data provides us with multiple rich viewpoints (see Andrews 2008). Reflexivity needs to incorporate the passage of time, as time continually mediates the ways in which we think about a research topic and our understandings of specific research questions (Doucet 2008). The influences on our choices and interpretations may only be apparent to us over time after we have moved out of the research space (Mauthner and Doucet 2003). I think that this method brings with it greater integrity and does narratives more justice, because it somehow feels more organic, flowing and honest.

Documenting Collective Voices of Trauma and Transition

My research draws on a series of workshops and group discussions conducted over a period of one year with the support group for abused African migrant and refugee women who are living in South Africa. The support group ran with the aim to strengthen, develop, and empower destitute and abused women by helping them become agents and gain their rightful place in South African society. The group aimed to provide spaces for women to network and tell their stories of abuse. Members included women from various parts of Africa; including Zimbabwe, Congo, Rwanda, Kenya, and South Africa. Most resided in low-income rental housing in poor suburbs in Cape Town, lower Woodstock and Salt River, an area which is situated between the Table Bay docks and the lower slopes of Devil's peak, which is affected by high levels of poverty, crime and drug abuse. Some group members lived in coloured and black townships in surrounding areas of the Western Cape. These include black townships in the areas Strand, Belhar, and Langa.

I had been doing volunteer work with the organisation for over a year prior to the data gathering. The insight that I gained from this prior involvement with the group meant that I could identify individuals who were interested in being involved in the research. My volunteer work with the group also provided me with useful insights about the workings of the group and the relationships between group members. 'Ma Wendy',[1] for example, was an older woman from Congo who served as the 'mother' of the group and who grounded the meetings in some way with her presence and her strong resolve to stand up for her rights as a woman. She encouraged the younger women through a firm and heartfelt validation of their experiences.

The research was carried out in different areas of the Western Cape; including the southern suburbs; the Cape Town black townships; and townships in the Helderberg area about 50 kilometres from the main central business district. In December 2010, a colleague invited me to a

[1] This name is a pseudonym, as are all the other participants' names documented in this book. The decision to use pseudonyms was made to ensure participants' rights to confidentiality and anonymity.

workshop in Woodstock, Cape Town. She had invited me as she knew of my interest in the field and my drive to do work with women who have experienced violence at the hands of an intimate male partner. At the workshop I sat and listened to the founder speak so beautifully and powerfully about women's strength and rights. What really struck me was her statement about the vision of the women's group. Here these women were with very limited funds and no support from the South African government, but they were dedicated to make the group thrive. This was a grassroots initiative that I knew would contribute brilliantly in the fight against such violence: it seemed to me that the group was already providing a much-needed platform for women to give voice to their experiences and they received acknowledgement from others during these tellings. In the context of limited social services for abused women and in the tide of racist, classist and xenophobic discourses in South Africa, this women's group functioned as a unique space of expression and engagement.

Participants

The women who took part in this study all self-disclosed as having experienced violence at the hands of an intimate male partner and other forms of gender-based violence. All the women came from disadvantaged backgrounds characterised by extreme poverty. They had all travelled from their home countries in Africa to South Africa and had been living in the country for an average of five years at the time of the research. Their current social location in South Africa was one in which they experienced the realities of social deprivation and unemployment combined with continued gender violence, racism, and xenophobia.

Apart from their shared experience of group membership as well as their shared experiences of abuse and foreigner status in South Africa, the women were from various cultures and African countries of origin. The term 'shared experience' as I use it in this book refers to the women's experiences of being part of the support group and their shared experience of gender-based abuses. As Israel et al. (1998) state, the term 'community' need not refer only to a geographically set out area but could also refer to a community of individuals who are part of an ethnically diverse group and who may share common identification, emotional connection, and common values—as is the case with this sample of women.

I utilised a convenience sampling approach (see Adames and Campbell 2005) with some use of snowball sampling when the core members introduced me to other members over time. During my time working with the women many new members came to try out the workshops and many became regular attendees of the group. The women's interest showed the need for such work in this context. It was rewarding hearing a new member tell her story. To witness women disclosing aspects of their gendered experience honestly and openly is so rare, because there are so few safe spaces for such disclosures. My previous research stimulated my awareness of the pressing need for such community-level sources of support for women living in South Africa.

My inclusion criteria for participants was that the women self-identified as members of the group (whether their attendance at the group's meeting were regular or not) and that they had experienced some form of gender violence in their lifetime. I did not initially set out to explore psychological violence associated with the oppression of female sexuality, this emerged organically and powerfully through the open-ended methods.

In total there were six women who took part in the selected group discussions which are documented in this book. Their ages ranged from 26 to 54 years. All the women had at least one child at the time of the research. All identified as heterosexual. Each woman did not attend every workshop or focus group session. This was based on their availability, which was often a challenge as many of the women were called for part-time jobs on the weekend. They had to earn money for their families. It would not have been ethical for me to expect the women to place the workshops before an opportunity to earn money for their families.

Data Gathering Aims

I find it disturbing that much feminist work from Europe and North America has resulted in cultural imperialism and further oppression of women who take part in research. Much research benefits the researcher while there are no benefits to individuals and communities. During my research I wanted to adopt an approach that would contribute in some way to addressing these issues. In line with the feminist concerns documented above, I aimed to conduct research that respects the validity of indigenous cultural knowledges. I wanted to engage in representations that do not merely replicate dominant patriarchal discourses. I wanted an approach that would help me explore women's collective voices, allowing for their own frames of meaning to emerge and evolve.

Women, and particularly disadvantaged foreigner women, have largely not been given a voice in mainstream psychological research: The methods adopted here aim to counter these restrictions, focusing on the women's intuitions, imaginations and the concerns central to their current existence. In line with an African-gender perspective (see van Schalkwyk and Gobodo-Madikizela 2015), I wanted to place the women in the centre of their own worlds, opening space for them to create and narrate their own self-representations that were not shaped by me, the researcher. The research spaces were naturalistic sites, similar to the spaces at which they gathered through their support group work, and therefore provided women with a comfortable and non-coercive context within which they could express their own concerns and frames of meaning.

Traditional qualitative methods such as individual interviews conducted with someone one has just met fall short in terms of their capacity to really capture the essence and complexity of participants' emotional and experiential worlds. Seidman (2006) says that interviewers who propose to study their interviewee's experiences by arranging a once-off fleeting interview 'tread on thin contextual ice' (p. 17). Such brief interactions lack context (focusing on decontextualised 'snapshots' of talk) and they do not provide fertile ground for the development of rapport between researcher and informant. Individual interviews do not allow for the development of meaning over time or the interviewer and interviewee's longitudinal reflections about the meaning of these experiences. How can we expect someone that we hardly know to divulge intimate aspects of their personal life and trauma? And, what kind of stories can we expect as a result? A person cannot begin to make sense of their trauma in one or two sessions—there needs to be time and space for 'digging out', analysing, and interpreting one's feelings and emotions. Often the interview questions shape participants' answers in ways that inhibit their own meanings from emerging and decontextualise their talk (Kitzinger and Barbour 1999).

During my previous work I have often felt unsettled doing research with women who I have mostly not met before the interview and who I will most often not meet again afterwards. What significance did my research have for these women's lives? In what ways was I upholding feminist aims? I wanted to conduct research that would 'give back' to the community of study in the form of actual change—through practical workshops which may prompt psychological healing/transformation. I wanted to establish long-term connections with the people who take part in the research, gaining all-round knowledge of the texture of their lives. It was my aim to capture the complexities of women's voices that I have witnessed during my years of volunteer work with women who have experienced gender violence and abuse.

Another problem with individual interviews is that they do not capture the collective dimension of meaning making. I wanted to adopt methods that would allow me to explore the ways in which women make meaning together through dialogue. I wanted to capture the collective texture of this talk and theorise about the potentials for agency within such a support group setting. Such an approach is more fitting with African-based views of the collectivist dynamic of identity construction—identity is most energetically forged through relational dynamics with community and family (Mkhize 2004).

I needed a methodological approach that would move beyond the limitations of conventional qualitative research—a unique methodology that would help me achieve these aims. In what follows, I unpack this distinct methodology, collective biography, which is longitudinal in its approach; collectively based; and which foregrounds my partnership and connections with the women. Such a methodology served a twofold purpose. Firstly, the collective research spaces (workshops and focus group interviews) provided rich data allowing me to theorise about the psychological processes at play and women's agentic strategies which emerged through their shared narratives. Secondly, the research facilitated practical spaces for change—spaces through which the women could negotiate new kinds of agency in their lives and narrate positive social identities. Through their talk they negotiated different realities for themselves and slowly broke away from the confines of patriarchal restrictions. Scholars have argued that such narratives have material implications for women's lives as the effects of narrating positive selves extends beyond the moment of telling, into the individual worlds beyond the research (Davies and Gannon 2006; Gavey 2005). The workshops and focus group research sessions were sites of actual change where the women were able to voice aspects of their subjectivities that they had not been able to voice before. Lynn, for example, speaks about how these collective sessions provided her with space to express previously silenced aspects of her gendered experience:

> **Lynn:** For me how I deal with it is okay talking about it in this space that is helping me, I am offloading ... you see the most important the most really big part in this is for me what happened in my childhood it never featured anywhere in my life at all until the time that we start to talk about it.
>
> (Focus group discussion 1)

Transformation Through Dialogue: The Collective Biography Methodology

For this study, I utilised a dynamic and creative methodology called collective biography drawn from theoretical insights offered by feminist poststructuralist scholars Davies and Gannon in their book *Doing Collective Biography* (2006). Collective biography is a postmodern methodology that encompasses epistemological assumptions and methods of memory-work research. Memory work is a social constructionist method that works with visual imagery (such as photographs) to stimulate the process of remembering. Annette Kuhn, a leading scholar in this field, describes memory work as 'an active process of remembering which takes an inquiring attitude towards the past and the activity of its (re)construction through memory' (2000, p. 186). The 'active' component of this work involves using images to reflect on one's past and to reprocess this past through one's current perspective.

Collective biography draws on feminist poststructuralist theories of agency and identity and is a useful methodology for recovering the past through creative ways and gaining knowledge about how this past is shaped by broader discursive structures within which narratives memories are situated (Cowman 2012). Such work is well suited for studying the collective, or intersubjective, dimension of meaning making (Stephenson 2001). The epistemological assumptions of the collective biography approach aided me in conceptualising relational selves and how I could go about studying such selves within the dynamics of these workshops. Collective biography focuses on understanding the *process* of constructing a self (Davies and Gannon 2006). Participants' stories no longer signify individual identities but are interpreted through the lens of a collective process, which makes visible the ways in which their understanding of their lived experience is discursively constituted (Davies and Gannon 2006). Selves are constituted in concert with others through the taking up and resisting of certain discourses (Davies et al. 2006b, p. 87). Thus, this dynamic methodological approach provides the means to explore the links between the individual and the social. I could explore how the women made sense of their gendered experiences *together* and how, through collective dialogue, they situated their experiences in relation to others' stories and in relation to broader social discourses, making meaning through the social and cultural 'threads' available to them.

According to Davies and Gannon (2006), such collective processes result in some level of transformation—a movement away from the restriction of dominant patriarchal discourses—a flight, during which one unmoors themselves from hegemonic discourses and takes up alternative discourses which provide new, more positive ways, of understanding oneself as a gendered being. Part of this process of transformation is listening to others' stories in the collective setting and, by doing so, gaining a bird's eye view of the unequal power dynamics infused in one's gendered experiences. Such engagement often leads to a shattering of certain commonsense notions about the world and, as Maria Tamboukou (2008) states, facilitates a process of 'detaching' from socially constructed 'truths' and discovering alternative ways of understanding one's existence. This capacity to transcend harmful patriarchal understandings and re-imagine oneself is central to Davies' (2000) notion of agency that I draw on in this book (outlined in Chap. 2). I unpack such strategies in the chapters that follow. Below I turn to my practical implementation of the collective biography methods.

Two-Phase Data Gathering Approach: Workshops and Group Discussions

As discussed above, I adapted methods drawn from the core principles of collective biography methodology outlined by the work of Bronwyn Davies and Susan Gannon. This method was first used to explore the gendered experiences of academics. The researchers conducted workshops with a group of academics using art and narrative to get their ideas flowing about their past experiences as gendered beings. The participants/researchers then drew on the workshop themes as a starting point for a collaborative writing process. They used feminist poststructuralist theory to analyse experience and to explore what selves emerged through this collective writing process. This was the way in which collective biography was initially used. However, scholars in the field suggest that these methods should be adapted and reinvented in ways that suit the specific group that is taking part in the research. For my research I drew on the collective biography guidelines offered by Davies and colleagues, while adapting the methods to suit the specific group of women involved. These women were economically disadvantaged women who have not been versed in the academic discourses of feminism or feminist poststructuralist theory. One of the core ways in which I adapted this methodology was that instead of collaborative writing processes, we engaged in processes of collective talk which functioned as the preliminary analysis. Creative workshops were conducted in phase one of the research. I then analysed major themes from these workshops and took the themes back to the women in phase two of the research (the group discussions) for further analysis through collective conversations.

My work is founded on the epistemology of emergence and the collective development of voices over time throughout the research process. It is important to comment here on the differences between collective biography research and participatory action research, as some of the central tenets of these approaches overlap—namely, the focus on collective inquiry and exploration of participants' social history. Participatory research privileges a community's knowledge but is still often driven by the goals and frameworks of the researcher. Often participatory researchers enter communities with the aim of improving communities' systems and knowledge. Researchers who adopt collective biography methods, on the other hand, immerse themselves in the community of study, becoming part of the emerging group processes. Participatory approaches posit that we should enrich the community's already existing strategies, while collective biography creates new strategies within the very moments of collective work (see Davies and Gannon 2006).

There were two distinct phases of data gathering. Phase one comprised of four interactive workshops with core members of the women's support group; these were followed by a series of smaller focus group discussions which comprised the second phase of the research. This two-phase method is common of the collective biography approach (Davies and Gannon 2006). The data gathering took place over a one-year period. Such a longitudinal methodology allowed the women to 'grow' into the space and become familiar with each other's stories and characters. Intimate memories were shared. Connections were created among the women. The spaces promoted women's deep reflection on their gendered experiences. The initial workshops and subsequent focus group discussions were not structured according to any pre-set questions. Rather, the women were given an opportunity to openly explore the themes through stories of their life experience and what was meaningful for them. Their meanings and imaginings were expressed in a naturalistic setting (as an extension of the workshops that were already being held with the group). All the women took part in several research sessions over the year-long period of data gathering.

Their involvement over time meant that I could piece together parts of their stories across sessions and theorise about individual life trajectory. This was further complemented by the fact that I had worked with the women for a significant period before the data gathering and had background contextual knowledge about each woman's life. I could piece together threads of experience as they connected it to different temporal moments and geographical spaces of their lives.

At the beginning of each workshop, I reiterated to the participants what the research was about and why it was important, and I asked them to sign a consent form. With permission from the women, the workshops were audiotaped with the use of digital Dictaphone. Two group members, Chadamwari and Akeyo, acted as co-facilitators of the workshops, assisting me with carrying out the workshop activities and in translating some sections of talk. Free counselling sessions were made available for the women during this time at the Saartjie Baartman Women's Centre and the Family and Marriage Association of South Africa (FAMSA) in Cape Town.

The workshops were based on themes of gender-based violence and utilised participatory methods. The first three workshops took place at the church hall. During the first workshop, I engaged in my own story about an experience of emotional abuse that I had witnessed in my circle of friends. This story had been sitting with me after witnessing an episode whereby my friend's male partner was abusing her severely emotionally and controlling her movements. I could not understand why the unequal power dynamics of the relationships were not visible to her. I could not understand why she did not break the ties with this abusive man. I felt in turmoil. I had knowledge that could potentially help this friend, but I could not communicate this to her. She was not ready to receive the knowledge. Through sharing my personal story and emotions I invited women to engage with my story, opening space for their perspectives and an opportunity for them to connect their own life experience to parts of the story. I then asked the participants to reflect on my story and to relate the scenario to their own witnessing and experiences. A rich discussion commenced taking as the starting point the unequal power dynamics between women and men that were, for all of us, powerfully visible in my narrative. I realised as the women began to speak that my story stood as an archetype for many stories which the women held, by identifying the similar points and repeating trends we were engaging in an analysis and critique of the patriarchal system, although we did not explicitly call it this.

In the second workshop I made use of images, a method in line with the memory-work approach (see Kuhn 2000). I presented a variety of images of women and girls in various scenarios, ranging from overtly abusive images to images which could be interpreted in different ways. One depicted a man with his hand raised in the air, about to hit a woman who crouched over and tried to protect the back of her head with her hands. Other photos conveyed more subtle but powerful meanings. Lynn was drawn to a captioned photograph of a young girl in remote western Sudan who had been captured and branded on the arm by Janjaweed militia. She is dressed in flowing garments hiding her body save for the mark on her upper arm. Her eyes have a hollow and distant stare. A third was of two young girls smiling and content standing under a tree. Some images were of distorted figures or shadows of human beings, and thus could be interpreted in multiple ways. Participants were given time to reflect on the images. I then asked them to comment on the relevance of the image to their own lives. When engaging with the visual texts, Akeyo voiced the following:

> **Akeyo:** (The images) remind me of the lives of refugees here in this country South Africa, because that's where I have been so far, and it just made me think how the people suffer to simply get a life.
>
> (Collective biography workshop 2)

Chadamwari picked up a black and white photograph of a woman crying holding her face in her hands. She says,

> **Chadamwari:** It reminds me of all the things that women go through and most of the times they will be alone, and they resort to crying and just weeping because they have a lot of issues that might be going on in their lives but then they don't have anyone to talk to. They don't have people supporting them or helping them. Or they don't even know where to go. Most of the time this is abuse from their partners or abuse from their family or any other abuse that they go through, and then they don't know who to go to, who to tell or what to do and then they end up just sitting there and crying with most of the time no one to tell.
>
> (Collective biography workshop 2)

A central thread of the collective narrative which the women developed through their emotional engagement with the images was men occupying what they termed 'the main chair' and a sense of the injustice that men have the privilege of doing what they want while women are restricted in so many ways. They engaged in a collective analysis of the unequal power dynamics infused in their own lives and how they experience these power dynamics as African women.

> **Chadamwari:** I also thought of something that just came up also our culture (Shona, Zimbabwe) doesn't encourage openness and uh expression of views for women. We are not supposed to say how we feel about a thing or whatever. We are not supposed to do that. You are just supposed to go on with what you supposed to do... It's also our culture and many other African cultures they don't have rights, the women don't have rights. They have little rights, or they don't have rights at all. So, you just go on with what you are supposed to do. You know already what you are told to do. If you are supposed to go on and get married. If you are supposed to do the chores or whatever.
>
> (Collective biography workshop 2)

The third workshop was centred around drama. Participants were divided into small groups and asked to come up with a short play related to their experiences of gender or things that they had witnessed in the world. The women then acted out the short skits. Each skit was followed by a reflection section. During the second half of the workshop we engaged in a larger group discussion based on our feelings and responses to the plays. Pratt (2004) says that role-plays are a powerful means of producing data that transcend the limits of traditional qualitative research convention. In her words, role-plays 'encourage flights of fantasy and are attuned not simply to documenting existing patterns of exploitation and social inequality, but to transforming them' (Pratt 2004, p. 10). Through role-play, women have access to an imaginary space and can engage with previous aspects of their experience which may be difficult to put into words.

During the fourth collective biography workshop, which was held in a small container[2] in a black township in the Helderberg, participants were presented with short vignettes about different violence against women scenarios. They engaged with the vignette in small groups. Discussion was stimulated via an analysis wheel with the following questions: What did you see? What do you think of this scenario? What did you feel? What could we/the community do in response to this abuse? After the feedback exercise we moved into a group storytelling session during which the

[2] The 'container' refers to a shipping container commonly used on the peripheries of townships in South Africa as schools or meeting venues.

women had a chance to narrate experiences that were most important to them.

As the workshops progressed, I became aware of the depth and multitude of abuses that the women had suffered throughout their lives at the hands of different men. They broke the entrenched silence surrounding much of their gendered experiences. The women's narratives were textured by shame and anger, and a sense of injustice that across their different African cultures men were deemed superior to women and men were 'allowed' to get away with harsh violations of women's bodies and spirits. The workshop activities—role-plays, dramas, dialogues—created spaces through which the women could engage with their gendered trauma on different levels, expressing meaning in creative ways. The space for creativity which these sessions opened up was paramount for setting the tone, allowing access to the women's unconstrained voices which provided me with rich insight into the women's lived realities. The open-ended and creative (unstructured) methods of data gathering allowed the women to talk in ways that they wanted about what they wanted; the women were able to take up the position of authority of their lives and realities. This notion of authority is a central aspect of Davies' (1990) concept of agency that I draw on in this book.

The workshop activities created what Munt calls 'landmarks' of recognition—sites at which the women recognised and identified with parts of other women's narratives. Listening to others' stories of their gendered experiences mobilised a critical awareness among participants as they caught a glimpse of the texture and 'truth' of their own gendered experiences, allowing them to engage with their own memories in different ways from what they had done before. The role-plays and dramas were scenarios that were 'invented' by the women themselves and then acted out in groups for the others. This provided an alternative way of expressing issues of trauma and pain that is akin to storytelling methodology—a process that allows for the emergence of people's contextually informed narratives and intuitions. Such a process may be more fitting for people who are more in tune with modes of meaning making aligned with collective energy, rather than more individualised (Westernised) approaches to accessing emotion. Munt elaborates below:

> Storytelling is a practise widespread in predominantly oral cultures, which tend to favour idiomatic fable, myth and allusion over the prosaic enunciation of feelings. Articulating one's emotions in words can appear brutal,

> selfish and rude to those not privileged enough to be familiar with 'therapy speak' and who may well prefer instead the more indirect iteration of their bodily phantasmagoria, every symptom and twinge corresponding to a stage of their journey. (Munt 2011, p. 4)

So, the workshops were a beginning point at which participants could engage with their memories in creative ways before moving towards deeper reflection. Through the creative and open-ended methods, women's own ideas, concerns, and frameworks of meaning about gender violence emerged. The initial workshops served a valuable base for orientating me towards significant emerging themes. A crucial part of this process was that the women had their stories and perspectives validated by the other women who had been through similar traumas. There were many moments when the women concurred with each other and encouraged each other to move deeper into their narratives or to move forward in some aspect of their lives. Most notably, at the time of reviewing their stories, this emerged as women validating others' intuitive feelings about unequal power dynamics between men and women and the felt injustices of sexual trauma. These connections stood as catalysts for the deep sharing that emerged and the narrative weaving of strong threads of shared meaning.

I analysed the workshop data drawing out the groundwork themes and then used these themes to structure the topics for the second phase of data gathering—the focus group discussions. Thus, the data was driven by the women's voices. The preliminary workshop themes were taken back to the women and each focus group functioned as a mode of collective analysis, moving deeper into the identified topic. Topic guides were used introducing the women to the theme of the day, rather than pre-set questions. So, what had usually been done by the collective biography academics through collective writing processes (see Davies and Gannon 2006) was done here through talk. These smaller group discussions were spaces within which the women could move into a deeper analysis of their gendered experiences. The data from these discussions was transcribed verbatim, after which I conducted the in-depth analysis.

Analysing Collective Voices

The collective biography method is a form of data gathering that sheds insight into the ways in which women generate practices and understandings that challenge patriarchal norms (Davies 1990). As women witness other women's stories in the collective setting through role-plays, drama and dialogue, the dominant masculine structures often become visible. They may then be able to find new ways of thinking about themselves by breaking free from patriarchal moulds, discovering new storylines about their lives, and reinventing old discourses (Davies 1992). Enriched with its feminist poststructuralist underpinnings, this methodology allowed me to explore how the women constructed their identities in relation to the other women members and in relation to broader strands of meaning that were generated in the collective research setting.

I utilised a narrative approach for understanding how the women participants constructed their realities within the context of the research. Rather than trying to understand any generalisable 'truth' of the women's stories, I explored the ways in which their narratives connected and interacted in the production of knowledge about the female self (see Tamboukou 2008). As is consistent with many approaches to narrative, my focus was not on the story in itself (as fact), but rather emphasis was placed on the 'narrativity' (see Rojas Silva 2017), or the narrative strategies used—and what these strategies tell us about how the women collectively engage with the social textures of their lives and memories linked to different spaces (back in their home countries; travelling through Africa; and living in current post-apartheid South Africa).

I adopted an ongoing process of memory talk rather than a collective writing process that is common of collective biography work. I read and re-read the transcripts searching for significant themes in the women's talk and I identified common thematic repertoires in these conversations. Such a process of qualitative analysis does not attempt to provide representative data, as it is maintained that all discourses emerging are important, no matter how often they appear. Specifically, I drew on a narrative-thematic methodology with a focus on the co-construction of identities, positioning, and the social patterns and functioning of stories (see Squire 2008). In line with a social remembering approach, I worked from the perspective that all narratives are fluid and contextual manipulations of memory (Reissman 1993) and memories are narrated in certain ways to achieve various social aims (Eisikovits and Winstok 2002; Haaken and Reavey 2012). Narratives are a way of practising certain types of identity in certain contexts during interactions with specific others (De Fina 2003), but at the same time they provide insight into the substance of lived reality, as they are the means through which life is made interpretable and livable (Davies 1991). Such a reading creates space to theorise about the psychological function of such narratives for the person who is doing the telling.

In this chapter, I have discussed the unique and valuable collective methodology which allowed me to work more comprehensively towards achieving African-centred feminist aims. I discuss the processes and practices of my research and put forward a 'new chapter' for African-centred gender research which moves beyond the limitations of traditional qualitative methods. In the chapter that follows, 'Mubobobo: Memories of the Past, Metaphors for the Current Self', I explore Zimbabwean women's narratives of mubobobo rape, what they described as a phenomenon that occurs when men obtain a magical substance which enables them to rape women from a distance. I theorise about the meanings around these narratives in terms of the women's experiences of, and resistance to, patriarchal oppression of female sexuality.

References

Adames, S. B., & Campbell, R. (2005). Immigrant Latinas' conceptualisations of intimate partner violence. *Violence Against Women, 11*, 1341–1364.

Andrews, M. (2008). Never the last word: Revisiting data. In M. Andrews, C. Squire, & M. Tamboukou (Eds.), *Doing Narrative Research* (pp. 86–101). London: Sage.

Bacchus, L., Mezey, G., & Bewley, S. (2006). A qualitative exploration of the nature of domestic violence in pregnancy. *Violence Against Women, 12*, 588–604.

Bohler-Muller, N. (2002). Really listening? Women's voices and the ethic of care in post-colonial Africa. *Agenda, 54*, 86–91.

Cowman, K. (2012). Collective biography. In S. Gunn & L. Faire (Eds.), *Research methods for history* (pp. 83–100). Edinburgh: Edinburgh University Press.

Davies, B. (1990). The problem of desire. *Social Problems, 37*, 801–816.

Davies, B. (1991). The concept of agency. *Social analysis, 30, Postmodern critical theorising* (pp. 42–53).

Davies, B. (1992). Women's subjectivity and feminist stories. In C. Ellis & M. G. Flaherty (Eds.), *Investigating subjectivity. Research on lived experience*. London: Sage.

Davies, B. (2000). *A body of writing 1990–1999*. Walnut Creek: AltaMira Press.

Davies, B., & Gannon, S. (2006). The practices of collective biography. In B. Davies & S. Gannon (Eds.), *Doing collective biography* (pp. 1–15). New York: Open University Press.

Davies, B., Gannon, S., Laws, C., Lenz Taguchi, H., McCann, H., & Rocco, S. (2006b). Reading fiction and the formation of feminine character. In B. Davies & S. Gannon (Eds.), *Doing collective biography* (pp. 35–60). New York: Open University Press.

Davies, B., Browne, J., Gannon, S., Honan, E., & Somerville, M. (2006c). 'Truly wild things': Interruptions to the disciplinary regimes of neo-liberalism in (female) academic work. In B. Davies & S. Gannon (Eds.), *Doing collective biography* (pp. 79–87). New York: Open University Press.

De Fina, A. (2003). *Identity in narrative: A study of immigrant discourse.* Philadelphia, PA: John Benjamins.

De Lauretis, T. (1987). *Technologies of gender: essays in theory, film, and fiction.* Bloomington: Indiana University press.

de Vos, P. (2015). The Limit(s) of the law. Human rights and the emancipation of sexual minorities on the African continent. In D. Higginbotham & V. Collis-Buthelezi (Eds.), *Contested intimacies: Sexuality, gender, and the law in Africa* (pp. 1–16). Cape Town, South Africa: SiberInk.

Derickson, K. D., & Routledge, P. (2015). Resourcing scholar-activism: collaboration, transformation, and the production of knowledge. *Professional Geographer, 67*, 1–20.

Doucet, A. (2008). From her side of the gossamer's wall(s): Reflexivity and relational knowing. *Qualitative Sociology, 31*, 73–87.

Eisikovits, Z., & Winstok, Z. (2002). Reconstructing intimate violence: The structure and content of recollections of violent events. *Qualitative Health Research, 12*, 685–699.

Fish, J. (2006). *Domestic democracy: At home in South Africa.* New York: Taylor & Francis Group.

Fox, A. M., Jackson, S. S., Hansen, N. B., Gasa, N., Crewe, M., & Sikkema, K. J. (2007). In their own voices. A qualitative study of women's risk for intimate partner violence and HIV in South Africa. *Violence Against Women, 13*, 583–602.

Fraser, H. (2004). Doing narrative research: Analysing personal stories line by line. *Qualitative Social Work, 3*, 179–201.

Gavey, N. (2005). *Just sex? The cultural scaffolding of rape.* New York: Routledge.

Gill, A. (2004). Voicing the silent fear: South Asian women's experiences of domestic violence. *The Howard Journal, 43*, 465–483.

Gqola, P. (2017). *Reflecting Rogue: Inside the mind of a feminist.* Johannesburg, South Africa: Jacana Media.

Haaken, J., & Reavey, P. (2012). Why memory matters: Disturbing recollections. In J. Haaken & R. Reavey (Eds.), *Memory matters: Contexts for understanding sexual abuse recollections* (pp. 1–13). New York: Routledge.

Harned, M. S. (2005). Understanding women's labelling of unwanted sexual experiences with dating partners: A qualitative analysis. *Violence Against Women, 11*, 374–413.

Hofisi, C., Hofisi, M., & Mago, S. (2014). Critiquing interviewing as a data collection method. *Mediterranean Journal of Social Science, 5*, 60–64.

Israel, B. A., Schultz, A. J., Parker, E. A., & Becker, A. B. (1998). Review of community-based research: Assessing partnership approaches to improve public health. *Annual Review of Public Health, 19*, 173–202.

Johnson-Odim, C. (1991). Common themes, different contexts. In C. T. Mohanty, A. Russo, & L. Torres (Eds.), *Third World women and the politics of feminism* (pp. 314–327). Indianapolis: Indiana University Press.

Kitzinger, J., & Barbour, R. S. (1999). Introduction: The challenge and promise of focus groups. In R. S. Barbour & J. Kitzinger (Eds.), *Developing focus group research: Politics, theory and practice* (pp. 1–20). London: Sage.

Kuhn, A. (2000). A journey through memory. In S. Radstone (Ed.), *Memory and methodology* (pp. 179–196). Oxford: Berg Publishers.

Macleod, C. (2006). Radical plural feminisms and emancipatory practice in post-apartheid South Africa. *Theory & Psychology, 16*, 367–389.

Macleod, C. (2008). 'Who? What?: An unindicted view of towards a new psychology of women from post-apartheid South Africa. *Feminism & Psychology, 18*, 347–357.

Macleod, C., & Durrheim, K. (2002). Foucauldian feminism: The implications of governmentality. *Journal for the Theory of Social Behaviour, 32*, 41–60.

Mauthner, N. S., & Doucet, A. (2003). Reflexive accounts and accounts of reflexivity in qualitative data analysis. *Sociology, 37*, 413–431.

Mauthner, N. S., Parry, O., & Backett-Milburn, K. (1998). The data are out there, or are they? Implications for archiving and revisiting qualitative data. *Sociology, 32*, 733–745.

Melucci, A. (1995). The process of collective identity. In H. Johnston & B. Klandermans (Eds.), *Social movements and culture* (pp. 41–63). Minneapolis: University of Minnesota Press.

Mkhize, N. (2004). Psychology: An African perspective. In D. Hook (Ed.), *Critical psychology* (pp. 24–52). Lansdowne, Cape Town: University of Cape Town Press.

Mohanty, C. T. (1991). Under western eyes: Feminist scholarship and colonial discourses. In C. T. Mohanty, A. Russo, & L. Torres (Eds.), *Third world women and the politics of feminism* (pp. 51–80). Indianapolis: Indiana University Press.

Munt, S. R. (2011). Journeys of resilience: The emotional geographies of refugee women. *Gender, Place & Culture: A Journal of Feminist Geography, 19*, 555–577.

Narayan, U. (2000). Essence of culture and a sense of history: A feminist critique of cultural essentialism. In U. Narayan & S. Harding (Eds.), *Decentering the center: Philosophy for a multicultural, postcolonial, and feminist world* (pp. 80–100). Bloomington: Indiana University Press.

Okin, S. M. (2000). Feminism, women's human rights, and cultural differences. In U. Narayan & S. Harding (Eds.), *Decentering the centre: Philosophy for a multicultural, postcolonial, and feminist world* (pp. 26–46). Bloomington: Indiana University Press.
Parker, I. (2005). *Qualitative psychology: Introducing radical research.* New York: McGraw-Hill.
Pereira, C. (2000). Feminist knowledge. *African Transitions, 490*, 77–85.
Pereira, C. (2002). Between knowing and imagining: What space for feminism in scholarship on Africa? *Feminist Africa, 1.*
Pratt, G. (2004). *Working feminisms.* Edinburgh: Edinburgh University Press.
Reissman, C. K. (1993). *Narrative analysis.* London: Sage.
Rojas Silva, B. (2017). Book review: Narrative imagination and everyday life. *Feminism & Psychology, 27*, 385–388.
Seidman, I. (2006). *Interviewing as qualitative research-A guide for researchers in education and the social sciences.* New York: Columbia University; Teachers College Press.
Sjoberg, G., & Nett, R. (1968). *A methodology for social research.* New York: Harper & Row.
Sokoloff, N. J., & Dupont, I. (2005). Domestic violence at the intersections of race, class, and gender: Challenges and contributions to understanding violence against marginalised women in diverse communities. *Violence Against Women, 11*, 38–64.
Squire, C. (2008). Experience-centred and culturally-orientated approaches to narrative. In M. Andrews, C. Squire, & M. Tamboukou (Eds.), *Doing narrative research* (pp. 41–63). London: Sage.
Stephenson, N. (2001). "Speaking like a woman": Agency in intersubjective communication. *Australian Psychologist, 36*, 19–26.
Tamboukou, M. (2008). A Foucauldian approach to narratives. In M. Andrews, C. Squire, & M. Tamboukou (Eds.), *Doing narrative research* (pp. 102–120). Thousand Oaks, CA: Sage.
van Schalkwyk, S., & Gobodo-Madikizela, P. (2015). Introduction. In S. van Schalkwyk & P. Gobodo-Madikizela (Eds.), *A reflexive inquiry into gender research: Towards a new paradigm of knowledge production & exploring new frontiers of gender research in Southern Africa* (pp. xi–xxxv). Newcastle-upon-Tyne: Cambridge Scholars Publishing.
van Schalkwyk, S., Boonzaier, F., & Gobodo-Madikizela, P. (2014). 'Selves' in contradiction: Power and powerlessness in South African shelter residents' narratives of leaving abusive heterosexual relationships. *Feminism & Psychology, 24*, 314–331.
Walshaw, M. A. (2010). The researcher's self in research: Confronting issues about knowing and understanding others. In L. Sparrow, B. Kissane, & C. Hurst

(Eds.), *Proceedings of the 33rd annual conference of the mathematics education research group of Australasia Incorporated 2010: Shaping the future of mathematics education* (pp. 587–593). Australia: Freemantle.

Wright, S., & Nelson, N. (1995). Participatory research and participant observation: Two incompatible approaches. In N. Nelson & S. Wright (Eds.), *Power and participatory development: Theory and practice* (pp. 43–59). Southampton; London: Intermediate Technology Publications.

Yuval-Davis, N. (1997). *Gender and nation*. London: Sage.

CHAPTER 4

Mubobobo: Memories of the Past, Metaphors for the Current Self

The 'Unspeakable': Normalised Violence and Silence in South Africa

Feminist scholars both globally and in the South African context have highlighted the severe extent of women's experience of vulnerability in public spaces. Women are expected to monitor their movement and their behaviour in such spaces or face negative consequences such as shaming or even direct physical violence. Writing about the South African context in her book *Rape: A South African Nightmare*, Gqola (2015) links women's sense of vulnerability to what she calls the 'female fear factory'—a repetitive theatrics, or playing out, of the powerful and the powerless in public spaces. Such theatrics, says Gqola, manufacture female fear through signals and recognisable cues understood by everyone, producing a constant sense of vulnerability for women. The metaphor of the factory used by Gqola eloquently describes the machinery functioning in social spaces with various components and 'assembly lines' manufacturing female fear. A crucial component or assembly piece (to use Gqola's term) of this process is social discourse about the inferiority of female sexuality and black female bodies. Social meanings surrounding the devalued (black) female body are infused into everyday life in this context. The effects of these meanings constitute violence, which is normalised in that it happens every day and in all spheres of life (Gqola 2015). It is such normalisation that makes the disruption of such processes unthinkable because they have been entrenched into everyday patterns of gender relations. This 'fear factory' effectively controls

S. van Schalkwyk, *Narrative Landscapes of Female Sexuality in Africa*, https://doi.org/10.1007/978-3-319-97825-3_4

women's expression of sexuality. It is often the ever-present threat of violence, or the sense of vulnerability, that curbs women's behaviour and the spaces that they occupy in South Africa (Dosekun 2007). Women are constructed as sexual objects, while male sexual entitlement is rendered a normal aspect of masculinity (Hassim 2014). Much of women's experience remains unspoken.

Globally, meanings around trauma scripts are structured around masculine language and strict definitions of 'abuse' and 'victim' (Lempert 1996). According to such scripts, abuse should be observable and nameable (rape, battering); abuse should be severe; and abuse should leave physical marks on the victim's body. In their well-known book chapter '"Nothing Really Happened": The Invalidation of Women's Experiences of Sexual Violence', Kelly and Radford (1996) suggest that in the absence of a severe physical assault, women find it difficult to make sense of their experiences of violence. The point is that such scripts often do not provide women the space to voice the complexity and extent of their gendered experiences.

Dominant scripts of gendered abuse often do not 'speak' to the fine-tuned textures of experience (Griffiths 2005, p. 19, as cited in Rajiva 2014, p. 147). In other words, nameable forms of violence do not convey the whole picture of women's experiences of patriarchal oppression of female sexuality. Many experiences affecting feminine subjects are continual and ever-present violations of the self—as such, they are normalised and unspoken. These are the 'ordinary traumas' that happen every day that are often considered normal because they are so woven into the fabric of society. Forter (2007) says that these experiences are emphatically social disturbances which have been thoroughly naturalised in ways that make it necessary to excavate and 'estrange' them in order to see them *as* social traumas. Many experiences related to the oppression of female sexuality are not visible to the uncritical eye, however, the effects of existing as a feminine subject within this web of power is disastrous. It is of critical significance that such experience is theorised.

Root (1992) introduces the notion of insidious trauma. This refers to continual, unrelenting traumas experienced because of one's social position—when a particular social position is devalued within the complex system of power structures. Insidious trauma is part of the collective social trauma of people who share certain gendered, raced, and classed subjectivities. The importance of such a view is that a multitude of forms of discrimination such as racism, sexism as well as life conditions such as poverty, are included in the concept of trauma. Also included in this expanded definition is acknowledgement that trauma is often repeated continuously (it is all around in daily life) and it is often not defined as abuse/trauma (such as everyday microaggressions). The effects of such traumas may be gradual and subtle, but they collectively work to erode the human spirit, having an impact on self and identity (Forter 2007). These 'small acts' of violence work to degrade the self because they deny women their full human subjectivity. The silencing around such experiences is deeply harmful. When one is not able to name and voice experiences of gender oppression, one often feels it in the body as an ever-present uncomfortable companion that tells us all is not well. When kept unspoken these feelings 'exist' as remnants guiding the sense we make of ourselves in the world. Telling is a form of agency because the narrator can work through negative emotions and incorporate these experiences into their identity (Gobodo-Madikizela et al. 2014). Women are not living a life of psychological freedom if they do not have an opportunity to voice these experiences.

A prominent theme that emerged through the drama, role-plays and memory-work methods during the initial workshops was women's experience of sexual degradation and violence in public spaces in South Africa. Infused in these discussions were accounts of men touching women's bodies on public transport, masturbating on parts of their bodies on trains and spaces where people are packed together, and men using violent language to degrade and violate women's bodies. Alongside these 'provable' acts of violence were accounts of women's sense of their bodies as constantly observed through the male gaze and powerfully *violated* through this very gaze. It seemed as if the latter stories surrounding sexualised experience were more difficult to articulate or pinpoint—constituting what has been outlined above as 'invisible' or insidious traumas (see Root 1992) that have no language through which to be spoken. One woman's statement in workshop 2 illuminates a sense of these hard-to-name experiences: *'People rape you when you are walking, even in their minds!'*

Mubobobo Rape

During the research, the topic of mubobobo emerged powerfully and persistently as a central motif of the women's collective narratives. They described mubobobo as an act whereby men obtain magical muti which enables them to have sexual intercourse with a woman without any physical contact. 'Muti' is a term for traditional medicine in southern Africa. It usually refers to herbs and other natural products such as parts of trees or plants and is prescribed by African traditional healers, or 'Izinyanga'. While some muti is considered healing, certain types of muti are associated with witchcraft and evil practices and thought to cause physical pain or sometimes even death. The women's stories about mubobobo were as follows: men obtain this muti so that they can rape women from a distance, just by watching a woman, or by thinking of them. They described this 'rape' as prevalent in public spaces where women can easily be observed—bus stops, train stations, market places, and other spaces where people come together in relative anonymity. Within these spaces, the mubobobo perpetrator (always described as male) can watch women and choose any woman he wishes. The women also described this practice happening at night in the privacy of women's own homes. In such cases, they spoke of women having sexual dreams and waking up feeling as if they had just had sex. The narrators used the words 'rape from a distance' and 'muti rape' to describe this practice. The mubobobo narrative emerged as a central motif of the women's collective memory. They wove rich narratives about the effects mubobobo has on women's lives.

> **Akeyo:** Ja, I think it's something that can cause trouble in their lifetime cause like there was some people they don't know about mutis and all that underworld, they are just innocent beings maybe young girls or what and those men they just prey on those people and then they don't know. They [the women victims] will be like having that feeling every morning like 'what was happening to me every night?'. You know, and they are troubled. Psychologically I think they are troubled as well. Every morning you wake up you don't know what is happening you don't know that feeling but it's that feeling that you get when somebody has been doing that to you [having sex] and if it goes on and on and you don't seek help because you don't know what it is, it can be damaging I think, psychologically.
>
> **SvS:** Ja, for the woman, ja.
>
> **Chadamwari:** For the woman because the man is enjoying it. They can't be damaged anyhow.
>
> (Focus group discussion 1)

And,

> **Cheney:** In Zimbabwe I also tell my daughters never to go where like there is something people are dancing in the street jho there are these large circles

people are watching. It is better to avoid those places because a lot of women, it was coming from the Herald our local newspaper, (they) will find (themselves) wet because a man will be busy with you. Busy with you and you just feel what is going on and yet somebody has already finished [ejaculated].

Chadamwari: Ja, those places and all the places that are crowded, men have been taking advantage too.

(Focus group discussion 1)

These accounts of mubobobo were rich and pervasive. In my efforts to contextualise these narratives, I engaged in further research on the topic. It became evident that mubobobo is an established narrative in Zimbabwean cultures. Mubobobo is a topical subject in Zimbabwean online media seen through various accounts of mob justice against perceived perpetrators. Interestingly, a common language used by the media draws on technology. Mubobobo has been dubbed 'the African bluetooth system' and 'The bluetooth version of rape'. Such sex is said to happen without consent and without physical contact. It has been conceptualised as a remote sexual intercourse which 'connects' male perpetrator and victim (Sibanda 2013). Others, such as Gwandure (2009), describe mubobobo as an electric current 'people can see the consequences of mubobobo and not the electric current itself' (p. 77). The 'electric current' or 'wireless' metaphor suggests that mubobobo is characterised by an elusive power, or force, whereby male perpetrators draw something from the female victims. Sibanda (2013) suggests that reports in Zimbabwe run rife documenting the negative psychological effects experienced by mubobobo victims. These include claims of hysteria, trauma, miscarriage, and hallucinations. In other words, mubobobo is often attributed as the cause when 'things go wrong', attributed to black magic or 'witchcraft rape', as mubobobo is sometimes called (Sibanda 2013). These representations of mubobobo in the Zimbabwean community media suggest that the practice, which used to be the subject of traditional sites of storytelling, has been entrenched in the realm of everyday discourse in Zimbabwe (Sibanda 2013). All this points to the broader social repertoires of understanding—the cultural narratives—that the narrators in my study draw on in their accounts.

In this chapter, I trace the women's narratives of mubobobo drawing from focus group discussions which consisted only of Shona women from Zimbabwe who are currently living in South Africa. Firstly, I outline my own meaning making about such a practice which was completely outside my own repertoire of understanding. I then unpack the women's stories of mubobobo which centre on juxtapositions of pleasure/vulnerability and power/powerlessness. I end the chapter by theorising about the psychological function that such narratives may play for the women and what these narratives tell us about their experiences of, and resistance to, patriarchal oppression of female sexuality.

Making Meaning of Rape from a Distance

When the women first mentioned mubobobo, I found it difficult to make sense of these narratives. It was the first time that I heard of anything like this and the stories of mubobobo were outside my cultural repertoires of understanding. When I first told one of my colleagues about it, I remember her laughing. As a black South African woman, the mubobobo narrative was also completely outside her experience and culture. Her reaction, I think, would be common to most who have not encountered mubobobo narratives. Western discourses structure ideas about what is rationally possible. These ideas define what we believe to be possible or 'true'. Taken at face value, ideas about rape from a distance do not fit the criteria of the possible, from a Western framework. My reflection on my colleague's reaction resulted in mixed feelings with some anxiety. How was I to make sense of such narratives? My position throughout the mubobobo discussions was one of outsider taking on a very distinct questioning role about the topic. This has been, and still is, a difficult topic to write about. However, over time through listening and re-listening, I began to get more of a sense of the meanings underlying the women's narratives.

According to Campbell (2003), memory and the self are historically braided concepts and she warns that it is possible to fall trap to attacking the selfhood of others by invalidating what they remember. Thus, I wanted to interpret the stories in a way that would be compatible with broader postcolonial feminist aims—to privilege the knowledge and culture of the women and to acknowledge the textured complexities of their realities. I had to contextualise the mubobobo narrative within the broader context of Zimbabwean culture and women's sexuality and the shared cultural resources that the women had at their disposal. I turned to the literature. However, I found that the scholarly work dealing with mubobobo was limited and unhelpful in providing an understanding of mubobobo that privileges the experience and collective knowledge of women.

Fortune Sibanda (2013) provides an outline of the terminology and topographies of mubobobo. He engages in some analysis of the complexities around mubobobo, particularly the incongruencies of this belief system with the law that make it difficult to define the act or hold male perpetrators accountable. However, his article lacks a gendered analysis. In other words, he does not examine what this witchcraft rape might mean for women themselves. In his article 'Mubobobo: Women Have No Sexual Fantasies in Their Sleep', Calvin Gwandure (2009) argues that Shona women are unable to make sense of their sexual pleasure or desire. He says that due to Zimbabwean cultural restrictions on female sexuality, women cannot understand themselves as sexual subjects. As a result, argues Gwandure, women interpret their sexual bodily sensations as mubobobo (unnatural occurrences cause by an outside force).

Gwandure's interpretation is problematic. He argues that women are not capable of making sense of their sexual pleasure/desire. This conveys a sense that Shona women are passive objects—that oppressive discourses about female sexuality stifle women to such an extent that they know nothing about their sexual self. Women misinterpret their own sexual desire as mubobobo, says Gwandure. Gwandure's view positions women as naïve about their bodies and their sexuality. It does not leave room for acknowledging women's agency. Cultural constraints may limit the sexual subjectivities of women, but women are able to negotiate sexual agency and resist harmful discourses. Women *do* have knowledge about themselves as sexual vehicles and they express this knowledge through complex and creative cultural avenues (Arnfred 2015; Tamale 2005, 2013). Ultimately, Gwandure's views about women's lack of capacity to engage with their sexuality, although perhaps not consciously intended, reflects a male perspective that resonates with patriarchal views.

Postcolonial feminist scholars consistently argue that women's experiences of sexuality in African contexts are more complex than suggested by Westernised frames of powerlessness (see Arnfred 2015; Tamale 2011, 2013). As scholars who are serious about promoting *new* knowledge, we must always look at the multiple meanings surrounding cultural narratives and the ways in which women work with these narratives in complex ways (Dellenborg 2004). To interpret the narratives of mubobobo at face value—that is, to take the narratives to portray aspects of women's static powerlessness—ignores important aspects of women's meaning making. In order to move away from Westernised hegemonic feminist stories, I needed to look critically at these women's narratives, beyond merely interpreting the mubobobo narratives as signifying another form of violence.

I interpret the women's narratives as products of a particular way of remembering socially which achieve certain aims. Memory is the thread through which we make our world known to ourselves and others (Haaken and Reavey 2010). It is the way through which we create a self in the world. From a social remembering perspective, I do not focus on whether mubobobo is 'true' or not. Rather, I examine the ways in which the women use the mubobobo narrative and what this tells us about their experiences of, and resistance to, patriarchal oppression of female sexuality. Narratively, I explore the ways in which women's narratives connect and interact with dominant knowledge surrounding female sexuality, while at the same time producing new knowledge (see Tamboukou 2008). Narratives are a way of practising certain types of identity in certain contexts during interactions with specific others (De Fina 2003), but at the same time they provide insight into the substance of lived reality, as they are the means through which life is made interpretable and livable (Davies 1990, 1991). I looked beyond women's words to explore the psychological and cultural significance of their accounts. I paid attention to what was being communicated subtly. This was a process of looking beyond the obvious.

Collectively Narrating Mubobobo: Voices of Shona Women from Zimbabwe

Considering the context of deep-rooted and harmful patriarchal oppression of female sexuality in Zimbabwe that suppresses women's sexuality and renders sexual expression taboo, what cultural meanings do these Zimbabwean women bring with them from 'back home'. Within the context of brutal violence against women who transgress modes of 'appropriate' sexuality and the strong undercurrents of xenophobia in South Africa, through what means can these Zimbabwean women express aspects of their experience within the current moment of telling? How can the narrators express their gendered experiences safely in such an environment? Culbertson (1995) reminds us that memory is always subjected to the socio-cultural meanings which define what can be said (and what is believed). I interpret the women's narratives of mubobobo in light of these severely oppressive cultural forces making their mark on women's sense of who they can be sexually, while acknowledging that women *do* have knowledge about their sexual bodies and they are able to express this knowledge by working with aspects of their culture in subtle yet powerful ways. I begin my discussion with an examination of women's narrative expressions of lingering memories of vulnerability, trouble, and desire.

Female Sexuality: Collective Expressions of Vulnerability, Trouble, and Desire

Cheney was 43 years of age at the time of the research discussions. She had been divorced from her husband for many years. Cheney's marriage was characterised by frequent emotional and sexual abuse at the hands of her husband. One of the many stories she tells is how this man used to bring home women and have sex with them in their family home. Cheney was present when this happened, sitting in the other room while her husband was having sex. However, Cheney said that the most painful part of her marriage was having sex with her husband. She describes how he engaged in sex with a lack of emotion often refusing to look at her while having sex. Sometimes, says Cheney, he would read the newspaper while having sex with her, indicating a lack of subjective engagement, rendering Cheney object status. It was clear throughout her narrative that Cheney experienced these actions as a violation of her sexualised body and mind. She disclosed that the experience left her 'hating sex' and avoiding sexual intimacy. She told us that this experience has resulted in her no longer having sex. In the discussion about mubobobo rape, Cheney says the following.

Cheney: What I know is in a dream you can have like those funny dreams. Like us maybe we get that, we have been sexually active yes. But maybe now we are talking three or four years without it (sex). Once in a while we would have that kind of dream and then those are called wet dreams.

Group: Yes.

Cheney: But to think it was someone using you (mubobobo) or it's just a dream ...

(Focus group discussion 1)

Through her use of language 'you can have those funny dreams' and 'those are called wet dreams', Cheney positions herself as sexual subject. 'Wet dreams' signify sexual needs and an imaginary element tied to sexual desire. Cheney uses the collective 'we' and 'us' connecting a sense of her individual experience with the experience of the collective. She insinuates that sexual desire is part of their biological repertoire and subjectivity as Shona women from Zimbabwe.

However, it is clear that Cheney does not express her sexual subjectivity here in a bold or definitive way. As I have shown, patriarchal discourse surrounding female sexuality often renders women's expression of their sexual subjectivity taboo. We see that while Cheney expresses aspects of her sexuality and desiring self (here the wet dream), it seems as if cultural prescriptions maintain some hold. In the last line of the excerpt she says, 'but to think it was someone using you (mubobobo) or it's just a dream'. In doing so, Cheney creates ambivalence in her account—right at the end she poses the question of what is really going on: Is it mubobobo rape or is it a dream stemming from one's own sexual desire, she asks. Mubobobo is an accepted cultural script through which Cheney can express aspects of her sexuality in a way that is safe for her. Davies et al. (2006c) suggest that such ambivalence is a common element of women's meaning making about their gendered subjectivity during collective biography work. Cultural messages are often so ingrained that a kind of 'culture' within operates to monitor talk according to socio-cultural conventions. In this sense the 'strong pull' of culture pushes Cheney back from expressing her sexuality outright. As scholars have illuminated, the subject goes though mo(ve)ments as she catches herself in the act of being subjected, while at the same time working to deconstruct this position in any way possible (Davies et al. 2006c). Davies et al. (2006a, p. 181) describe this process from a feminist poststructuralist perspective.

> She is above all, in process, vulnerable to inscriptions that may be opaque to her and yet developing the powers to make the discourses and their inscriptive powers both visible and revisable.

The mubobobo narrative is a means through which Cheney can express aspects of her sexual subjectivity. This narrative provides her with language to express these aspects of her sexuality while at the same time producing ambivalence, which 'protects' Cheney from any negative consequences related to the disclosure. Through mubobobo, Cheney is able to position herself as sexually desiring subject—a position which may not be so easily achievable in other settings.

Akeyo narrates similar textures of her gendered experiences through the use of mubobobo. At the time of the research she was 26 years old. She was married with one young daughter. A persistent theme throughout Akeyo's narrations was her memories of life on their family farm in Zimbabwe. Earlier in the discussion, she provided rich detail about her childhood visits to the farm and described her grandfather as a man that utilised many different forms of muti to enhance crop growth. She reflected on her mother's constant warnings to be careful of mubobobo, an intergenerational narrative among the women that signalled to young girls that they were always vulnerable.

> **Akeyo:** I lived around it, but I never directly experienced it. Maybe I did, and I didn't feel it. I don't know. Because my grandfather had a lot of muti stories.
>
> (Focus group discussion 1)

Akeyo conveys meaning that she was exposed to mubobobo while growing up, she knew about the practice but did not experience it directly. She then contradicts this statement with 'maybe I did, and I didn't feel it. I don't know.' Through her description of her grandfather who used muti a lot, she suggests that she was always potentially vulnerable to mubobobo. We see through the texture of her narrative that she conveys a sense of uncertainty. This was a common element throughout the women's narratives of this abstract cultural practice. It was clear that mubobobo is difficult to define or thread into a cohesive memory of experience.

Below Akeyo elaborates on the elusive nature of mubobobo.

> **Akeyo:** He (the mubobobo perpetrator) will just be walking simply or maybe just look at you with the eyes. It is something that we grew up hearing and something that maybe happened around us you know. So, they will just sit and look at you, maybe with the eyes and then they are busy. So, I think it has got levels that maybe they are busy undressing you. So, it could be a psychological thing. You know undressing you while they are staring at you.
>
> (Focus group discussion 1)

Through this narrative thread, we gain a sense that the signs of mubobobo mirror everyday activities such as men's observations of women. Mubobobo is difficult to identify as it is often performed through subtle extensions or 'normal' and common male behaviours. Akeyo's narrative helps us better understand her constructed confusion about whether or not she has experienced mubobobo. We also gain a sense of the ever-present possibility of mubobobo in public spaces where women's bodies are always in a sense prey-objects subject to be invaded by men's 'eyes'.

Although Akeyo says that she is not sure if she has experienced mubobobo, she narrated a detailed account of the ways in which the ever-present possibility of mubobobo has shaped her life.

> **Akeyo:** Mubobobo makes one feel scared, it makes you feel very scared. Like I am saying I don't know if my grandfather slept with me.
>
> **Elinah:** Mmm.
>
> **Akeyo:** You know? And if I look at my grandfather the relationship between us how I feel about him you know the love I have for him as my mother's father. You know it (mubobobo) *disturbs* relationships, especially family relationships it disturbs a lot. It gives like confusion and conflict and you know hatred. It affects a lot. You really not sure who to trust anymore.
>
> (Focus group discussion 1)

Akeyo conveys a rich sense of the complexities of living a life in which mubobobo is always a possibility. Living in an environment in which mubobobo is practised pervasively, she says, has an effect on her psyche. It deeply affects her sense of self in relation to others. She constructs a vulnerable self in relation to her grandfather, a patriarchal male subject ('I don't know if he slept with me'). Here Akeyo aligns with dominant scripts of female subject positions as 'fearful' and 'powerless' in relation to males (see Lamb 1999)—she provides us with a sense that her experience as a woman in relation to mubobobo is coloured by a sense of powerlessness and uncertainty. Her focus on the family context is powerful. The contradictions are clear. She narrates her feelings of 'confusion' and 'conflict'—someone whom she loves, the male leader of the household, is at the same time someone that she doubts. These contradictions, narrated as the result of the ever-present possibility of mubobobo, disrupt normal family relations. It 'disturbs relationships', in Akeyo's words. She suggests that this conflict has affected her by generating feelings of hatred and lack of trust of male family members.

Exploring possible deeper meaning behind Akeyo's narration, I had a sense that something was being communicated implicitly. Earlier on, Akeyo states that concerns around mubobobo were communicated to her from a young age by her mother ('that's what they claim'; 'That's what we just grew hearing'). Such a feeling of *self as vulnerable* may have been a core part of the experience of female family members on the farm in Zimbabwe. I wondered if Akeyo's narrative could reflect broader concerns of female family members—a feeling of vulnerability that has been passed on from the older generations of women to convey their experience and to protect their young. Perhaps the cultural script of mubobobo is a socially accepted way through which women can express these concerns. According to my interpretation, Akeyo is narrating her collective feminine consciousness and experience through the mubobobo script. Such a consciousness was sown by her mother through social messages when she was young and strengthened throughout Akeyo's life through witnessing violent abuse in her family and social context.

Elaborating on the effects that the ever-present possibility of mubobobo has on her life, Akeyo says the following.

> **Akeyo:** Even some of my mother's brothers who do muti. Even if I get a wet dream I will hurt them for no good reason. I will suspect him. And you know once I suspect someone did something evil to me there is something behind my head, even if I don't want to accept it.
>
> **Chadamwari:** In your consciousness.
>
> **Akeyo:** In my head you know and maybe that will affect my kids. You know like at home (in Zimbabwe) we really like draw family relationships we draw them close. Extended families we keep them. So that would affect maybe to an extent that my child would never visit my uncle. I don't hardly talk to him because I am not sure what he is up to. Even if he didn't do it to me (mubobobo), I have a girl child, maybe he will do it to my child, you know? So, it affected me a lot.
>
> (Focus group discussion 1)

Akeyo tells us that her sense of constant vulnerability in relation to mubobobo significantly shapes her sense of identity as woman, mother, and female family member. Firstly, she says that if she experiences a wet dream, sexual fantasies or pleasure while sleeping, she will blame her uncle and 'suspect' him of practising mubobobo on her. This thread of her narrative conveys a powerful message. She talks openly about her experiences of wet dreams but infuses a sense of ambivalence once again through the use of the mubobobo script—when she experiences such a thing, her mind is drawn to suspicion about the cause of this sexual desire. This is how she presents this aspect of her sexual desire to us. This suggests that her sense of sexuality is intricately connected to her sense of vulnerability. Perhaps within the context of telling—a South Africa within which female sexuality is deeply connected with shame and silence (Artz 2009; Gqola 2017)—this is one of the only ways in which Akeyo can speak openly about her desires. Here we see Akeyo drawing on an account of her sexual desire (wet dreams) but at the same time, and very quickly, she projects blame onto her uncle, the male other, who signifies patriarchal control. Akeyo projects this shame onto her uncle—an image of manhood which is the source of her desire, and an image of patriarchal power which is ironically the source of such shame.

Secondly, we see a continuation and strengthening of this sense of *self as vulnerable* 'inherited' from her mother and other female family members. Akeyo voices that she now tries to protect her daughter by keeping her away from the uncle who uses muti. What is evident is Akeyo's sense of men's ever-present capacity to violate (mubobobo can happen at any time). We see this knowledge translating into a violation of Akeyo's mind, through her description of the effects of this constant suspicion. It affects her relations with her family members ('something behind my head') and she chooses to be a 'good' mother in spite of cultural pressures which value the family collective (see Mkhize 2004). This is important for Akeyo, she emphasises 'it affected me a lot'. There is a sense of the clash between cultural expectations to value family ties and her desire to protect her daughter from potential abuse. These narratives raise important questions about female sexuality and the experience of vulnerability. How can women protect their young in contexts within which family ties are valued? How can mothers negotiate a positive sense of self within this context?

Interestingly, infused into the accounts of mubobobo as harmful were descriptions of sexual pleasure and desire experienced by mubobobo victims. Akeyo succinctly describes the experience.

> **Akeyo:** You just feel like you are in bed with a man and you feel something is happening. You don't know what is wrong with your hormones or whatever, you just feel like you are in the middle of crazy business.
>
> (Focus group discussion 1)

Later in the discussion she elaborates on this feeling,

> **Akeyo:** Um this muti caressing, you don't feel a hand touching your boob; you just feel the hormones, like crazy hormones.
>
> **SvS:** Aah, so not in a specific place?
>
> **Akeyo:** Not in a specific place. You feel like the rush or whatever you know the body is relaxing and you can really feel you are like having sex and you can enjoy the feeling of sex. You don't really feel the in and out part (laughs) of the thing [penetration]. You just feel the feeling of what happens after the in and out and then later on you just come, the pants are wet.
>
> (Focus group discussion 1)

And,

> **Akeyo:** I remember I was with (friend's name) she said she had such an experience, but she didn't know what it was you know.
>
> **Chadamwari:** But it's nice.
>
> **Akeyo:** You know your body would respond to the feeling it's nice like when you are having sex you are enjoying the sex. It is nice, you like it even though you are not participating in the sex. But you feel the feeling is good. It is not a bad feeling. It is a good sexual feeling and then when it is done you come. And you don't know what is happening, you are still surprised.
>
> **Chadamwari:** That shows it is very *strong* muti (group laughs) for the lady to feel everything and even come and everything … finish on her part.
>
> (Focus group discussion 1)

The accounts above show that the negative descriptions of mubobobo were juxtaposed with descriptions of physical pleasure. The women narrated that female victims often experience pleasurable sensations in their bodies, as if they are engaged in sexual intercourse. Importantly, through their narratives of mubobobo they position women as sexual agents who have knowledge about sex and who enjoy sex. They are voicing previously silenced aspects of sexual pleasure/desire.

The ambiguous narratives including pleasure/vulnerability, power/powerlessness, and not knowing/knowing the body signified something beyond mubobobo itself. These descriptions provide signposts that map out a deeper terrain of meaning. These narratives provide insight into the subjectivities of women who are situated within a particular African culture (Shona from Zimbabwe) that restricts the expression of sexuality and sexual desire. So, these narratives tell us something meaningful about women's experience as subjects within the nexus of violent discourses surrounding the oppression of female sexuality.

As the discussions progressed, I experienced an increased sense of understanding—more and more I felt that the texture of the narratives resonated somewhat with my own experiences of femininity. When reviewing the data with a sensitivity to the topic of female sexuality, I immersed myself in a re-reading/re-listening of the women's audiotaped voices. During this time, I had a vivid dream about men, different men—images of men which were blended into one. In my dream, I had a feeling that I was trying to communicate something to these men, but I just couldn't. I felt restricted and trapped. When I woke up, I was sitting for a while with the feeling of this dream, trying to piece together what it could mean. The feeling was unsettling and difficult to define. In retrospect, I think that this dream stands as a rich example of the way in which the women's voices affected me. The women's stories energetically connected me with my own subjective world and past experiences. Specifically, I think that this dream was all about my own experience of patriarchal oppression of female sexuality—my sexual subjectivity and position as woman within this matrix of oppression. The complexities around how and when to express aspects of sexuality; the sensitivities of how as a girl/woman we are perceived; and the pain of sometimes acting in ways that are not true to one's own wants/desires. These are all textures of female-sexualised experiences that are difficult to engage with in a world infused by patriarchal oppression of female sexuality. This speaks importantly to the reciprocal effects of power and knowledge that are a result of patriarchal discourse. My dream provided me with felt knowledge about the deeper meanings surrounding mubobobo. The mubobobo narratives were giving voice to the complexity and texture of women's gendered experience as sexualised subjects in the world. It is through mubobobo that the women could voice this unspeakable aspect of female experience.

Considered through a feminist poststructuralist lens, narratives do not convey an essential 'truth', but rather provide insight into the construction of self through language. This in turn conveys meaning about narrators' subjective experience, or the *feeling* of inhabiting the social world (Davies and Gannon 2006). Along these lines, I consider the mubobobo narrative in terms of what it means for these women's sense of self as black, foreigner, Zimbabwean women living in current South Africa. Scholars have argued that we need to consider the multiple and pervasive everyday acts of continuous trauma that affect people's lives due to devalued positions associated with gender, race, class, citizenship, and other socially-constructed categories of being (Root 1992; Forter 2007). Everyday experiences of 'small' acts of violence, or what Root (1992) calls insidious trauma, shape women's experience and subjectivities in powerful ways. They are an integral part of the functioning of patriarchal oppression of female sexuality (Gqola 2015). These intersecting positions also shape what forms of resistance are available to women.

I also consider these narratives in light of the limited language encompassed in dominant discourses surrounding 'abuse' and 'trauma' (see Lamb 1999). Dominant conceptualisations of trauma are structured around 'visible' events—such events need to be observable to others, they need to leave marks on the body, and, for women to achieve the status of 'true victim' they need to seem unequivocally powerless in relation to the abuser. These dominant scripts do not speak to the textured experiences of many women (Rajiva 2014). Any hint of female sexual agency invalidates women's accounts (Reavey and Browne 2007, 2009; Reavey 2010). In the South African context, women's agency is often met by patriarchal forces which shame women (Gqola 2015), as discussed above.

The complexities around dominant definitions of 'abuse' and 'victim' significantly shape what experiences are considered violent in a patriarchal world. This has a powerful impact on women's storytelling and what sense they can make of their gendered experiences. Women do not have the language to speak about their constant experience of vulnerability and the many everyday violations experienced within a patriarchal system. This is particularly true when such experiences are intricately tied to the sexualised body. In this light, I interpret the mubobobo narrative as a metaphor for the women's complex and conflicted gendered experiences in a patriarchal world in which oppressive discourses run rife. Mubobobo is a means to express the textures of this vulnerability, which often have no language. The narrators could express their subtle and often overwhelming sense of vulnerability; contradictions experienced with the position 'woman'; and the complexity around their sexual subjectivities (seen through the juxtapositions of pleasure and vulnerability). Importantly, by drawing on mubobobo, they could discuss these things 'safely' without the threat of shame or blame. Mubobobo is a metaphor for the 'unspeakable' aspects of these women's experience as feminine subjects.

My findings resonate with an important study done by African cultural studies scholar Katrina Thompson. In her article 'Zanbari Women's Discursive and Sexual Agency: Violating Gendered Speech Prohibitions Through Talk About Supernatural Sex', Thompson (2011) examines how women navigate patriarchal restrictions about talking about sex and female desire by drawing on narratives of supernatural sex. A prominent discourse in coastal Tanzania is that of popobawa, a sexual demon which sexually assaults people and leaves them to tell this sexual story, sometimes even demanding that they do so (Thompson 2011). Thompson argues that through talk about popobawa, the women challenge hegemonic ideologies which silence them. In this way, she interprets these narratives of supernatural sex as examples of the women producing resistance narratives.

Along a similar vein, I argue that the women in my study worked with the mubobobo narrative in a way that resists hegemonic patriarchal discourses which silence women. They voiced previously silenced aspects of their sexual subjectivity/experience. The core threads of both research, mine and Thompson's (2011), point to women's use of culturally accepted narratives to destabilise dominant power structures. The women use these cultural narratives in their own way for a particular function—to express aspects of their feminine subjectivity, albeit in a form which may be 'disguised' to themselves and others. In the next section, I discuss another core aspect of mubobobo—narrators' linguistic images of men who perpetrate this 'rape from a distance'. I also theorise about the psychological function of such narratives.

'You Would Never Imagine Touching Them': Re-creating Selves Through Images of Mubobobo Perpetrators

During their stories, the women collectively constructed the social and psychic world of mubobobo perpetrators as 'other' and lacking in value. In what follows, I explore the women's language and the specific ways that they chose to present these men. I then theorise about the narrative and deeper psychological function of these constructions.

In the extracts below, Chadamawari and Akeyo construct mubobobo perpetrator types by drawing on common-sense aspects of these men's psychology.

> **Chadamwari:** But is it true what I heard that um like men who are shy they can't approach women, they go out to get the muti and men who stay unmarried because you know there are men who don't want to get married they just stay single bachelor whatever until forty fifty years. They go and get that muti for that pleasure and then they keep it and don't get married. Maybe they don't want the responsibility of a family or what. They just want to stay single.
>
> **Akeyo:** Isn't that a modified version of sexual toys and whatever because now days like the modern men are buying women, things that don't talk back, they can put them in whatever place.
>
> **SvS:** That is interesting.
>
> **Akeyo:** People who don't want responsibilities, no women in their house, homosexuals who don't want women anyways. They just need sex, but they don't want women in their space.
>
> (Focus group discussion 1)

In the talk above, Akeyo brings in the theme of sexual toys. Sexual toys are often caricatures of women's body parts onto which men can perform various sexual acts. Akeyo likens the body of female mubobobo victims to sexual toys. According to her representation, muti, like sexual toys, can be bought by men to achieve sexual gratification from a passive or powerless female figure. Here they construct women as powerless, passive, objects of men's desire. This is significant when considering that the women conveyed that mubobobo victims are usually unaware that someone is violating them, and they are powerless to identify the perpetrator or resist in any other way. So, in other words, both sexual toys and muti enable men to control the feminine and render the female body a site onto which men can perform perverse imaginings and desires. This is true for *all* men, even those who have relatively little social power.

The meanings that come through here provide rich insight about the ways in which these women perceive their bodies to be used by men. This reflects the nature of their subjective experiences in a patriarchal world within a culture that severely restricts women: a world where every man is a potential threat. On a surface level, the concept of mubobobo served as a metaphor for women's feelings and intuitions associated with various forms of bodily and psychic disruptions of feminine boundaries.

In the first extract above, Chadamwari sets the scene for the type of man who utilises muti to have sex with women. She conveys that her understandings about these types of men have been shaped by stories she has heard from others ('is it true what I heard?'). In doing so, she opens space for the other women to engage with her descriptions of mubobobo perpetrators. Her first description is that these men are shy. Here she connotes the sense of someone who cannot assert themselves socially and who may not have the capacity to establish certain relations, such as marriage. Behaviourally, says Chadamwari, these men are not able to approach women and they are not able to cope with the responsibility that marriage entails.

Akeyo voices the second characteristic of these men—they are unconventional men in that they don't want women in their house. She then goes further to say that these men are homosexuals who are not interested in establishing relations with women ('they just need sex, but they don't want women in their space'). In the Shona culture of Zimbabwe, there are negative connotations attached to men who are unmarried (Gwandure 2012), homosexual men (Hodza 2015), and men who do not overtly express their sexual needs. These positions connote the failure to achieve culturally 'appropriate' African manhood.

Below Akeyo, Elinah, and Cheney contribute to this co-constructed image of the typical mubobobo perpetrator type by narrating what they represent to be common aspects of these men's materiality.

> **Akeyo:** And in most cases it would be the worst people that you would never imagine even touching (group: Yes!) ja and these people they go around with pride like something like I am going in and out you know I am always sleeping with you.
>
> **Elinah:** But if you saw this person he doesn't bath all the time, he was smelling. But just imagine.
>
> **Cheney:** Imagine that person on top of you. Oh my God!
>
> (Focus group discussion 1)

Immediately evident in the talk above is the women's descriptions of the low personal hygiene of mubobobo perpetrators. Through this image of dirty, stinking men who do not have the resources to take care of their body and their dress, the women convey the message that these men are very poor and may be beggars who live on the streets. Akeyo, Elinah, and Cheney narrate a sense that they are disgusted by such men. This can be seen through their words, 'worst people', 'never imagine touching', and, 'imagine that person on top of you. Oh my God!' It is through these narratives that the women position themselves as different from men who perpetrate mubobobo. Implicit in their talk is a sense that they, as women, have access to more social power than these men. Akeyo says that the men are proud that they have a strategy that will enable them to obtain women sexually, as in usual circumstances they would be rejected by respectable women.

The women narrate the typical mubobobo perpetrator type as 'shy', 'homosexual', 'disgusting', and 'smelly' men who do not occupy social positions that afford them power in the African context. They infer that these men need to engage in alternative means by which to achieve the standards of appropriate masculinity. So, according to the women's view, these men turn to muti because their social situation is worse than women who are often helplessly stuck in the position of feminine roles, because like women these men have to fit the standards of traditional masculine roles, which their subject positions of gayness and shyness do not allow them to do. Thus, according to Chadamwari and Akeyo's interpretation, men's decision to use muti stems from a position of *weakness*, it is all that is left for them to do as men who are unable to face the world with women in it. Why did the women choose to represent mubobobo perpetrators as shameful and powerless? Could these constructions serve a particular function for the women who narrated them? I turn to this question next.

Akeyo, Chamadwari, Elinah, and Cheney are all Shona, a culture which largely restricts women's expression of their sexual desire. Often women who do not adhere to conservative sexual codes are constructed as bad and/or tainted in some way (see Potgieter et al. 2012). Many women are constantly under the threat of what McFadden (2003) terms 'brutal socialisation' (p. 54) through which female sexual memory and instinct is suppressed or 'muted'. Such suppression may be more complex when women have undergone repeated abuse across their life trajectory, as is the case for the women whose voices are documented above.

Women often internalise these negative messages about their bodies and their minds and such schemas may become toxic in the sense that they have a profound impact on women's sense of themselves in the world. As a result of these toxic social residues women may have deeply embedded intuitive feelings of shame, inadequacy, and unworthiness associated with their feminine sexual self (Enander 2010). With this in mind, the women's descriptions of mubobobo perpetrators as 'shy', psychologically and spiritually lacking, and 'dirty/disgusting' could represent the women's own sense of shame—a sense of themselves as somehow psychologically and socially inadequate and as unable to reach the status of 'respectable' femininity. The women's descriptions of mubobobo perpetrators as physically 'dirty' and 'smelly' are of significance when considering the ways in which poor women's bodies are degraded by the meanings that are generated through dominant social scripts. Perhaps these descriptions signify the women's internal information about their bodies as worthless, blameworthy, and tainted?

So, according to my interpretation, the participants' constructions of the social and material bodies of mubobobo perpetrators signify a process whereby they narratively project their negative feelings about sexuality onto these men. In other words, these images of the male perpetrators are a symbol of the women's suppressed sexuality/sexual desire. These images represent the 'tainted' parts of themselves that they have internalised through cultural messages. Importantly, by narratively 'getting rid' of these 'tainted' aspects of themselves the women can negotiate more positive selves in their tellings—selves that are more powerful in relation to the male perpetrators and selves that are not 'weighed down' by the negative aspects of female sexuality and desire.

From a feminist poststructuralist theoretical viewpoint, these narratives provide important insight into the process of agency and the narrative (re-)creation of selves that emerges among economically disadvantaged, migrant Zimbabwean women who have experienced a multitude of forms of abuse. Davies (2000) says that collective biography research comprises of imagined stories or creative narratives of a combination of various 'truths'. These resources are valuable for the participants as the act of speaking such things holds powerful potential for the disruption and decentring of discourses that one has been bound to. In this way, the speaker is able to 'unstitch' themselves from the confines of patriarchal meanings, slowly piece by piece. This is the essence of the process of transforming the feminine self (Davies 2000).

As seen in the analysis above, Akeyo, Elinah, Chadamwari, and Cheney utilised the mubobobo cultural script to mobilise negative feelings and intuitions about their bodies and their sexualities. They did this by narratively projecting these feelings onto the image of the typical mubobobo perpetrator type. During this particular narrative moment, they were able to create new selves that are not shaped by socio-cultural messages about female sexuality and violated bodies. They were thus able to work towards the disruption of subjectivities that have been moulded onto them by society. Davies et al. (2006d, p. 79) draw on Roland Barthes' concept 'decomposition' to theorise about a process observed in their own work. They write about a subjective move through which the narrator unmoors themselves from the confines of dominant discourses—a collective process of undoing the composition of social life. It is through such collective processes that individuals creatively shape new meaning about themselves in the world.

These (re-)constructions of self may also have an important impact on the ways in which the women *experience* the world. Gavey (1989, 2005) argues that by resisting certain discourses and by constructing the self in different ways, one shapes the ways in which they experience themselves in relation to others. Breaking gendered silence, even via metaphor and narrative projection, is a crucial step in the complex process of moving towards a position of agency. As women mobilise previously 'hidden' embodied emotions, they can begin to engage with these aspects of the self and work towards an integrated self and a position of fuller humanity. This kind of narrative mobilisation—the mubobobo narrative strategy—provides important insights into the creative ways in which abused, migrant women may enact agency in the world.

Scholars have argued that local, community narratives can function as a valuable resource for members of a collective, particularly when dominant cultural narratives fail to represent their lived experiences as individuals (Langellier and Peterson 2004; Mankowski and Rappaport 2000). There is often a divide between what is known and what can be said. Narrators need to find a way of making sense of their experience in such a way that it is legitimated and comprehendible (Culbertson 1995). The past is 'another country' through which women can voice 'unspeakable' aspects of their oppression by seeking landmarks—culturally accepted descriptions and explanations that provide orientation for approaching the self (Haaken 1999). Drawing on the mubobobo narrative, the women engaged with the landmarks and cultural information at their disposal, with powerful effects.

In this chapter, I have critically examined a central storyline of the women's collective narratives—mubobobo. I have considered these narratives in light of what they tell us about women's experience of, and resistance to, patriarchal oppression of female sexuality. Using a feminist poststructuralist lens, I do not view the women's language as a transparent tool conveying the 'facts' of experience (see Weedon 1987). Rather, I interrogate the social meanings surrounding mubobobo to find deeper meaning about the narrators' construction of identity. The women narrated certain selves collectively, in concert with others, allowing me to explore the links between their personal experiences and broader social meanings/ repertoires (see Davies et al. 2006d, p. 87). I have examined how the narrators make meaning *together* and how they negotiated meaning through the cultural resources available.

I interpret Mubobobo as a narrative strategy through which the women break the moulds of patriarchal power. It is through the culturally-accepted script that the women voice their memories of vulnerability, trouble and desire. They subtly communicate their experiences of patriarchal oppression of female sexuality and the effects of such oppression. Psychologically, the women 'get rid' of culturally entrenched negative feelings around female sexuality. Mubobobo is a symbolic way of communicating these things. The narrators voiced these complex aspects of their experience of female sexuality, the 'unspeakable', in a way that creates positive selves. Scholars working in the field of trauma and memory consistently argue that telling is an act of agency. The very act of telling positions women as authors of their own meaning, provides opportunities to create something new, and allows women to negotiate their own discursive agency (see Davies 1991). Expressing embodied experience is of critical importance, says Culbertson (1995), because remembering itself, 'creates a "me", finally, rather than a disembodied, confused recipient of harm' (p. 184).

In current South Africa, the context within which these women told their stories, there is limited language available and few opportunities through which women can express these aspects of their 'everyday' oppression. For many, the safer route is to remain silent. However, women continue to feel the 'truth' of their gendered experience, although this 'truth' may be sometimes imperfectly known. The core elements of these women's narratives—a sense of fear, suspicion, uncertainty, and negative feelings of shame and hatred, struck me on an emotional level. The textures of their narratives speak to their experience of inhabiting their social world as women. They provide us with insight into their complex experiences of patriarchal oppression of female sexuality. At moments we see resistance to such discourses, cracks or fissures whereby they position themselves as sexual agents and carve positive identities in the face of such oppression.

Mubobobo was a narrative tool through which the women could express complex aspects of the self. Within the nexus of patriarchal power systems, mubobobo allows these women to narrate their experiences in a 'disguised' form in a way that is safe, drawing on a cultural narrative that is shared by the other participants. It is through these narratives that the women break patriarchal moulds about what can be spoken. The women are able to integrate certain embodied feelings and emotions as part of their selves and, by doing so, they re-narrate themselves anew. The voices documented here stand as narratives of resistance in the sense that the narrators carve positive identities through their telling—identities which are often closed off in patriarchal cultures. Such voices illustrate the powerful act of *resisting* dominant patriarchal scripts that define what one can know about oneself and who one can be (Davies et al. 2006b). In the next chapter 'Crossing Borders in Africa: Collectively Narrating the "Foreigner" Within', I examine the women's stories of their travels through Africa and the physical and psychological borders they crossed to get to South Africa.

References

Arnfred, S. (2015). Female sexuality as capacity and power? Reconceptualizing sexualities in Africa. *African Studies Review, 58*(3), 149–170.

Artz, L. (2009). The Weather watchers: Gender, violence and social control. In M. (Ed.). Research Council.

Campbell, S. (2003). Respecting rememberers. In S. Campbell (Ed.), *Relational remembering. Rethinking the memory wars.* Oxford: Rowman & Littlefield Publishers.

Culbertson, R. (1995). Embodied memory, transcendence, and telling: Recounting trauma, re-establishing the self. *New Literary History, 26*, 169–195.

Davies, B. (1990). The problem of desire. *Social Problems, 37*, 801–816.

Davies, B. (1991). The concept of agency. *Social analysis, 30, Postmodern critical theorising*, 42–53.

Davies, B. (2000). *A body of writing 1990–1999.* Walnut Creek: AltaMira Press.

Davies, B., & Gannon, S. (2006). The practices of collective biography. In B. Davies & S. Gannon (Eds.), *Doing collective biography* (pp. 1–15). New York: Open University Press.

Davies, B., Brown, J., Gannon, S., Hopkins, L., McCann, H., & Wihlborg. (2006a). Constituting 'the feminist subject' in post-structuralist discourse. In B. Davies & S. Gannon (Eds.), *Doing collective biography* (pp. 167–181). New York: Open University Press.

Davies, B., Gannon, S., Laws, C., Lenz Taguchi, H., McCann, H., & Rocco, S. (2006b). Reading fiction and the formation of feminine character. In B. Davies & S. Gannon (Eds.), *Doing collective biography* (pp. 35–60). New York: Open University Press.

Davies, B., Dormer, S., Gannon, S., Laws, C., Lenz-Taguchi, H., McCann, H., & Rocco, S. (2006c). Becoming schoolgirls: The ambivalent project of subjectification. In B. Davies & S. Gannon (Eds.), *Doing collective biography* (pp. 16–34). New York: Open University Press.

Davies, B., Browne, J., Gannon, S., Honan, E., & Somerville, M. (2006d). 'Truly wild things': Interuptions to the disciplinary regimes of neo-liberalism in (female) academic work. In B. Davies & S. Gannon (Eds.), *Doing collective biography* (pp. 79–87). New York: Open University Press.

De Fina, A. (2003). *Identity in narrative: A study of Immigrant discourse.* Philadelphia: John Benjamins.

Dellenborg, L. (2004). A reflection on the cultural meanings of female circumcision: Experiences from fieldwork in Casamance, Southern Senegal. In S. Arnfred (Ed.), *Re-thinking sexualities in Africa* (pp. 79–94). Sweden: Almqvist & Wiksell Tryckeri AB.

Dosekun, S. (2007). 'We live in fear, we feel very unsafe': Imagining and fearing rape in South Africa. *Agenda, 21,* 89–99.

Enander, V. (2010). "A fool to keep staying": Battered women labelling themselves stupid as an expression of gendered shame. *Violence Against Women, 16,* 5–31.

Forter, G. (2007). Freud, Faulkner, Caruth: Trauma and the Politics of Literary Form. *Narrative, 15,* 259–285.

Gavey, N. (1989). Feminist poststructuralism and discourse analysis. Contributions to feminist psychology. *Psychology of Women Quarterly, 13,* 459–475.

Gavey, N. (2005). *Just Sex? The cultural scaffolding of rape.* New York: Routledge.

Gobodo-Madikizela, P., Fish, J., & Shefer, T. (2014). Gendered Violence: Continuities and transformation in the aftermath of conflict in Africa. *Signs: Journal of Women and Culture in Society, 40,* 81–99.

Gqola, P. (2015). *Rape: A South African nightmare.* Johannesburg, South Africa: Jacana Media.

Gqola, P. (2017). *Reflecting rogue: Inside the mind of a feminist.* Johannesburg, South Africa: Jacana Media.

Gwandure, C. (2009). Mubobobo: Women have no sexual fantasies in their sleep. *The Open Anthropology Journal, 2,* 74–81.

Gwandure, C. (2012). Sexual desire and expression among girls in a traditional Shona context. *Anthropologist, 14,* 415–423.

Haaken, J. (1999). Heretical texts: the courage to heal and the incest survivor movement. In S. Lamb (Ed.), *New versions of victims: Feminists struggle with the concept* (pp. 13–41). New York: New York University Press.

Haaken, J., & Reavey, P. (2010). Why memory still matters: Disturbing recollections. In J. Haaken & P. Reavey (Eds.), *Memory Matters: Contexts for understanding sexual abuse recollections* (pp. 1–14). New York: Routledge.

Hassim, S. (2014). Violent Modernity: Gender, Race and Bodies in Contemporary South African Politics. *Politikon: South African Journal of Political Studies, 41*, 167–182.

Hodza, F. (2015). Beyond heteronormativity: Doing gender and sexuality in university contexts. In S. van Schalkwyk & P. Gobodo-Madikizela (Eds.), *A reflexive inquiry into gender research: Towards a new paradigm of knowledge production & exploring new frontiers of gender research in Southern Africa* (pp. 27–45). Newcastle upon Tyne, UK: Cambridge Scholars Publishing.

Kelly, L., & Radford, J. (1996). 'Nothing really happened': The invalidation of women's experiences of sexual violence. In M. Hester, L. Kelly, & J. Radford (Eds.), *Women, violence and male power: Feminist activism, research, and practice* (pp. 19–33). Bristol, USA: Open University Press.

Lamb, S. (1999). Constructing the victim: popular images and lasting labels. In S. Lamb (Ed.), *New versions of victims: Feminists struggle with the concept* (pp. 108–138). New York: New York University Press.

Langellier, K. M., & Peterson, E. E. (2004). *Storytelling in daily life*. Philadelphia: Temple University Press.

Lempert, L. B. (1996). Language obstacles in the narratives of abused women. *Mid-American Review of Sociology, XIX*(1& 2), 15–32.

Mankowski, E. S., & Rappaport, J. (2000). Narrative concepts and analysis in spiritually-based communities. *Journal of Community Psychology, 28*, 479–493.

McFadden, P. (2003). Sexual pleasure as a feminist choice. *Feminist Africa 2: Changing Cultures*, 50–60.

Mkhize, N. (2004). Psychology: An African perspective. In D. Hook (Ed.), *Critical psychology* (pp. 24–52). Lansdowne, Cape Town: University of Cape Town Press.

Potgieter, C., Strebel, A., Shefer, T., & Wagner, C. (2012). Taxi 'sugar daddies' and taxi queens: Male taxi driver attitudes regarding transactional relationships in the Western Cape, South Africa. *Journal of Social Aspects of HIV/AIDS, 9*, 192–199.

Rajiva, M. (2014). Trauma and the girl. In M. Gonick & S. Gannon (Eds.), *Becoming girl: Collective biography and the production of girlhood* (pp. 137–158). Toronto, ON: Women's Press.

Reavey, P. (2010). Spatial markings: Memory, agency and child sexual abuse. *Memory Studies, 3*, 314–329.

Reavey, P., & Brown, S. D. (2007). Rethinking agency in memory: Space and embodiment in memories of child sexual abuse. *Journal of Social Work Practice, 21*, 5–21.

Reavey, P., & Brown, S. D. (2009). The mediating role of objects in recollections of adult women survivors of child sexual abuse. *Culture & Psychology, 15*, 463–484.

Root, M. P. P. (1992). Reconstructing the impact of trauma on personality. In L. S. Browne & M. Ballou (Eds.), *Personality and psychopathology* (pp. 229–265). New York: Guilford Press.

Sibanda, F. (2013). Experiencing sex via the 'blue tooth': Phenomenological reflections on the nature, use, and impact of mubobobo in Zimbabwe. *Greener Journal of Social Sciences, 3*, 84–90.

Tamale, S. (2005). Eroticism, sensuality and "women's secrets" among the Baganda: A critical analysis. *Feminist Africa, 5*, 9–36.

Tamale, S. (2011). Introduction. In S. Tamale (Ed.), *African Sexualities.* Cape Town, South Africa: Pambazuka Press.

Tamale, S. (2013). Eroticism, sensuality and 'women's secrets' among the Baganda. In S. Jolly, A. Cornwall, & K. Hawkins (Eds.), *Women, sexuality and the political power of pleasure* (pp. 265–285). London: Zed Books.

Tamboukou, M. (2008). A Foucauldian approach to narratives. In M. Andrews, C. Squirre, & M. Tamboukou (Eds.), *Doing narrative research* (pp. 102–120). London: Sage.

Thompson, K. D. (2011). Zanbari women's discursive and sexual agency: Violating gendered speech prohibitions through talk about supernatural sex. *Discourse & Society, 22*, 3–20.

Weedon, C. (1987). *Feminist practice and poststructuralist theory.* New York: Basil Blackwell Ltd.

CHAPTER 5

Crossing Borders in Africa: Collectively Narrating the 'Foreigner' Within

There was a lion and we pass the border there and we get into South Africa. We get in tough at night. We don't know where we are going to go but we are inside South Africa now because we see light … so when you pass into South Africa there is light, like heaven.
(Wendy, focus group discussion 7)

In this chapter, I explore the women's narratives of their journeys from their home country to South Africa. These are stories about crossing borders—both geographical and psychological. The geographical borders that these women crossed refer to the border posts, or physical entry points between countries in Africa. The psychological borders are evident through the women's narratives as borders of morality and sexuality that the women had to cross in order to survive in the space of transit—and their grappling with the meanings of these experiences in their retrospective accounts. The main theme of this chapter is women's narratives of sexual encounters with men at these border posts between African countries. Evident in the narratives is a potent tension between the strong 'cultural pull' towards the position of 'good' female sexual subject and on the other hand situations of poverty and desperation which 'push' women into engaging in sexual acts regarded as shameful/deviant. Throughout the narratives this tension plays out as the women constantly negotiate available identities.

S. van Schalkwyk, *Narrative Landscapes of Female Sexuality in Africa*, https://doi.org/10.1007/978-3-319-97825-3_5

I begin the chapter with a brief outline of my interpretive framework through which I make sense of the women's narratives. Here I outline silences in the narratives and examine what these mean through a social remembering lens. I then move into a deeper analysis of the women's narratives of self in transit. I end off this chapter providing theorisation about the psychological function such narratives play for the women's sense of self in the world. I focus on how they tell their stories of experiences at the border posts and what these narratives suggest about their experience of, and resistance to, patriarchal oppression of female sexuality.

'It Was Another Chapter of My Life': Encounters at the Border Posts Through a Social Remembering Lens

Sitting in the lounge at a group member's home drinking tea Lynn, Chadamwari, Wendy, and I discussed their experiences of travelling from their home countries to South Africa. Lynn travelled from Kenya, Chadamwari travelled from Zimbabwe, and Wendy travelled from Congo (DRC). Often their journeys took many days and were emotionally and physically exhausting. They arrived in South Africa with no idea where they will sleep that night. Lynn describes her travel from Kenya to South Africa. She told us that she came to South Africa in search of better employment opportunities, so she could provide for her family. Lynn's motivation to move to the country resonates with the motivation of many other African migrants (Daimon and Nyamunda 2013). South Africa has promised, and still does to some extent, a better life with greater social and economic opportunities for people from different parts of the African continent. At the time of her travels, Lynn was still married to her husband who abused her physically and emotionally. However, she travelled alone to South Africa to set up base for her family, leaving her three young children and her husband to join her at a later stage. Lynn narrates that she was short of money for her journey through which she had to travel from Kenya, through Tanzania, Zambia, Zimbabwe, and finally entering South Africa. She listed all the countries she had to pass through, conveying a deep sense of the enormity of her journey.

Lynn provides an account of her experience at one border post. She had run out of money and needed to present 500 US dollars in order to pass through. She explained that she met a man at this border post who helped her go through without having to pay. Lynn says that after this engagement she and the man 'became close'. He bought her breakfast at a restaurant and Lynn spent the day with him, as her bus was only arriving that evening. Besides this broad-brush narrative sketch, Lynn did not provide any further details about what happened with this male stranger. I wanted to know more about the gendered dimension of this experience—did the man perhaps want something in return for these favours? How did Lynn feel about this experience? When I attempted to delve further, Lynn responded as follows.

> **Lynn:** Look Sam I have a lot of experiences at those borders. If I start talking about it now we will sit until midnight. From the hour that I got into that Nissan bakkie[1] leaving Kenya it was another chapter of my life.
>
> (Focus group discussion 7)

However, straight after this Wendy provided more detail about these gendered encounters at the border posts.

> **Wendy:** You know that problem? That man helps you. It is not for free.
>
> **Lynn:** Ja [yes].
>
> **Wendy:** Ja, you know it's not for free. He wants to buy you things. You pay only your body. No other payment. Only your body. So, you must pay. Nothing is for free.
>
> (Focus group discussion 7)

Lynn's account of what happened with this man at the border post lacks information and through her language she skirts around the details of her experience. She says, 'I have a lot of experiences at the border posts' and she does not have time to unpack what happened in transit ('we will sit here until midnight'). Further, she narrates the time of transit as 'another chapter of my life' closing off any further discussion of the details. Lynn actively chooses to represent her experience in such a way within the particular moment of telling of the group discussion. I have termed such lack of disclosures narrative silences. Wendy's description of relations between women and men at border posts, on the other hand, 'fleshes out' Lynn's

[1] A South African word meaning a light truck or pick-up truck.

account and provides us with evidence that there is more to the story. In Wendy's account, we gain a sense of the contextual detail of transit—a social environment in which women's bodies are objectified as sources of exchange. In these spaces, exchanges (women paying with their bodies) happen often and for most women this is a way of surviving in transit. In this account Wendy affirms her status as an older and more knowledgeable group member, painting a linguistic picture of their common knowledge about transit. It is significant that Lynn affirms what she is saying. This made me wonder: what meaning can be made of Lynn's narrative silence?

Rather than interpret such lack of disclosures as insufficient data, I drew on the theoretical source guiding my study—feminist poststructuralist understandings of language and identity. Bronwyn Davies provides useful insights. Davies (2000) says that we must examine the discourse and practices through which gendered experience is articulated. She adds that it is equally important, though, to examine the absences and silences in accounts. Such silences, says Davies (2000), provide crucially important insights about subjectivity. Silences tell us about what narrators are 'allowed' to say in any given context and provide further rich theorisation of agency and identity within the narrated moment (Davies and Gannon 2006). I began to think about what Lynn's narrative silence suggests about her subjectivity, and what function such silence strategically plays in her management of a sense of self in the world.

Through a social remembering lens, I acknowledge that a survivor's relationship to their past is never immediately settled but rather continuously managed in the present moment of telling (Haaken and Reavey 2012). Identity and agency are constantly managed through different moments of telling. An important part of the process of narrating our memories is to construct the self in ways that manage the moral judgements that others can make about you/your story (Reavey and Brown 2007). The ways in which narrators choose to tell, and what they choose to narrate, is, of course, shaped by broader social-cultural scripts.

In her fascinating text, *The Trouble with Blame: Victims, Perpetrators, and Responsibility*, Sharon Lamb (1999) critically discusses contemporary meanings around victimisation, blame, and responsibility. She argues that limited and decontextualised social scripts of 'victim' deny women their power and shut down the potentials for human dignity and healing. Social scripts provide narrow scope of who can be classified 'victim' and under what circumstances victimhood can be ascribed (Lamb 1999). Women must fit certain criteria in order to achieve the status of true victim (Lamb

1999). Women who are passive non-agents and who act in line with 'appropriate' femininity are more easily believed and more readily accorded a victim status. On the other hand, women who are seen to exhibit agency or some level of choice in certain circumstances are most often blamed and considered culpable in their own abuse (i.e. they are not so easily afforded a victim status). Such discursive meanings are particularly pronounced when it comes to sexuality—women who exert agency as a sexual subject are positioned along the lines of 'bad' feminine subject (Macdonald 1995). Subject positions such as these encompass meanings and labelling of 'prostitute' or 'whore' (Gavey 2005), degrading women psychologically and sometimes even rendering them vulnerable to physical danger (McFadden 2003). I outlined these trends in detail in Chap. 2 of this book.

Patriarchal discourses surrounding blame and responsibility are infused into normative meanings around sex and violence. We only have to think of the ways in which rape victims are often scrutinised via the criminal justice system. This brings to mind the rape trial of former South African president, Jacob Zuma, whereby the accuser, a woman dubbed Khwezi who was close family friends with Zuma, was subject to much scrutiny about her sexual history. She was also accused of wearing sexually alluring clothing (the African Kanga). All this was to 'prove' that what had occurred was consensual sexual relations and not rape. Jacob Zuma had hordes of supporters, both men and women, who stood outside the court room in solidarity. He was acquitted of the rape in 2007.

In her work in another context, Liv Haram (2001) provides rich information about discursive processes of blaming women. In her fieldwork with the Meru tribe in northern Tanzania, Haram explores the question: Why are women seen as the cause and transmitters of HIV/AIDS? Haram (2001) found that emerging patterns of migration of single women from rural to urban areas in search of income-generating activities generates moral discourses around these women's sexual behaviour. Discourses centre on constructed binaries of unclean/dangerous (polluted) women and safe/clean women. Directly addressing the link between female sexuality; movement/mobility; and stigmatisation/blame/shame, Haram (2001) argues that women who travel for a better life, particularly those who travel alone are transcending the borders of 'appropriate' gendered behaviour outlined by patriarchy.

Haram (2001) argues that within the context of the HIV/AIDS crisis, single women's spatial mobility is intricately connected with discourses around respectability. Haram found that unmarried or single mothers were gossiped about in the community and labelled *Malaya* ('loose' or promiscuous). Some women who are rumoured to have multiple lovers are gang raped by groups of men. Actions which blame/shame, punish, or brutalise women for displaying active sexuality reflect underlying tensions in society between female sexuality and male control (Haram, 2001). The result: women who do not adhere to the normative patriarchal codes of femininity cannot achieve victim status and will most likely not be believed if they experience abuse. Within such discursive environments, it is very difficult for women to discuss aspects of their sexual agency/choice.

Within the context of socio-cultural dramas of abuse, women may have to negotiate *alternative* linguistic means to express and give meaning to their experiences. The reconstruction of memory is, in essence, the taming of embodied memories of the past (Culbertson 1995). In representing experience, narrators have to manage the kind of identities they present. This constitutes an important aspect of agency through which narrators may find their voice and reclaim a sense of identity (Culbertson 1995; Gobodo-Madikizela et al. 2014). Lynn's narrative silence about the details of her experience with the man at the border post is situated within such discursive frameworks. Lynn may have engaged in this narrative silence to avoid any negative connotations associated with her sexuality and her moral self. Any information that may suggest that Lynn engaged aspects of her sexuality for material gain in transit may compromise and render unstable her status as victim of gendered abuse across the lifetime.

My presence in the research space impacted the way in which Lynn told her narrative. I have never travelled through Africa and when entering these discussions, I had no knowledge about this experience and the stressors of survival. My lack of knowledge played a powerful role in co-constructing the meanings generated in the discussions (Melucci 1995). The narrators were the authority on the topic. I could only gain a sense of their experiences through listening to the women's stories and, more specifically, through what they chose to tell and the ways in which they chose to tell it. My position as white South African woman 'outsider'/researcher trying to understand their experience may have meant that narrative silences were necessary—the power dynamics may have set up a need for the women to manage potential shame or stigma from me. An important point is that my lack of knowledge meant that the women were able to utilise narrative silences (I did not know anything about transit). They were thus able to manage their identities though such specific 'codes' of shared information—they had shared knowledge about sexual relations with men at border posts but managed how they presented this knowledge to me.

While Lynn did not fully disclose the details of her encounter at the border post, in the rest of the discussion she described the context of transit in rich detail. The women collectively narrated the social context at the border posts as a space of chaos, confusion, and compromise. A subtext through their narratives was that women are hyper-vulnerable in this space and poverty and desperation motivate women to engage in sexual relations with men in exchange for money. The women utilised narrative strategies to communicate their experiences of travelling through Africa in ways that would not compromise their position as 'good' feminine subjects. I explore these narratives in detail in the next section, paying attention to what these stories tell us about the women's experiences of and resistance to patriarchal oppression of female sexuality.

Narratives of Transition, Powerlessness, and Place

All the women travelled alone through the spaces of Africa, except for Akeyo who travelled with her mother. They utilised many modes of transport including private vehicles or trucks and buses, carrying all their belongings with them. The stories that follow are encompassed by themes of financial deprivation; danger; forests rich with human bones; risking their lives to illegally pass gun-clad officers at the border posts; and being stranded in the dark with lions.

> **Lynn:** But then the other thing which I felt that really you know we kind of really put ourselves at risk during the seven days that I travelled. Apart from the map that I had if anything happened if there was an accident or if anyone killed me, nobody would have traced me.
>
> **Wendy:** Ja (yes).
>
> **Lynn:** And you don't think of that. And later I was just imagining how many women fall trap and they never reach their destination.
>
> (Focus group discussion 7)

And,

> **Chadamwari:** There are quite a lot. That's what I was going to talk about. Other women and especially women who die on the way from Zimbabwe.

> As short as it is, there is a lot that happened in those forests. Somebody was even telling me that those forests are rich with human bones. Those forests, because you know what they did it was a lot of pressure for people to go [to South Africa] so it was like a lot of people wanting to cross there to the other side of that border, that distance. There is a river and there is a forest. So, they would go through the forest. So, they would do a lot of things. I heard there were points where they were told to remove their clothes and you are with men, and you are a woman. You have a child now already you are not a girl you are a woman.
>
> (Focus group discussion 7)

The narrators co-construct a thick description of the social world of transit. It is significant that they do not discuss their own experiences directly at this point, rather they draw on 'things that they have heard' and general images of what occurs in transit, piecing together 'bits' of knowledge through their retrospective reflections. Their narratives convey rich meaning about their actual and symbolic consideration of these border posts—what these spaces mean for them now. Risk, uncertainty, chaos, and gendered violation were core elements of these stories. They described transit as a space in which normal social rules do not apply.

Lynn describes transit as 'another world'.

> **Lynn:** I was just thinking being on transit is another world. It is another world. And if you get to the border that place is so busy, and everything is there.
>
> **Chadamwari:** It is also very active.
>
> **Lynn:** Mmm ... it is *busy* twenty-four hours people going up and down. Everything is happening. So, you can imagine.
>
> **Wendy:** In the business that business of sexuality is too much.
>
> **Lynn:** It is too much! People are compromising too much. It is too much. You go and see, and you sit like this you watch, and you see this is like another life altogether.
>
> (Focus group discussion 7)

Lynn starts off by describing the space within which women travel through Africa as 'another world'. She provides a sense that such spaces are 'busy' with human interaction with people going up and down doing their business. Through her statement 'everything is happening', we get a sense that in this space a person witnesses or experiences things that are not part of normal life. Chadamwari concurs with her that such spaces are 'very active'. Wendy then moves deeper, specifically giving name to sexual behaviours. She conveys a sense that sex in the space of transit happens often and explicitly—'that business of sexuality is too much'. There is a sense that Wendy does not agree with the kinds of sexual activity that she witnesses in transit. Their narratives seem linked to undercurrents of morality and social values. We see this through Lynn's words 'it is too much! People are compromising too much.' Here there is a sense that the people who engage in sexual activity at these border posts are surrendering their values and human worth in transit by engaging in this business of sexuality. The 'business' of sexuality suggests a link with money and materiality. The linguistic picture painted is of a social environment within which the normal rules about the intimate nature of sex are inverted. People do not hide these sexual relations, it is out in public for all to see, as reflected through Lynn's comment 'you sit like this you watch'. The women narrate the space of transit as very different from their lives back home where sexuality is private and silenced.

The women also described connections that they witnessed on buses while travelling the long route to South Africa.

> **Lynn:** You see Chadamwari and Wendy I don't know whether you saw this Wendy when you travelled very long distance like the passengers in the bus they start connecting because the journey is long.
>
> **Chadamwari:** It is long. It is like you are living together.
>
> **Lynn:** Ja, the people like start trusting each other and you are *strangers*. And at night you know the people are already comforting themselves.
>
> (Focus group discussion 7)

Above the women discuss an example of social interactions that they witnessed while travelling on long distance buses through Africa. Lynn conveys that people start 'connecting' on these long journeys, *strangers* in fact start comforting themselves. Chadamwari concurs that she witnessed the same thing. Her words 'it is like you are living together' suggest that the nature of such connections is not like usual interactions that happen between people who have never met each other. Rather, she provides a sense of the intimacy involved. These strangers even start trusting each other, says Lynn. Drawing on their shared experience and what they witnessed travelling through Africa, Lynn and Chadamwari reinforce this image of transit as a place in which usual social boundaries are dissolved. The women's narratives of the *context* of this 'other world' of transit stood as the foundation for more complex stories through which the women co-constructed very particular kinds of identities.

'You Are Desperate, and You Want to Cross': Narrating the Desperate Self in Transit

A pressing theme throughout the women's narratives was that of severe financial deprivation and strain—simply not having enough money to travel through Africa safely in a way that could provide for their sustenance and accommodation needs. This was juxtaposed with a sense of their urgent need to get to South Africa to start a life making money or to set up a base for their children who were still in their home countries. Being stuck in Africa on the way was narrated as a central concern—anything could happen in this unknown space. These narrative threads of experience were utilised by the women together and formed the backdrop for their co-construction of 'desperate' selves in transit.

> **Wendy:** You are in that *need*. When you are travelling you are in that need and we don't have sometimes enough possibility for your travelling. So, it is like, I *want* to arrive in South Africa, but I don't have a possibility (resources). But I must use it all the way for me to arrive there.[2]
>
> **Lynn:** Arrive there [spoke simultaneously with Wendy].
>
> (Focus group discussion 7)

Using the words 'you' and 'we', Wendy positions the others in the group (and perhaps all women who travel through Africa) in the same category according to their dire economic circumstances during transit. She conveys a sense of a deep tension—they wanted to get to South Africa to gain access to a better life but did not have enough money to complete their journey successfully. We see through these stories that urgency

[2] Italics in this excerpt indicates Wendy's original emphasis.

and desperation are central features of these women's narratives of their experiences of travelling through Africa. The need to reach South African soil was urgent. Wendy told us in another discussion how she was stuck in Angola for a significant period of time because she did not have enough money to complete the rest of her journey. She described this as a terrifying time during which she felt increasingly vulnerable being in a foreign country. The descriptions of women's desperation and need in transit stood as a backdrop, an explanation if you will, for why women might engage with men sexually for money. Wendy's words, 'I must use it all the way for me to arrive there' suggest that while travelling through Africa women need to use what they have (their bodies) to ensure that they have enough money to successfully complete their journey to South Africa.

Along a similar discursive frame of desperation and need, Lynn narrates the following.

> **Lynn:** Ja (yes), like, for example, I travelled from Kenya through to Tanzania, Zambia, Zimbabwe, South Africa. And I experienced a lot of stuff. It was a journey for seven days but the things that I went through I think is two chapters of a book [Lynn: giggling]. If I start explaining to you one by one you will say, 'No, how did you go through that?' You know its really not easy as an African woman travelling through countries because one you have got limited finance or things have been tough for you at home. You are moving into another country you are going to look for a better life. But in the process of doing that you know you experience a lot of things. For example, myself I had R1800[3] from Kenya to South Africa. And those are how many countries that I had to go through? It was difficult. It was very, very difficult. There are some things that happened at the border posts it is just you know things you really don't want to do, but you are desperate, and you want to cross. And so, you are forced to like compromise with yourself.
>
> (Focus group discussion 7)

Lynn draws on her collective identity of 'African woman' to colour her description of her experiences in transit ('It is not easy as an African woman travelling through countries'). She discusses the severe financial strain she experienced in transit. She only had R1800 to complete her

[3] R1800 rand is equal to approximately 134 US dollars.

seven-day trip. With this money she had to cover her food, accommodation and bus fare. She also says that 'things were tough at home', emphasising her need to get to South Africa in search of a life with better opportunities. Lynn narrates that in the face of her hardships and financial need transit was 'very, very difficult'. It is because of this desperation that she had to do things that went at odds with her morals and values ('things you really don't want to do'). The underlying meaning she conveys is clear: Within the context of lack of money and resources, engaging in sexual relations with men for money is not something that she wanted to do, but it was one of the only options which allowed her to gain resources to successfully complete her trip to South Africa. It is through her description of her poverty and desperation in transit that Lynn conveys that sexual engagements with men in exchange for money are not a choice, it is something that one must do to survive. Lynn states that she was 'forced' to compromise with herself—she had to go against her morals and values about sex/sexuality to cope with the challenging environment of transit. There is a sense of a potent tension between the strong 'cultural pull' to be a good sexual subject while at the same time doing what you have to in order to survive. What would have happened if she had not compromised her morals and values? Many women get 'stuck' in transit, while some may be forced to return home to dire situations in their country of origin.

Evident throughout the stories was a deep sense of the psychological effects of this desperation in transit.

> **Chadamwari:** It's a coping mechanism because sometimes you don't really want to do it. You are not that kind of person that can do such a thing. Things like prostitution. But you end up when you reflect, and you think I actually had sex for this you know, or I actually did this for that. You know something that you wouldn't do in normal life.
>
> **Lynn:** Exactly!
>
> **Chadamwari:** You compromise.
>
> **Lynn:** You compromise, and you block your mind. And you don't even know what's right or wrong. Your sense of decision making kind of like shuts down. So, ja (yes), it is not a good experience. It is terrible.
>
> (Focus group discussion 7)

It is significant that Chadamwari names these 'things' that happen in transit (sex with men for money) as prostitution. This act of naming attaches an additional layer of meaning for these described encounters. From the frame of reference of her culture (Shona from Zimbabwe), women who engage in prostitution are heavily stigmatised and shamed (Tamale 2011). However, she distances herself and other African women ('you') from any responsibility for such an act. Firstly, she describes their innate characters by saying, 'you are not that kind of person who can do that thing. Things like prostitution'. Here, she implies meaning that such behaviour is not normal for them; it is not something that they would do in 'normal life'. Rather it is a coping mechanism to survive in the chaotic and oppressive space of transit. Women like them are forced to have sex with men as a coping strategy, but they 'really don't want to do it'. The oppressive space of transit, according to Lynn and Chadamwari, mean that women have to compromise their morals and values, 'blocking their mind' to what they are doing. They had to consciously block off meanings of 'appropriate' femininity from their cultures of origin and dissociate from the world they knew. This involved entering an unknown place where their minds were thrown into another mode of mental functioning. The desperate self was functioning in transit. This desperate self was presented as a 'foreigner' self in that it behaved in ways that are very different to what the true self would. By constructing the true self as absent in transit, the narrators convey meaning that they are not accountable for their actions within these spaces. They narrate that within this space of desperation they experienced a loss of their capacity to view the world as they used to. This is evident through their words, 'you don't even know what is right or wrong' and 'your sense of decision making kind of like shuts down'.

Lynn then expands on this description of lack of choice in transit by connecting her personal experiences with the experiences of other women who travel through Africa.

> **Lynn:** I think … a lot of men take advantage of you know those kinds of situations. Especially (of) young women who are going through. And personally, I have experienced bad things being on transit. And I have also watched other women what they go through and how they compromise and the things they do. You just look at it and say it's also another form of abuse that you never even kind of classify.
>
> (Focus group discussion 7)

Lynn presents this financial hardship as a common experience of 'African women' travelling through the border post. We get a sense that oppression is magnified for all women in the space of transit and that such oppression shapes women's behaviour. She says that she has observed this—'I have also watched other women that go through and how they compromise and the things they do.' Men easily take advantage of travelling women who do not have money. Women's lack of choice in transit and the circumstances that force them into compromising their values is another form of abuse, says Lynn. She explicitly names these experiences as abuse. She suggests that there is not sufficient language to acknowledge women's oppressive experiences in transit, evident through her words ('it's also another form of abuse that you never even kind of classify'). Lynn conveys powerful meaning about the unique and intersectional oppression of migrant women who are faced with financial challenges, physical burden and stress, and the compounding psychological effects of uncertainty and the will to set up a 'good life' for their children.

By narratively connecting her own experience to other African women, or recognisable feminine subjects, Lynn emphasises their shared experiences in transit. She links her personal experience to the broader social context of this space, drawing on discourses of unequal gendered power dynamics. Men have the power to take advantage and women do not have the power to choose differently. Men are active and responsible for their actions while women's responsibility is softened—their actions are shaped by the oppressive context of transit. The connection of personal experiences with the realities of others is a critical resource for women for analysing their own experiences of oppression (McFadden 2003). The narratives served to situate the encounters at the border posts within the broader social context of women's oppression. Importantly, it is through such narrations that the women were able to linguistically frame their experiences at the border posts as *abuse* and position themselves as victims of the oppressive social forces at play.

Social discourses structure meaning about what experiences constitute abuse. This deeply influences meanings around who can position themselves as victims (Lamb 1999). Women have to fit certain criteria to achieve the status of 'true victim'. To be considered 'victim', women need to convey a 'neat' picture of the context of their experience. Importantly, the boundaries between men's patriarchal power as perpetrators and women's powerlessness should not be blurred. If women exhibit any level of agency they are considered culpable. If, for example, such sexual relations between men and women at the border posts were framed as mutually beneficial—men receiving sex and women receiving money—women would not be able to position themselves as victim. This then opens women up to stigma and shame surrounding their engagements in sex for money.

In spite of such discursive challenges, the women are able to name their experiences as abuse through their narratives of their desperation in the chaotic and confusing world of transit. Naming abuse is an important part of the processes of healing (Hage 2006). The ability to name these experiences as abuse is important for the women narrators. It has powerful implications for their subjectivities, as they are able to protect themselves from the shame surrounding the action of utilising their sexuality for material gain. The women are thus challenging patriarchal scripts and negative definitions of female sexuality by strategically positioning themselves as victims of the oppressive system in transit. They are collectively crafting a different reality for themselves through their specific ways of remembering these events in this collective biography discussion. In the next section I discuss Lynn, Chadamwari and Wendy's talk about another kind of 'foreigner self' in transit—a psychologically damaged self.

'I Just Became Another Person': Narrating a Damaged Self in Transit

Through the collective stories of the space of Africa, the border post confusion and conflict, there emerged another narrative thread which spoke powerfully to the kinds of selves the women presented during these discussions. Drawing on broader psychological discourses, the women spoke about a 'damaged' self that functioned in the space of transit. Intricately connected to this sense of self was the women's past experiences of abuse and violation at the hands of various men in their families and communities. They narrated that past effects of abuse 'revisited' powerfully at the border posts.

> **Lynn:** I think also the other thing that makes it worse is you are from a family that is not functioning properly, or you are coming from an abusive relationship. For example, myself, travelling in between those countries you have got that unhealthy bond that you always want to be attached to someone. I don't know if you experienced what I did? Ja like (you just want) to feel protected.
>
> **Chadamwari:** There is somebody there for you.

> **Lynn:** Yes! And you really don't know yourself, so it is very, very difficult for you to make your own decisions as a person. You kind of keep leaning and what I experienced, I can't speak for everyone, but I can just speak out my experience. What I have watched and what I think, most of the people that come from broken families that are running from country to country, they are much more vulnerable to the men that take advantage of them on the way. And this is something that I have watched.
>
> (Focus group discussion 7)

Lynn conveys meaning that particular versions of the past—abuse and trauma in families—heightens women's already vulnerable position in transit. Lynn had experienced years of violent abuse at the hands of her husband and repeated sexual abuse as a child. As a result of this abuse, says Lynn, she has a damaged self which is not strong enough to face the world alone. This self is always in need of someone there to 'be attached to'. Her words 'you keep leaning' signify a sense of her own powerlessness. She conveys a sense that the abuse has broken her down to a level of constant dependency. This self that strives for the 'unhealthy bond' is weak, vulnerable and traumatised—a fitting example of a 'true' victim of abuse, as outlined by dominant cultural scripts (see Lamb 1999). This self is not functioning in a normal way, it is detached ('you don't know yourself') and lacking agency ('it is very, very difficult for you to make your own decisions as a person'). This self may seek out the wrong people, such as men in transit who want to take advantage of the feminine body.

From a social remembering perspective, we cannot say that these narratives unequivocally suggest some kind of innate pathology caused by an abusive past. Of course, this does not negate years of research that suggests that abuse harms women psychologically (see Dutton and Painter 1993; Walker 1979a, b). Rather, we need to look below the surface of language to explore deeper meanings and what this means for the narrators' sense of themselves in the world (see Weedon 1987). This allows us to avoid falling into the trap of assuming powerlessness as the only feature of women's lives (see Mohanty 1991; Reid and Walker 2005). The women chose to tell their stories in these ways for a certain social/psychological purpose. Such narrations are of crucial importance to their project of the self within the collective biography research settings.

Reavey and Gough (2000) provide important insights here. In their work with women who have experienced sexual abuse, they found that women strategically work to 'dis/locate' blame. Women draw on their past experiences of abuse to explain their current behaviour, and, in doing so, they manage dilemmas about their agency in the present. So, by drawing on psychological discourses of 'typical' abused woman—traumatically bound to her past in a cycle of repetition (O'Dell 2003)—the narrators are working to ensure that moral judgments cannot be made about their actions.

Lynn and Chadamwari elaborate on this damaged self in transit.

Lynn: And then you go beyond your boundaries ...

Chadamwari: You don't have any boundaries at that point.

Lynn: I don't think you have any boundaries at that point.

Chadamwari: And you regain them when you get to the other side (South Africa).

Lynn: To the other side. And then it is funny because now I have just remembered and when you reach your destination (South Africa) then you become another person. So, it is kind of a personality split. I don't know whether this is coming from the abuse that somebody has experienced. Especially in childhood where maybe you have had uh assault and stuff. You know it kind of splits you. Then it's like again when you reach South Africa then that person is gone. You become somebody else. Now you are in South Africa, you are good.

(Focus group discussion 7)

Lynn and Chadamwari co-narrate an image of blurred boundaries of the self in transit. Once again, they use the pronoun *you*, framing their description as part of the broader experience of African women migrants. The boundaries that they refer to here seem to suggest psychological boundaries. As they moved through the geographical spaces of the border posts, their morals, values, and rules of behaviour dissolved. They repeat 'you don't have any boundaries' and strongly reinforce the idea that what they have learnt about femininity and ways of being proper sexual subjects did not apply in transit. Ways of behaving and relating to others was different in this space.

The narrative of the 'damaged self' in transit emerges powerfully. Lynn draws on trauma discourse, or what O'Dell (2003) calls the 'language of trauma', to give meaning to their story. '[Y]ou become a different person' and 'it is kind of a personality split' reflect broader meanings related to trauma, compartmentalisation of identities, and a betrayed self. Lynn refers to the 'splitting off' of positive and negative parts of themselves—the self with no boundaries in transit and the 'good' self that they 'become' when they reach South Africa. The self in South Africa is morally correct and abides with the rules of sexual engagement.

The narrators draw on rich moral landscapes associated with female sexuality. Importantly, this damaged self is constructed as not part of the true self. The damaged self emerges in transit; it is the self that goes beyond moral boundaries while the true self is not implicated. Interestingly, their meanings about morality were closely tied to particular spaces. The 'bad' damaged self is associated with the dark chaotic world of transit while the 'good self' is associated with South Africa. Space has been identified as an important feature of women's agency. Spaces are imbued with social meanings and are an important narrative resource for women to make meaning about themselves in the world (Taylor 2010). Paula Reavey (2012) suggests that women make meaning about their power/powerlessness through the use of space associations. Such associations have important implications for identity. What we see above is that the women clearly narratively associate the space of transit with powerlessness and the space of South Africa with increased power and morality. They are thus able to present their current self is South Africa in a positive way as 'good' and morally correct.

At the core, patriarchal oppression functions around harmful meanings related to 'bad' sexual behaviour versus 'good' sexual behaviour (McFadden 2003; Gavey 2005). The women powerfully resist these discourses refusing to take up the position of bad sexual subject. The damaged self that had sex with men in transit was a transitory self and not part of the core identity. This is the self that is implicated, not their true self. Importantly, while the women position themselves as powerless through the narrative of the damaged self in transit, they do not own this position.

Scholars have argued that women need to more rigidly adhere to proper rules of conduct (sexual restraint and passivity, proper dress, etc.) in public spaces because these very spaces are associated with *sexualised* meanings around men's entitlement to punish women who act out of line (Doeskun 2007; Haram 2001; McFadden 2003). Women are vulnerable to scrutiny, shame or violence if they openly display aspects of their sexuality in public spaces (Tamale 2011). However, the narrative of the 'damaged self' was useful for the women. It was a way of making meaning about sex with men in transit that minimises their culpability. In the next section, I theorise about the deeper psychological function of such collective narratives.

The Psychological Function of Collective Memories of Transit

The women's heart-wrenching stories about the psychological and physical dangers of transit bring into light their meaning about the unpredictability of transit and women's increased vulnerability within these spaces. Their collective analysis of the unique manifestations of patriarchal oppression within these spaces contributes important knowledge. It provides insight into the ways in which these women experience patriarchal oppression of female sexuality. Their accounts were infused with meanings about the intersections of poverty and citizenship and women's bodies as a means for exchange—as objects that exist to pleasure men. Their narratives also tell us much about the kinds of identities that are available to these women. Their accounts 'map out' and colour their experiences of the oppression of female sexuality as migrant women who have travelled through Africa.

South African feminist scholar Catriona Macleod (2008) reminds us that it is of critical importance to study gender within the 'patchworks of global patriarchies' (p. 348)—how patriarchal oppression manifests differently in different contexts and how women have unique experiences of such violence. Space, temporal moment and individuality are important elements of such an analysis (Macleod, 2008). The narrators weave their own unique story as authors—a story intricately connected to their identities. They are contributing their own unique patchwork of meaning to global knowledge and binding these threads of meaning as an important part of their past. Their narratives of transit are their own representations of the space that they travelled through. They speak for themselves. The linguistic images they create extend beyond understandings or prescriptions offered by (Western) scholars in the field, because here there is something new, something specific to their lives and interpretations.

On the one hand the women's narratives highlight elements of their agency seen through their choice to leave their homes and pursue a better life in South Africa. However, in order to survive during their travels, many women are forced to have sex with men in exchange for money.

There are negative connotations associated with selling one's body. The act of utilising one's body for material gain is out of line with dominant patriarchal scripts of women's passive sexuality and is therefore highly stigmatised in most African cultures. Women do not have the space or the language to discuss aspects of their sexual agency as this often places them in a dangerous position where they are blamed or shamed for their actions (McFadden 2003; Tamale 2011). In the face of such complexities (and dangers), the women adopted alternative narrative strategies. The 'foreigner' self in transit (desperate and damaged) was a core narrative resource through which the women linguistically displaced shame or potential negative meanings about sex with men in transit. The linguistic image of the 'foreigner' self was a means through which the women could express their complex experiences in transit while at the same time presenting positive selves in the moment of telling.

Importantly, such narrations of identity are not mere linguistic achievements. Gavey (2005) reminds us that constructing the self in certain ways shapes the ways in which narrators experience themselves in the world. All subjects are situated within the linguistic realm and to change discourses is, for the large part to change oneself (Davies and Gannon 2006). In other words, it is through such discursive practice that people actively produce social and psychological realities. There were deeper psychological processes at play for the women narrators. Through these ways of remembering the narrators were able to psychologically manage negative emotions associated with patriarchal oppression of female sexuality.

Women's engagement in sex for money is a topic heavily loaded with cultural meanings of shame. In the face of harmful discourses surrounding female sexuality, this is a dangerous topic for the women because they could open themselves up to shaming or judgement. Many of the women discussed that they had never spoken about these specific experiences in transit. The research discussions were, for most, the first time that they had voiced these experiences. The central motif of the women's collective memories, the 'foreigner' self in transit, seemed to provide a socially acceptable way of explaining their actions in transit. They were able to tell their 'messy' stories in a way that is intelligible to others—to themselves and to me, the researcher. These 'foreigner' selves represented a symbolic scapegoat for the narrators' actions. Telling these kinds of stories may have helped the women downplay a sense of their own culpability in transit. They managed the aura of shame that is so powerfully and intricately linked to female sexuality.

My presence in the group discussions may have influenced the ways in which the women told these stories. On many occasions, I told the women how I valued the gender-based violence work that they were collectively doing in their women's group. They may have wanted to strategically present such good moral selves to me—the 'other', the outsider, the researcher who was going to write about their stories. The narrative images of 'true' victim and moral agent are compatible with their identities as support group members. Perhaps they were concerned that any hint at their sexual agency or culpability would have complicated my view of their integrity and sincerity with regards to the gendered abuse they have experienced throughout their lives?

The 'foreigner self' narrative strategy emerged at the moment of telling and is deeply connected to the collective dynamic. The space of the collective biography discussion played a significant role in the women's resistance of patriarchal meanings around female sexuality. The women shared the experience of travelling through Africa. These shared experiences allowed them to make sense of these experiences while at the same time making positive meaning about themselves in the world. This is something which may not be imaginable on an individual level. The power of collective telling cannot be underestimated (Davies and Gannon 2006). Haaken (1999, p. 24) says of such spaces,

> Some of the pleasure in social remembering, in the sharing and creation of a common stock of stories, is in the sense of strength that the group provides in protecting against previously overwhelming experiences, thus making them more emotionally manageable.

The act of agency lies not only in the capacity to tell but in taking up the position of author of your own story (Davies 1991). Agency lies in the action of choosing to tell your story in your own way. Agency is about shaping your own reality through these modes of telling. This is exactly what the women did. They were able to recreate their past and find their voice in the face of patriarchal oppression. Importantly, they disrupted hegemonic scripts about female sexuality, inverting the binaries of this dominant narrative in their own way for the narrative purpose of finding meaning about their experiences. Through this process, they co-created selves that are not defined by patriarchal shame.

In this chapter, I have traced women's narratives of their travel through border posts in Africa with a specific focus on women's stories of having sex with men in exchange for money. The monitoring of one's sexuality takes on a very different image in strange environments where women are often hyper-vulnerable to abuse and judgement. Evident in the women's narratives is a potent tension between the strong 'cultural pull' towards the position of 'good' female sexual subject and the realities of poverty and desperation which 'push' women into engaging in sexual acts regarded as shameful/deviant. However, the women work collectively to construct a positive sense of self through their stories. They avoid the danger of negative categories generated by harmful patriarchal discourses about female sexuality. As is consistent with the collective biography approach to language and subjectivity (see Davies and Gannon 2006), I focus on the women's words and collectively constructed repertoires but also their silences. Silence is a powerful piece in this chapter. In such collective work, silence can often be as important as words themselves. Moments when narratives lack information tell researchers much about participants' inner world and the battles that they are fighting. The first section outlines narrative silences during which the women skirted around the details of their encounters with men at border posts. However, later on, as the narratives in the second section show, the narrative of the 'foreigner' self—both the desperate and damaged aspects—'filled' in the gaps of what very well may have been silence.

I identify a central motif of the women's narratives, the 'foreigner self', as a linguistic resource which the women used to talk about their experiences in transit. It is through this narrative that the women were able to manage potential blame or shame about having sex with men in exchange for money. The co-constructed narrative allowed the women to position themselves as powerless in transit; however, they did not own this powerless position. They were able to narrate their experiences without being 'weighed down' by shame or blame associated with selling the body. Ultimately, the women were able to narrate the full complexity of their experiences, as authors of their story, and make new meanings about themselves in the world. Such collective telling is of critical importance considering the deep stigma, shame and silence connected to female sexuality and women's bodies in current South Africa. In the next chapter I explore women's stories of living in South Africa. I focus on their narrative imaginings of the sexual world of black South African women—symbolic female 'others'—which shed important insight into the ways in which the narrators experience patriarchal oppression of female sexuality in post-apartheid South Africa rife with xenophobia, racism, and deep-seated poverty.

References

Culbertson, R. (1995). Embodied memory, transcendence, and telling: Recounting trauma, re-establishing the self. *New Literary History, 26(1)*, 169–195.

Daimon, A., & Nyamunda, T. (2013). *Smuggling through fluid and porous African borderlands and the state's response: The case of the Zimbabwe-South Africa border during the crisis in Zimbabwe, 1998–2009*. Unpublished Manuscript.

Davies, B. (1991). The concept of agency. *Social analysis, 30, Postmodern critical theorising* (pp. 42–53).

Davies, B. (2000). *A body of writing 1990–1999*. Walnut Creek: AltaMira Press.

Davies, B., & Gannon, S. (2006). *Doing collective biography*. New York: Open University Press.

Doeskun, S. (2007). Don't be sexy, don't be there. Discourses of space, danger, and women's sexuality in South Africa. In *Sexuality in Africa magazine* (pp. 7–9). Lagos, Nigeria: Africa Regional Sexuality Resource Centre.

Dutton, D. G., & Painter, S. (1993). Emotional attachments in abusive relationships: A test of traumatic bonding theory. *Violence and Victims, 8*, 105–120.

Gavey, N. (2005). *Just Sex? The cultural scaffolding of rape*. New York: Routledge.

Gobodo-Madikizela, P., Fish, J., & Shefer, T. (2014). Gendered violence: Continuities and transformation in the aftermath of conflict in Africa. *Signs: Journal of Women and Culture in Society, 40*(1), 81–99.

Haaken, J. (1999). Heretical texts. In S. Lamb (Ed.), *New versions of victims: Feminists struggle with the concept* (pp. 13–31). New York: New York University Press.

Haaken, J., & Reavey, P. (2012). Why memory matters: Disturbing recollections. In J. Haaken & R. Reavey (Eds.), *Memory matters: Contexts for understanding sexual abuse recollections* (pp. 1–13). New York: Routledge.

Hage, S. M. (2006). Profiles of women survivors: The development of agency in abusive relationships. *Journal of Counselling and Development, 84*, 83–94.

Haram, L. (2001). 'In sexual life women are hunters': AIDS and women who drain men's bodies. The case of the Meru of northern Tanzania. *Society in Transition, 32*(1), 47–55.

Lamb, S. (1999). Constructing the victim: Popular images and lasting labels. In S. Lamb (Ed.), *New versions of victims: Feminists struggle with the concept* (pp. 108–138). New York: New York University Press.

Macdonald, M. (1995). *Representing women: Myths of femininity in the popular media*. London: Edward Arnold.

Macleod, C. (2008). 'Who? What?: An unindicted view of towards a new psychology of women from post-apartheid South Africa. *Feminism & Psychology, 18*, 347–357.

McFadden, P. (2003). Sexual pleasure as a feminist choice. *Feminist Africa 2: Changing Cultures*, 50–60.

Melucci, A. (1995). The process of collective identity. In H. Johnston & B. Klandermans (Eds.), *Social movements and culture* (pp. 41–63). Minneapolis: University of Minnesota Press.

Mohanty, C. T. (1991). Under western eyes: Feminist scholarship and colonial discourses. In C. T. Mohanty, A. Russo, & L. Torres (Eds.), *Third world women and the politics of feminism* (pp. 51–80). Indianapolis: Indiana University Press.

O'Dell, L. (2003). The "harm" story in childhood sexual abuse: Contested understandings, disputed knowledges. In P. Reavey & S. Warner (Eds.), *New feminist stories of child sexual abuse: Sexual scripts and dangerous dialogues*. London: Routledge.

Reavey, P. (2012). The spaces of memory. In J. Haaken & P. Reavey (Eds.), *Memory matters: Contexts for understanding sexual abuse recollections* (pp. 131–141). New York: Routledge.

Reavey, P., & Brown, D. (2007). Rethinking agency in memory: Space and embodiment in memories of child sexual abuse. *Journal of Social Work Practice, 21*(1), 5–21.

Reavey, P., & Gough, B. (2000). Dis/locating blame: Survivors' constructions of self and sexual abuse. *Sexualities, 3*(3), 325–346.

Reid, G., & Walker, L. (2005). African sexualities: Editorial introduction. *Culture, Health and Sexuality Journal, 7*(3), 185–194.

Tamale, S. (2011). Introduction. In S. Tamale (Ed.), *African sexualities: A reader* (pp. 1–7). Cape Town: Fahamu Press.

Taylor, S. (2010). *Narratives of identity and place*. London: Routledge.

Walker, L. E. (1979a). How battering happens and how to stop it. In D. Moore (Ed.), *Battered women* (pp. 59–78). Beverly Hills, CA: Sage.

Walker, L. E. (1979b). *The battered woman*. New York: Harper & Row.

Weedon, C. (1987). *Feminist practice and poststructuralist theory*. New York: Basil Blackwell Ltd.

CHAPTER 6

Psycho-Social Borders and Imagining the South African Female 'Other'

This year marks the 24th year since the end of apartheid in South Africa. The new democratic era promised hope and change for all. Many people began moving to South Africa from other African countries in search of work and a better life (Chigeza et al. 2013). All the women migrants whose voices are documented in this book mentioned that they made the decision to travel to South Africa to improve their life circumstances and the lives of their families. The promises of hope and change for a new South Africa unfortunately were not fulfilled. Not much has changed in terms of poverty and job creation. Today, the socio-spatial landscape of South Africa remains very much the same as during the apartheid era, with poor townships segregated away from the main city hubs. Black people still represent the most marginalised and poor groups in the country (Boonzaier and de la Rey 2003). Many black South Africans and African migrants living in the country struggle with access to housing and employment. Vast overcrowding and poor service delivery in the townships mean that most people do not have access to basic human needs such as electricity, running water, and sanitation (Hayem 2013). This is arguably the result of corrupt governments and mismanagement of government resources which affect the poor the most. Women disproportionately face the burden of poverty in the country, many of whom act as breadwinners of their family or sole supporter of their children and other extended family members (see Moore 2013; Pereira 2002).

S. van Schalkwyk, *Narrative Landscapes of Female Sexuality in Africa*, https://doi.org/10.1007/978-3-319-97825-3_6

In addition to the devastating rates of violence against women, the past decade has seen increased documentation of a relatively new form of violence—xenophobia. Xenophobia literally translates to a distrust or fear of non-citizens who are perceived to be foreign or strange. This manifests in certain in-group perceptions of an out-group. In South Africa, this has resulted in strained relations between many black South Africans and black African migrants living in the country. Spates of violent actions have been documented against black African migrants and refugees (Harris 2002). Prominent examples in the media are the burning and looting of foreigner-owned 'spaza'[1] shops and other incidents of mass violence. The underlying psychological features of xenophobia is to view African foreigners in terms of a homogenous category lumping them as the same (it is 'us' vs 'them'). Black African foreigners are perceived as 'others' who do not belong in South Africa and who are not deserving of a socially valued existence (Strauss 2011). They are seen as a threat stealing valuable resources such as jobs and housing from South African citizens (Sinclair 1998). Some scholars have argued that xenophobic attitudes are a result of a change in the idea of citizenship and belonging encompassed in the idea of *African ubuntu*, or one-ness, an important principle in the nation-building process of the 1994 democratic elections (Strauss 2011), towards a more exclusionary process that differentiates along the lines of South African citizenship (Hayem 2013).

Ultimately, through xenophobic speak, black migrants from other parts of Africa are constructed as a threat to the transformative post-apartheid project because they deprive black South Africans of their rightful opportunities (Strauss 2011). Black African foreigners in the country are the scapegoat, the outsider, the 'Other' perceived as people who contaminate life and stunt progress in post-apartheid South Africa (Morris 1998). Xenophobic violence in the country reached critical stages in May 2008 and then again in 2011. Evidence from the media and academic arena suggests, however, that xenophobic attitudes are still pervasive today (Chigeza et al. 2013; The South African Press Association 2013). Narrative evidence from my work with the group for abused women suggests that

[1] Spaza shops refer to informal shops run from the owner's home in a township or low socio-economic community. These shops usually sell small household items. The success of such businesses lies in the fact that due to unreliable public transport, it is difficult for people to travel from the townships to larger shopping centres which are in more affluent areas. Most people living in townships do not own their own vehicles and have to rely on costly and unreliable mode of transport in the form of mini bus taxis, buses, and trains.

discourses around foreign-ness and inferiority shape the lives of the African migrants in powerful ways. This was evident through their narratives of a constant sensitivity in the workplace; struggles to secure accommodation rentals; and a general perceived atmosphere of mistrust experienced while moving through everyday life.

In this chapter, I draw on the voices of six African migrants. Four women of the Shona culture from Zimbabwe; one woman of the Lou culture from Kenya; and one woman from the Democratic Republic of Congo (DRC). I use data from two group discussions that included only migrant women. The first discussion was based on the women's narrations of mubobobo and is an extension of the discussions documented in Chap. 4. This discussion took place in a small seminar room at a church in a low-income area of Woodstock, Cape Town. All the participants were from Zimbabwe. Akeyo and Chadamwari had been living in South Africa for eight and five years respectively. Akeyo worked part-time assisting a local NGO with fundraising activities. Chadamwari was unemployed and had been looking for work for quite some time. It was her goal to earn enough money to send to family members who are raising her child in Zimbabwe.

Elinah and Cheney had both been living in South Africa for three years working part-time as domestic workers, with a minimal wage and no benefits or job security. All the women except Akeyo were divorced and thus had to deal with the stigma that is so often attached to single women who travel by themselves (see Haram 2004). These women also experienced the financial challenges involved with being single mothers and often sent most of their money back to their extended family members who were raising their children in Zimbabwe.

The second discussion also consisted of foreigner women. Lynn from Kenya was 42 years old at the time of the interview and she had three children who were approaching teenagehood. At the time of the discussion, she had been living in South Africa for seven years and worked full time at a non-profit organisation. Lynn had travelled from Kenya to South Africa alone and later had arranged for her children and husband to join her. Her husband had been abusive throughout their marriage, but the abuse became more severe when her husband joined her in Cape Town. Eventually, she managed to leave him with the children and, after years of harassment as her husband tried to return to the family on multiple occasions, she was finally settled leading a life separate from him. She had to bear the hardship of paying the rent and making ends meet as a single mother. We met at Lynn's home for the discussion. It was always a welcoming space. Sitting around a low coffee table drinking tea, we discussed the women's experiences of living in South Africa.

The other participants were Wendy from Congo and Chadamwari from Zimbabwe. Wendy was 52 at the time of the discussion. She had been living in South Africa for 11 years and ran a small food business making meals and selling food dishes near the public transport ranks in Cape Town central business district. According to Wendy, some days were good; these were mostly the days when she was supported by a network of people from her country. Other days she reported selling only two or three plates of food. I was in awe of how Wendy kept the business running at her age and with no transport of her own. She had to prepare the meals at home and rely on public transport or friends to help her transport the food to her stall in the central business district. Wendy had five children and rented out rooms in her rental home for extra income. I discuss Chadamwari's life details above; she took part in both discussions.

The women whose voices form the weave of narrative in this chapter exist in a complex space of contemporary South Africa, which significantly shapes their experiences and their subjectivity. Subjectivity, according to Blackman et al. (2008), refers to the experience of 'multiple positionings' and how these play out in a given context (p. 6). The participants in this study must continually negotiate power dynamics related to the intersections of gender, race, poverty, and foreigner status in South Africa. The alienation, exclusion and heightened sense of vulnerability associated with being a foreigner in an era of xenophobia intersects with the hopelessness and shame of poverty, which in turn colours these women's experiences of, and opportunities for, healing. The very position of 'abused woman' is intricately connected to stigma and shame (Reavey and Brown 2009). These factors significantly shape the manifestation of patriarchal oppression of female sexuality in this context. As detailed in Chap. 2, such oppression manifests through dominant discourses which pathologise the female body or render it 'dirty' or deviant. Rules for appropriate femininity spanning many African cultures promote the ideas that proper women should be sexually passive, and they should not openly express aspects of their sexual desire (Kambarami 2006; Mupotsa and Mhishi 2008). Negative consequences abound for women who transgress these patriarchal scripts of female sexuality. Consequences range from blame and shame to the threat of overt violence as a means of social control.

As is consistent with the main theme of this book, in what follows I focus on the women's narratives and what they tell us about their experiences of, and resistance to, the patriarchal oppression of female sexuality in the context of South Africa. I foreground the women's narrative strategies that they utilise in their negotiations of agency which emerged through their collective meaning making. My analysis is framed around the three central questions of the study: (1) How do the women transform the past together within these collective spaces? It is important to emphasise that during the selected group discussions, there were no South African women present (except for me, the researcher); (2) What identities do they construct during their tellings?, and (3) What function could these ways of remembering have for participants' sense of self in post-apartheid South Africa? The focus of this chapter is narrators' constructions of black South African women's sexual character narrated through their stories of everyday life in the country.

I frame my analysis through a social remembering lens that posits that people tell their stories in particular ways to achieve a certain social purpose. That is, people remember their experiences in certain ways so that they can present certain kinds of identities to others (see Eisikovits and Winstok 2002). As Davies and Gannon (2006) argue, 'truth' is always a creation linked to self and agency. In other words, the stories that we choose to tell and the ways in which we tell these stories have powerful meaning for us. It is through these stories that we create certain identities (Taylor 2010). I therefore do not interpret the foreigner women's constructions of South African women as representing any true perceptions. Rather these narratives about the 'other' represent something about the inner psychological world of the women who are doing the telling.

Collectively Constructing the Sexual Character of the South African Female 'Other'

During the group discussions, the foreigner women animatedly discussed what they constructed as their common-sense knowledge about South African women. Dominant themes were that of sexual excess, lack of sexual restraint, and open sexual desire/behaviour—descriptions which position South African women as examples of bad femininity in relation to dominant patriarchal discourses. Below, Akeyo and Chadamwari from Zimbabwe narrate their common perceptions of South African women.

Akeyo: The South African women we regard them as people who love sex a lot. They love to sleep (around) they can't do without their sex. You know (laughing) they can't do without their sex. So, they need the sex. So, if obviously a man approaches you like that [in a sexual way] the South African women we regard them they will say yes. They will respond.

Chadamwari: They will respond [to men that approach them sexually]. I am sure they do.

(Focus group discussion 1)

Akeyo had been living in South African for 11 years at the time of the discussion. When she first arrived in the country, she lived and worked in a small farming village on the outskirts of Cape Town picking grapes for the process of wine-making. Akeyo describes that on the farm she encountered many people of different backgrounds, races, and cultures. It is in this social environment that she began to learn about South African culture. At the beginning of the except above, it is significant that Akeyo uses the word *we* linguistically situating her, and the other women present as part of a collective, afforded by the fact that they are Zimbabwean. She narrates the sense that they share common perceptions of South African women's sexuality. Although they each have their own individual experience in South Africa, they share similar knowledge and witnessing of South African women's sexual character. This speaks to what has been identified in the field of community psychology as the construction of shared realities that occur when individuals connect their experiences/ memories to others' narratives in a collective storytelling setting (see Langellier and Peterson 1992, 2004).

Akeyo represents *their* view that South African women 'love sex a lot'. Her repetition of the phrase 'they can't do without their sex' brings home the point about South African women's sexual appetites and conveys a sense that South African women are active sexual subjects who are driven by rampant sexual appetites. She then goes further to unpack South African's women's relational engagements with others on the sexual terrain. She says that these women love to sleep around, meaning that sex is not limited to their husbands or partners. She suggests that they have multiple partners and through her use of language conveys meaning that South African women are sexually promiscuous—they will have sex with many men with little or no regard for the sanctity of marriage. Chadamwari validates what Akeyo is saying ('They will respond [to men that approach them sexually]. I am sure that they do'), strengthening the believability of their collective perspective about South African women.

Both women theorise about the typical South African female's response to men's sexual advances—they will definitely respond in a positive way because of their easy sexual character. The Shona culture, to which Akeyo and Chadamwari belong, is still very much defined by patriarchal discourses regarding gender and sexuality (Hodza 2015) and, as such, values passive female sexuality; women's sexual restraint; and sex for the purposes of reproduction or satisfying a husband. In other words, sex for the purposes of female pleasure is not valued. Sexual restraint and the denial of female sexual pleasure and enjoyment are key requirements set up by dominant discourses in the matrix of power linked to the oppression of female sexuality (McFadden 2003). Akeyo and Chadamwari's narratives of South African women's sexual character must be read in relation to this cultural lens.

The narrators convey a sense that female South African citizens border on the pathological—they have no capacity to restrain themselves sexually, they are promiscuous, and they misuse their sexuality for their own selfish hedonistic aims. In this way, Akeyo and Chadamwari position South African women as faulty feminine subjects who do not/cannot abide by cultural strictures of gender and sexuality—what Ferguson (1996) in her analysis of motherhood and sexuality calls *inferior female* types. Quite clearly, in other words the participants construct black South African women as just not good enough. They narratively position them in a devalued social position through their meaning that they do not fit neatly into the required modes/roles of femininity. Black female South African citizens, according to the narrators, transcend these roles in ways that threaten the nuclear family and the moral fibre of the patriarchal project. As we saw in Chap. 2, defying respectable femininity has particular consequences for women. Women are blamed and shamed and placed in a position vulnerable to serious devaluation and disrepute if they fail to meet these standards. It is no coincidence that these foreigner women are positioning black South African in such a way, something which I hint at here and will unpack after an examination of additional narratives.

Later in the discussion, Akeyo and Chadamwari build on their descriptions of South African women's sexuality providing examples of incidents they remembered witnessing in their everyday life in the country. Akeyo begins by providing examples of some of the sexual relations that she witnessed in the space of public transit—here specifically while travelling by train.

> **Akeyo:** And in a couple of negotiations like if you are sitting around like I understand Xhosa you know if someone start to do that then the Xhosa lady would say, 'Oh bhuti uyenzani?' [meaning] 'What are you doing?' Then the guy would say, 'Ja, you know hayi its cold, let's do it you know I like you. I like your bums. You are beautiful.' And this one [the South African woman] is like, 'Oh, yes bhuti ngoku singayaphi?' [oh yes, now we go brother] and then they are negotiating now 'Let's go. Let's go.' And the people would get off at the wrong station maybe in the bush do it [sex] and then they are done, and they go back to the train, and it is something normal.
>
> (Focus group discussion 1)

In the first extract above, Akeyo narrates her observations while travelling on public transport. Akeyo does not own a motor car and thus needs to utilise public transport every day. She narrates a sense of the behaviour of South African women on the South African trains and at train stations. These are not any South African women—she refers specifically to Xhosa-speaking black South African women. This group of women still today are the poorest demographic group in the country. They are working-class women who utilise public transport daily. The women's constructions of South African women are based on raced and classed categories.

Akeyo provides a hypothetical example of South African women's interactions with men on the train. She makes it clear that these are men and women who do not know each other, they are strangers in the public space of the train station. Akeyo says that if a man approaches a woman with a sexual proposition ('let's do it') or a flirtatious compliment about her body ('I like your bums') then a typical black South African woman will usually start negotiating with the man about sex. She presents a likely response: 'Oh yes, bhuti ngoku singayaphi?' ('Now we go brother'). It is significant that Akeyo conveys women's responses as something that occurs regularly. In fact, she states that such occurrences are *normal*. She constructs this behaviour as a usual part of South African women's repertoire. Her account is infused with the backdrop of patriarchal discourses which provide scripts of sexual restraint and passivity (McFadden 2003). Traditional moral codes of sexuality in the Shona culture of Zimbabwe convey that it is wrong for women to initiate sexual contact with a man (Kambarami 2006). As Liv Haram (2004) reminds us in her study of social meanings about women in northern Tanzania, women's respectability is deeply tied in with notions of marriage and monogamy. Women who do not adhere to such prescriptions of behaviour risk ridicule or even the label 'prostitute' (Haram 2004). Women in most African contexts need to monitor their sexual behaviour even more strictly and diligently in public spaces.

Ayeko's narrative must be considered in light of this dominant patriarchal narrative of female sexuality. It is through this narrative that she provides clear meaning about the character of black South African women. These women who, she says, will often get off at a train station and have sex 'in the bush' with a strange man are lacking in self-restraint. They cannot control their sexuality or 'tone down' their sexual urges. They are driven by an uncontrollable urge to have sex. Importantly, the meaning that comes through is that this sexual behaviour is linked to South African women's lack of morals regarding sexuality. This is textured by Akeyo's description of sex happening in the space of the dirty ground and vegetation out in the open next to the train tracks. She provides little room for question about these women's sexual moral fibre.

Following on in the same discussion, Cheney conveys similar meaning about South African women's sexual characters.

> **Cheney:** In South Africa like there is no way for them [men] to use muti because it is something easy just approach like when people can just meet on the train and they agree [to have sex]. They meet like what he was doing if she was somebody loose then there won't be any need of using muti here. So, I think in South Africa there is a low level of mubobobo.
>
> (Focus group discussion 1)

Once again, we see the narrative of muti rape emerging. Mubobobo, which the women described as a practice through which men obtain a magical substance to rape women from a distance, was discussed in detail in Chap. 4. The women discussed men's use of muti as a way of gaining sexual access to women in Zimbabwe who are out of their reach materially and socially. However, in the excerpt above, Cheney provides a firm stance that such a practice would not be necessary in South Africa. The underlying meaning here is that men will not have to use this 'magic' to have sex with women because South African women are 'loose' sexually and sex is freely available to any man who wants it. Previously in their narratives, the women described mubobobo as an ever-present part of Zimbabwean culture.

However, Cheney says that there is a low level of mubobobo practised in South Africa ('there won't be any need of using mubobobo here'). Implicit in her account is the sense that Zimbabwean women are very different from South African women. Zimbabwean women have sexual restraint, they have appropriate sexual morals; therefore, men require muti to indulge their sexual fantasies and wants. South African women, on the other hand, give sex freely and therefore muti is not required.

In the talk outlined above, the women collectively narrate their insights about the common sexual character of black South African women. They construct the inner world or innate characters of black South African women. Painting a linguistic picture of these women as sexually without morals, unable to control their sexual urges, and as 'loving sex'. According to patriarchal rules which dominate in the Shona culture (of the narrators), women who behave in the afore-described manner cannot be placed within the valued position of 'appropriate woman' (see Mupotsa and Mhishi 2008). The narrators' meaning comes across clearly—black South African women do not meet the standards of respectable femininity. They position them in the category of 'bad women'. This resonates with the well-described binary of 'good woman'/'bad woman' described by MacDonald (1995) in her book *Representing Women: Myths of Femininity in the Popular Media*—patriarchal discourses offer limited options beyond a black/white approach; women are labelled as either pure 'Madonna' or as deviant 'whore'. Here, the women are narratively working with images that are placed at different poles of value against the backdrop of patriarchal scripts of female sexuality—'appropriate sexuality' (them) versus immoral sexuality (South African women). In the next section, I unpack similar themes during which the foreigner women narrated South African women as blameworthy in terms of their own sexual abuse.

'Put Some Eggs Where They Can See, They Will Volunteer to Spend the Night'

This section is based on a smaller group discussion with women from three African countries—Lynn from Kenya, Chadamwari from Zimbabwe, and Wendy from Congo. The women were discussing their transition from their home countries to South Africa and the discussion led to women speaking about ways in which the people in South Africa are different to people back home. Lynn narrates her experience of living in South Africa for more than seven years.

> **Lynn:** What I found most women here (in South Africa) mainly the black and coloureds but not everyone, they want money, but they want free money. They want quick money and that's why you find that even these Nigerians that are trafficking more often than not they use South African women. They can't come to abuse you because you won't accept, and you are working for yourself. They kind of like take advantage of South African women.
>
> **Wendy:** Ja, that people here.
>
> **Lynn:** So, what I have observed most ladies [from South Africa] they don't want to work. They want to dress nice and to look nice and buy everything. Ja, but not to work. So, then you become ...
>
> **Wendy:** easy ...
>
> **Lynn:** You know people who do bad things it is easy for them to use you because it's not taking them an effort or anything.
>
> (Focus group discussion 7)

Lynn and Wendy create an image of South African women drawing on their position as residents living in the country for several years. Lynn narrates that South African women want 'quick money' and 'free money', money that can be gained from minimal work or effort. These women want to look nice and buy luxuries, she says, but they don't want to work for their money. They construct (most) South African women as lazy and unambitious. Importantly, they infer that South African women behave in certain ways which compromise good behaviour and ultimately their own safety. South African women open themselves up to abusive relationships because they are lazy and want quick rewards, say the women. The narrators suggest that these negative attributes are somehow a fundamental part of South African women's characters. In the words of Wendy, South African women are 'easy' to abuse because they put themselves in situations where men can take advantage of them. Lynn concurs, 'it is easy for them to abuse you'. The meaning evoked is that South African women are to blame for much of the sexual abuse that they suffer. Lynn uses the example of human trafficking—the trade of women for sexual slavery and exploitation whereby women are often recruited based on false pretences for monetary gain. Human trafficking is a prevalent reality in southern Africa especially across the borders of Zambia, Zimbabwe, Mozambique, and South Africa (Bennett 2011).

It is significant that Lynn conveys that such abuses are not likely to happen to them. She says, 'they can't come to abuse you because you won't accept, and you are working for yourself'. She uses the pronoun *you* to address the other women in the discussion. Essentially, she signifies a sense of a collective, homogenous 'us'/'we' for the non-South African women, even though all three come from very different African cultures. The women narrate a contrast between the characters of South African women and their own characters. While South African women are constructed as lazy, fickle, and immoral, they narrate themselves, non-South Africans, as having more pride and moral standards. The implied message is that if South Africans were to have the same standards and moral high ground, they could protect themselves from various forms of abuse. It is through this collective comparison that the narrators construct positive social identities in relation to these 'other' women.

An important point is that the narrators refer to a certain raced and classed group of South African women. Lynn says, 'mainly the *blacks and coloureds* ... they want money, but they want free money'. The racial categories black and coloured represent the former apartheid government's system of racial classification of non-white groups. Although the apartheid system was officially abolished more than 24 years ago, black and coloured people (and particularly women) still represent the poorest and most marginalised groups in the country (Boonzaier and de la Rey 2003). The point here is that in the face of joblessness and severe poverty, women's choices to engage in exploitative sexual exchanges for money are more complex than the ideas presented by the narrators in this discussion. This was something I was acutely aware of as the conversations progressed. I pick up on this point later in this chapter.

Continuing along a similar vein, the narrators turned to discuss the views of non-South African black men—men from their own countries.

Lynn: Men from other African countries they really enjoy it here in South Africa. They say it is easier ...

SvS: What? To get sex?

Lynn: Mmm. You know, and *pretty* women just give them sex and they get so excited when they come here and there's a lot of pretty women.

Chadamwari: (laughing). You know what this other guy was saying? This guy was telling me, "Oh women here [in South Africa] when you want them

> you just invite them to your place and buy a crate of eggs and put them there quietly. When they see them you just ask, 'Are you spending the night or are you going?' and she will say 'No, I am staying'. So, they wake up the next morning you just say, 'Make yourself breakfast'. And they just take six eggs they break them all." This guy was just standing there saying, "Jho, you don't know about these local ladies, you can get a lot of sex from them because it's easy".
>
> (Focus group discussion 7)

Lynn and Chadamwari's co-constructed narrative of the experience of men from other African countries is based on their afore-mentioned descriptions of South African women's innately 'loose' sexual characters. We get a sense that the behaviour of these women creates an open sexual environment where sex is always possible and easily obtained. Furthermore, the narrators suggest that this sexual environment is specific to South Africa. She says, 'men from other African countries they really enjoy it here in South Africa' and 'they get so excited when they come here'. Here she draws on discourses of men's rampant and active sexuality, what Hollway (1984) identifies as the male sexual drive discourse. This refers to a well-established script globally and in the African context that conveys meaning about men's insatiable biological drive for sex. The South African environment, according to the narratives outlined here, is a suitable place to fulfil men's constant need for sex. The core narrative thread is that men are perhaps excited about this context because the sex is more freely available than back home in other African countries. This is because women in other African countries (women like themselves) are more sexually restrained and do not readily provide men with sex.

Chadamwari backs up this point about men from other African countries narrating her memory of a conversation with a Zimbabwean man who had been living in South Africa for a short period. The constructed scenario is about men using food to persuade women to sleep with them. South African women, says Chadamwari's information source, will give men sex in return for hardly anything, like six eggs. Through this re-narrated story Chadamwari conveys meaning that South African women often and easily sell themselves short, because of their opportunistic nature ('they take six eggs and break them all').

A bit further on in the discussion, the narrators add to their descriptions by drawing on the topic of prostitution.

> **Chadamwari:** You don't have to give them anything because it's not like prostitution. Prostitution is different because they [South African women] don't get paid but they enjoy …
>
> **Lynn:** It's the attention.
>
> **Chadamwari:** Not only. [they sleep around] so that they can be in a better place there because maybe they sleep somewhere else different
>
> **SvS:** So now they are in a nice bed.
>
> **Chadamwari:** It's a nice bed and you just show them milk or whatever and they just keep quiet. Somebody said he was just telling me the story and we laughed it off and I was thinking like, 'Okay, so that's what you do. When they are there you just put some eggs where they can see, some milk too. You just sit quietly, and they will volunteer to spend the night.
>
> **Lynn:** Oh, my goodness! That is how women are being reduced. It's terrible.
>
> **Chadamwari:** You have no value after that.
>
> (Focus group discussion 7)

My reading of the women's narratives is that they represent these sexual arrangements as a form of abuse—the element of men using women sexually for their own gain. This is illustrated through Lynn's statement 'That is how women are being reduced. That is terrible.' However, and perhaps this is why Chadamwari is able to 'laugh it off', the narrators also convey meaning that South African women *choose* to be in such situations. Chadamwari's statement is loud and clear: 'South African women don't get paid but they enjoy.' Once again, South African women's promiscuous sexual character and love of sex is highlighted. It is through the collective construction of this image of South African women's sexual character that the narrators position these women as being complicit in their own abuse.

The emerging theme here resonates with a prevalent practice in current South Africa—women (mostly young) trading sex with older men for financial reward or material gain. South African feminist scholars have termed these arrangements 'transactional sex' or the 'sugar daddy' phenomenon (see Gqola 2017; Hunter 2002; Shefer et al. 2012). While feminist scholars agree that such practices run rife in contemporary post-apartheid South Africa, there is heated debate about women's motivations for engaging in such sex with men. Some argue that within the context of severe poverty and lack of hope for real transformation in South Africa, these women's actions make perfect sense. They are engaging in transactional sex to survive and perhaps also to bring home money to their families. Others interpret these acts as performances of women's agency whereby women choose to engage in these acts to obtain a stylish image and access to material goods that would not otherwise be available to them (Hunter 2002). Pumla Gqola (2017) provides rich discussion about the complexities of interpreting these sexual relationships through a feminist lens. I agree with Gqola that such relations are highly unequal and exploitative and that to interpret these acts as women's choice or agency glosses over important elements of patriarchy and capitalism functioning in contemporary South Africa.

In reviewing the women's narratives from my current viewpoint, I am faced with the task of making sense of what I now clearly see was a discursive tension between me (the outsider) and the women (the insider-participants). This discursive tension mirrored the discourses inherent in the debates described above. Let me elaborate. The women participants clearly align with a view that South African women engage in sex with men to obtain a stylish image and a 'good life' (not merely for survival). Their co-constructed view triggered negative emotions for me. I was reminded of the extent of poverty that I witness every day in South Africa through my personal life and research. I felt that it was insensitive and even violent to ignore women's situations of poverty as a factor that could motivate them to have sex with men for money. My feelings evidently came out in a previous draft of my writing. Feedback from a prominent feminist scholar in the field alerted me to the fact that I had repeatedly tried to defend the South African women. She commented that it was clear to her that I had problems with the migrant women's framing of South African women. She reminded me that my narrative approach is not about finding any 'truth' about South African women.

I had to take a 'turn back' and revisit my work with different eyes. What I found on the second reading has given me much insight about my own subjectivity. In my initial writing, I had inserted paragraphs about the poverty and underprivileged life in South African townships repeatedly and with a harsh tone. Over and over again I critiqued the participants in my study for glossing over these realities of the South African women's lives. Below is a case in point where I reflect on some of my friendships that have developed through research and activism.

> Lynne's comment about women engaging in these sexual acts for attention really struck home for me. It led me to think about my many young black South African friends who live in deeply impoverished situations, some sharing a two-roomed shack with at least five other family members. The majority of these young women face daily challenges of unemployment, crime, deprivation of basic necessities, as well as abuse. I have witnessed many of these women engaging in sexual relations with men—many men, strange men, older men. Sometimes I find myself falling into the trap of judging and blaming these women, particularly when I accompany yet another woman to a clinic for an HIV test or when one of my friends falls pregnant by mistake, having no means to look after a baby. But then, on my next visit to their homes, I am reminded of the state of hopelessness that many of these women live in. I am reminded that such sexual relations with men may be the only way that these young women can mobilise any sort of power in their lives.
>
> (Samantha reflections; initial writing)

In my previous draft, I included varied statistics about women's poverty in South Africa and repetitive critique that the narrators so blatantly ignored the social context of these women's lives. What drove my obvious need to defend black South African women in my writing? I felt uncomfortable in the research conversations when the migrant women constructed South Africans in this way. I am aware of the negative associations and stigma attached to the identities of 'loose woman' and felt that I had to protect the South African support group members in their absence—and in extension other South African women to which these generalisations were referring. It was quite evident that during these particular research discussions I was an outsider to the women narrators. Even though I lived in South Africa, I could not contribute to the main thread of the discussion, as I did not necessarily agree with the way in which they were representing South African women.

It is also evident that the narrators did not position me as South African woman. Their focus was on black and coloured South African—my whiteness set me apart. I share citizenship with the black South African women, but my white privilege and related middle-class social position mean that I occupy very different identities to these women—in fact, one could say that I exist in another world. I wonder now if my need to defend black South African femininity was somehow linked to deep-rooted and mostly unacknowledged white guilt about my inheritance of privileges as a beneficiary of the apartheid system—benefits which still exist today. This has something to do with the constant trauma of witnessing extreme poverty and a way of life and hardship among many black people that is so different from my own life and so devastating. Reflections on this could constitute another paper in itself and is beyond the scope of this chapter. The point that I am making is that my second engagement with the data has attuned me to the ways in which such power dynamics play out in complex ways during the process of interpreting such narratives. In my second reading of the data I was better equipped to look deeper, beyond a search for any 'truth' related to these representations. In the next section, I explore the women's narrative descriptions of different socio-cultural worlds. The women narrated images of the broader social world of South Africa constructing cultural archetypes 'us' and 'them'.

'To Them Sex Is a Need, *That Is Obvious': Narrating Socio-Cultural Worlds*

This section of the book chapter is based on data that was drawn from the discussion around mubobobo. Three Shona Zimbabwean women took part in this discussion—Akeyo, Cheney, and Chadamwari. I detail information about these women earlier in the chapter. The women drew on their common-sense views of the social world of South Africa providing rich descriptions of the sexual climate of the country. Evident in their stories were neatly constructed binaries of 'us' (foreigner women) and 'them' (black South African women). They narratively established clear psycho-social borders between 'their' culture and the culture of South African women. Firstly, I analyse the content of these narratives, exploring the collective selves that these women construct *together* within the space of the collective biography sessions. I then theorise about the functions that such threads of meaning play for the women's sense of self in their current home—South Africa.

Drawing on her experience in the country, Akeyo opens up discussion about the sexual culture in South Africa.

> **Akeyo:** By the time we came [to South Africa] it was a normal thing. In (town's name) that's where I lived first, it was a normal thing. You would see a woman you know at the tavern drinking with friends. And she would go to her girlfriend's house you know with a part time boyfriend and have sex there. The husband is aware maybe he is at home and this woman will come home there's no fighting, there's no shouting. Life goes on as normal.
>
> (Focus group discussion 1)

Akeyo draws on her memory of the open sexual environment that she witnessed in a small wine-farming town in the country. She describes that cheating and promiscuous sexual behaviour is a normal part of South African life. It is significant that she mentions that such behaviour is condoned by others in the social sphere—the people in the tavern, the friend, and the husband. She insinuates that there are no negative consequences for the woman who sleeps around and cheats on her husband. The sense of this as the normal way of doing things is emphasised by her assumptions of what will happen when this woman gets home—'there's no fighting, there's no shouting' and 'life goes on as normal'. Presumably, Akeyo has witnessed such behaviour in the public spaces of the bars and tavern. However, it is less likely that she would have witnessed such interactions between husband and wife in the private sphere of their home. However, she postulates about the texture of these intimate interactions in the home, based on her witnessing of life in this town. Akeyo positions herself as knowledgeable about the sexual climate.

She then describes a more specific example of an encounter at the home of people she knew.

> **Akeyo:** I remember this other friend of ours it was a coloured family. The boyfriend came to the girl's house and they had sex. And when they came out of the house the mother asked the boyfriend if she [the daughter] was good in bed.
>
> **Cheney:** The boyfriend?
>
> **Akeyo:** Ja (yes), the parents went outside and then this daughter they knew it was the first time [having sex]. It was an excitement. It was good news for the family. She is going to have sex for the first time. She has just turned twenty-one. And then they get into the room the parents are outside smoking chatting to the neighbours knowing that their daughter is having sex for the first time in the house. And when they finished in the *daylight* when they come out the mother asked, 'Was it good?'. And my mother asked her, 'What culture is that? We don't do that in our country'. We were shocked.
>
> (Focus group discussion 1)

Once again, Akeyo describes the sexual climate of South Africa drawing on the behaviour of people of a particular race and class—poor coloured people in a small farming community in South Africa. These people form part of a community of labourers who work on the neighbouring farms. Akeyo represents a sense of shock. Her mother and herself were not used to witnessing such overt and permissive sexual behaviour. She weaves together factors which contributed to her sense of incredulity at the time. Firstly, she explicitly states the age of the woman ('twenty-one'). This young woman was having sex in the *daylight*. The family and neighbours were aware that the girl was having sex for the first time and they were gathered outside waiting for the act to take place 'smoking chatting to the neighbours'. In fact, Akeyo describes that the social atmosphere seemed to her like a celebratory event ('it was good news for the family'). Initially, we might say that the public nature of this sexual act and the permission granted by the young women's parents signifies an inversion of dominant patriarchal scripts about female sexuality (reserved for marriage, restrained, to be kept private). However, Akeyo states that after the couple had sex the mother asked the boyfriend if her daughter was good in bed. The picture that we get here is more of one tied to the objectification of women—the role of women to please men. It signifies something around a culture in which poor people may have to use their daughters' sexuality as a means to establish some sort of power in the community.

However, Akeyo's focus is placed mainly around her sense of disbelief about the public nature of the sex. This is seen through her statement 'we were shocked' and her account of her mother's response 'What culture is that? We don't do that in our country.' Dominant patriarchal discourses in Zimbabwe set up certain rules around female sexuality. Young girls having sex out of marriage is not morally correct and such girls will often be stigmatised or shamed (Kambarami 2006). Women should be virgins when they get married, according to the Shona culture. The subtext of Akeyo's narrative is that no proper mother in Zimbabwe would condone her young daughter's sexual activity out of marriage. A 'good' woman would definitely not condone such a situation and treat it as a celebratory occasion. The underlying message is that Akeyo and her mother observed this sexual behaviour from a place of better morals. Their culture is more morally correct and facilitates 'good' femininity as opposed to the open sexual culture of South Africa.

Cheney moves deeper into a description of their cultural values.

> **Cheney:** For a Zim[2] woman there has to be a relationship for you to have sex. That's why men would rather go for what—muti—for them to do whatever. Unlike *here* [South Africa]. In South Africa it is just 'I do, I do' [indicates agreement between the woman and man to have sex]. And then they take each other and just go. So, in our country like my sister had a baby at twenty-six. She was a virgin at that time. Unlike here [in South Africa] they consent a twelve-year-old on her own to go and have an abortion. Of which it is a thing she agreed to go and have sex. She will also consent to what—*abortion, termination of pregnancy.* Unlike in our country, even abortion you will go straight to jail.
>
> **SvS:** Is it?
>
> **Cheney:** Yes, you are not allowed. Abortion you will go to jail. And we have that thing when you are married, and the husband finds out you are not a virgin. They will make a hole on the blanket to show that your child *was not what—was not a virgin.* Of which it is taboo to go on your marriage bed without being a virgin. So that is why men maybe they crave muti in Zimbabwe. For him to have that whatever [sexual availability].
>
> (Focus group discussion 1)

Cheney begins her narrative drawing once again on the topic of mubobobo. She narrates her view of why the mystical practice is more prevalent in Zimbabwe. For Zimbabwean women, there has to be a relationship to have sex. This, she says, is why men require muti in Zimbabwe to obtain sex. In South Africa, according to Cheney, things are very different. Her words 'I do, I do' signifies that there is most often agreement between men and women about sex, regardless of a relationship. Interestingly, her words also parody the vernacular of official marriage vows. It seems as if she draws on these words to make her point about the lack of values in South African culture. She ends this off with 'then they take each other and go'.

Cheney draws on two controversial issues, underage sex and abortion, to construct her clear comparison between Zimbabwean culture and South African culture. Firstly, she says 'in our country' women do not engage in sex before marriage because it is taboo for women to marry a man if she is not a virgin. She draws on the example of her younger sister

[2] 'Zim' is short for Zimbabwean.

in Zimbabwe who was a virgin when she got married at the age of 26 years old. Cheney presents her observations that female sexual practices in South Africa follow different moral standards. She narrates that twelve-year-old girls agree to have sex. Secondly, she emphasises that abortion is illegal in Zimbabwe ('you will go straight to jail') but in South African culture they will consent to a 12-year-old going to abort a pregnancy 'on her own'. Cheney clearly links underage sex and abortion in South Africa to an immoral and 'other' sexual climate. She presents her common-sense view of South African-ness and constructs clear psycho-social borders between Zimbabwean women ('we'/'our country') and South African women ('they'/'here').

Cheney's representation of clear boundaries between the two cultures is very simplistic. Such strict dichotomies are not likely to represent the realities of women living in these contexts. Biographical detail that emerged through the storytelling spaces of the research also suggests that these women's experiences are more complex than outlined by their narratives of sexual cultures.

Cheney married when she was in her late teens, due to her impoverished situation she had no other means of survival. Her husband was much older than her. He repeatedly abused her emotionally and sexually throughout their marriage. Many of the other women who took part in this discussion experienced repeated sexual abuse in childhood. They were not virgins when they got married. I wondered about these women's experiences in relation to morality when they did not represent 'appropriate' femininity. I wondered how the women who had been raped in childhood felt on their wedding night when they could not present themselves as virgins. The point here is that there is always a backdrop of patriarchally condoned abuse and poverty that shape women's sexual experience and the positions they can occupy. In the narrator's constructions of binary 'us' and 'them', they do not engage with these complexities. In her narrative above, for example, Cheney does not leave room for discussion about the ways in which sex in Zimbabwean culture is often not morally correct.

Similarly, there is no acknowledgement of the fact that often South African women do not choose to engage in sex with men, such sex may be one of the only options available for them. An examination of patriarchal power and women's lack of choice was an ever-present thread of meaning when the women examined their own experiences (see Chap. 5). However, such a critical view was absent when they were discussing the experiences and behaviours of South African women. I wondered why they chose to ignore such complexities, I wondered why they chose to represent the cultures of Zimbabwe and South Africa in such static ways.

> **Akeyo:** To them [South African women] like the cultures we have stayed with sex it's a *need*, that is obvious. It is not something that (they) can shy off like we do. You know if someone is having a boyfriend they will ask you, 'Are you having sex? Is it good?'. If you are not having sex, then there is something wrong with you. With *us* if you are having sex when you are not married then there is something wrong with you (women laughing).
>
> **Chadamwari:** It's the other way around now.
>
> **Akeyo:** It's the other way around. So, it is not really a surprise why men do that [make inappropriate sexual advances towards women]. Because they just think that sex will happen because they do that with their women and they expect every woman to be like that. So [South African men] tend to wander away from their women and that's why they are now more and more like wanting to marry foreign ladies because they know that these people have respect for their bodies, they don't just do it with anybody.
>
> (Focus group discussion 1)

Evident in the talk above is representation of a South African cultural environment consisting of a web of attitudes that promote open sexual relationships 'if you are not having sex there is something wrong with you'. Such social pressures to engage in sex, according to the narrators, promote an inherent *need* for sex among people of the South African culture. Interestingly, Akeyo says that South Africans cannot 'shy off' sex like they do. 'Shy off' connotes meaning about an active movement away from something; of avoiding something one dislikes or fears. In this context this signifies energetically avoiding sexual urges and desires. Here Akeyo implies that Zimbabwean women have learnt to respond correctly to their sexual urges—a quick pulling back or withdrawal from sex and behaviours that are deemed inappropriate. She represents Zimbabwean women as 'good' feminine subjects. This use of language is significant and speaks to a core element of the narrators' experience of patriarchal oppression of female sexuality. Their representations of themselves as appropriate feminine subjects shows the powerful ties of patriarchal discourse—women align with these discourses to present themselves as good moral subjects. However, behind the scenes the narrators are negotiating a deeper sense of their belonging in the world. We see this through the meaning that the women make about the choices made by South African men.

Akeyo says that South African men have free sexual relations with their women, but they are recently choosing to marry foreigner women instead. Insinuated here is that the immoral sexual behaviour of South African women has caused men to be doubtful of their capacity to be good wives. Important, she says that South African men want to marry foreign ladies like themselves because they 'have respect for their bodies and they don't do it [sex] with anybody'. Situated within the backdrop of xenophobic attitudes in South Africa, the foreign women narrators may gain a sense of belonging and worth through their narratives of being wanted by South African men. It is significant that they did not mention foreigner men in this discussion.

When revisiting these narratives during the writing of this book, I was struck by the binaries and generalisations that the women drew on, even more so than in my first reading of the data. From my observations and experience in this context, sexualities and sexual values are diverse, multiple, and contextually based. Research shows us that cultures are morphing with boundaries becoming more fluid (Tamale 2011). Women are not static cultural subjects—they can and do resist aspects of culture if such practices do not serve their modern life or current beliefs (Tsanga 2011). New 'zones' of sexual norms are constantly emerging in a globalised world, spurred on by media and the internet (Bennett 2011). Emerging literature has and continues to show that sexual cultures are changing, and more space is available to negotiate new forms of sexual behaviour that transcend traditional patriarchal and cultural prescriptions (see Haram 2004). With this in mind, it is crucial to examine the women's binary descriptions of South African women (inappropriate sexuality) versus non-South African women (appropriate moral sexuality) in a critical way. In my second reading, my understanding deepened about the 'hidden' psychological agenda driving such 'either/or' narratives.

Resisting the Oppression of Female Sexuality: Narratively Weaving Positive Social Selves

The narrators' individual insights living in South Africa for a number of years coalesce into a unified collective knowledge about black South African women. Such a transcendence of the 'facts' of individual stories into a cohesive representation or common viewpoint of knowing the world is a common element of collective biography work (Davies et al. 1997). Individual insights merge with the insights of others in the collective setting, forming a thread of common meaning. Individual histories and experience become intertwined with the experience of other narrators in the setting generating 'tapestries of growing understanding' about the self (Davies et al. 1997, p. 75). It is my work as author to critically examine this consensus in meaning making—the collectively generated perspective about South African women—as such representations of a unity of perspectives and experience provide rich insights into the discursive process which drive such talk.

So, the women narrators collective weave a narrative of black South African women as *faulty feminine subjects*. They constructed clear psychosocial borders between their collective self and the selves of the imagined female 'others'. Their narratives were centred on South African women's deviant sexuality and immorality. As someone who had worked with the group for quite some time before the data gathering, I found this element of the women's talk particularly interesting and sometimes unsettling. The group for abused women consisted of black women from different African countries including many South African women. The South African women were active group members accepted into the group because of their experiences of abuse and maltreatment. Many of these women were close confidants and had established strong connections with the women who speak in the excerpts above. Importantly, during the sessions from which the talk above is drawn there were no South African women present (except me). Their absence allowed the foreigner women narrators to speak in this way. It need not be stated that such narrations did not occur in the sessions when South African women were present as participants.

During the talk I wondered about the contradictions and what such narrations meant for group solidarity and respect. Where these undercurrents always there throughout the women's engagements? What does such talk mean in terms of the notion of sisterhood? Constructing South African women in this way in front of me, the researcher, could have also been 'risky' for the women. Hypothetically, my view of the group's cohesion could have been tainted and this could potentially negatively affect their reputation as a successful support group. In retrospect, I do not remember these narrations influencing my view of the group's success. Rather, I felt as if these narratives represented something about the narrators' position in current post-apartheid South Africa. I do remember feeling anxious though when the women spoke, as if we were somehow colluding behind the backs of the South African women members. At the time I chose not to confront the women in any way by mentioning the

South African members or by challenging their views. This was not a conscious decision, but one that I identify now at the stage of writing. This is perhaps another example of how I existed outside of the women's own process.

With all this in mind, I wondered why the narrators chose to represent South African women in this way. I was interested in the psychological processes that were at play 'behind the scenes'. Below I address the analytical questions: What do these ways of remembering tell us about the narrators' experiences of, and resistance to, the patriarchal oppression of female sexuality? What identities do they construct and what function could these ways of remembering play for the narrators' sense of self in current post-apartheid South Africa?

On a surface level, the narratives resonate with what could be called reverse xenophobia—the women drawing on negative discourses about foreigners in South Africa that are infused in their social environment, internalising these discourses and projecting them back onto the image of South African women. However, this is only one element. It is crucial to look deeper at the intersections at play. The signal for me to look deeper was the women's persistent focus on *sex* and *sexuality*.

From a feminist poststructuralist view, I did not take these narratives to signify any 'true' perceptions of South African women, but rather something about the subjectivity of the narrators. Their words signify meaning about their experience in a patriarchal South Africa. These women constantly have to negotiate certain kinds of selves within the limited spaces possible within a country rife with gender violence, racism, and deep-seated xenophobia. All these women had experienced repeated gendered abuses throughout their lifetime and throughout the spaces of Africa through which they travelled on their journey to South Africa. Cultural constructions of femininity function around the shame and blame of women (Enander and Holmberg 2008; Reavey and Brown 2009). In her chapter 'The Weather Watchers: Gender, Violence and Social Control', South African feminist scholar Lillian Artz (2009) states that within the system of social control of female sexuality the female body is constructed as to blame for abuse—as 'willing', provocative, and guilty. The very label 'abused woman' has negative connotations. Colonial remnants of discourses around 'dirty' and 'dangerous' black female bodies abound in current South African culture (see Gqola 2015). Within such a system of power women need to find alternative, more positive, ways to make meaning about themselves in the world.

The women's foreigner status in South Africa is another deeply intersecting social position that plays a role in shaping the participants' inner psychological worlds. A persistent part of the social climate within which they live deny foreigners the right to a socially valued existence—manifested in everyday (discursive and other) experiences of ridicule, lack of respect, and attacks on self-worth (Harris 2002). These discourses have a powerful impact on the different intersectional social identities that are available to the participants (woman; abused woman; African female sexual subject; black; foreigner/non-South African). Their inner psychological world is shaped by these multiple oppressions and restrictive meanings. Such intersecting oppressions of the psyche need to be considered as backdrop to these women's experiences of, and resistance to, patriarchal oppression of female sexuality.

I documented in-depth detail of the patriarchal oppression of female sexuality in Africa—it's manifestations and resounding effects—in detail in Chap. 2 of this book. However, it is worthwhile to reiterate here a central point made by Swaziland-born feminist scholar-activist, Patricia McFadden (2003). In her Feminist Africa article 'Sexual Pleasure as a Feminist Choice', McFadden highlights that women's sexuality is largely repressed throughout the African continent. Although it must be noted that the manifestations of and possible responses to such oppression differ according to the history and politics of specific contexts. We must be cognisant of the fact that the oppression of female sexuality does not manifest in the same way for all women across the continent and across racial, ethic, and class lines (Pereira 2002).

The result of the oppression of female sexuality is that many women experience powerful restraints (discursive and symbolic) with regards to expressing aspects of their sexuality/sexual violation. Often aspects of female sexuality are rendered taboo and not designated the appropriate terrain for female engagement. McFadden (2003) terms this the 'muting' of female memory and instinct. Decades of work in the field of trauma and psychology tells us that such suppression of socially unacceptable aspects of our realities result in a build-up of, often unrecognised, shame and guilt (see Herman 1992). Such negative internalisation is the violent effect of patriarchy. I call these negative embodied emotions of shame and guilt 'residues of gendered oppression' in that they constitute what remains as an ever-present effect of cumulative experiences of gendered abuse and patriarchal restrictions. These residues constitute an uninterpretable known—many women do not have the interpretive repertoires available to express these embodied sexualised aspects of the self. At the same time, these 'residues of gendered oppression' have a powerful effect on women's subjectivities and sense of self-worth in the world (Herman 1992).

According to my interpretation, the participants are expressing aspects of their own sexual subjectivity through the core narrative of South African women as faulty feminine subjects. They do this in a disguised form because they are in tune with the dominant patriarchal discourses which convey meaning that female sexual agency is 'bad' and deviant. Their narratives connected and coalesced in the production of knowledge about the female self—the self of South African women and, in extension, their own selves (see Tamboukou 2008). In response to the patriarchally constructed social anxieties and fears around female sexuality, these women find an alternative means to express these aspects of the self.

I realise now that my presence as 'other' white women/researcher could have played a role promoting these 'disguised' ways of telling. Narrative scholar Corinne Squire (2008) reminds us that the kind of stories that narrators tell is always mediated by the audiences present (imagined or actual audiences). And, we must be aware that research narratives are intricately shaped by engagements between researcher and researched in the context within which narratives are produced (Mauthner and Doucet 2003; Melucci 1995). The social power attached to my whiteness and academic identities could have shaped the women's stories. My presence could have inhibited the women and resulted in less direct narrative routes for engaging their sexual subjectivity. This provides important information about power and the possibilities of representation with regards to the oppression of female sexuality.

Informed by a social remembering lens (see Haaken and Reavey 2010), I interpreted participants' narratives as a means through which they could manage their identity in the moment of telling. It has been well documented in the field of narrative psychology that narrators adopt linguistic repertoires to achieve certain social aims (Eisikovits and Winstok 2002; Reavey and Brown 2009). The women participants were narrating their experience/perceptions in certain ways to manage the moral judgments that others could make about them (imagined others and myself). This constitutes a collective process of constructing positive selves within the context of the oppressive discourses surrounding female sexuality.

According to my interpretation, the narrators linguistically transferred socially generated negative aspects of the self, residues of gendered oppression, associated with female sexuality onto the image of black South

African women. These are women whom they may identify with on a number of levels related to poverty, race, and gendered powerlessness. One important difference, however, is that South African women are in a relatively powerful position in relation to these foreigner women in terms of their citizenship. In this sense, they functioned as an important threat image infused with meanings related to citizenship and social value.

The narrators' collective constructions of South African women as shameful, deviant, and blameworthy (faulty feminine subjects) within the nexus of power of hegemonic discourses surrounding female sexuality, signify parts of their own embodied selves that may have been 'concealed' due to the very same discourses. This image of South African women is a screen onto which they project 'inappropriate' aspects of their sexual subjectivities—shame, a sense of blame, feelings of sexual desire—things which may not be so easily expressible for them in the current South African context. These are aspects of the self which they may not have fully integrated into their sense of self, purely because such integration involves expression. The narrators express these things *through* their core narrative of South African women as faulty feminine subjects. Such expression may even be in a disguised form to themselves.

In her work on the projection of negative images onto the feminine body, Judith Butler (1990) argues that the disavowal and consequent projection of negative embodied aspects of the self (here masculine onto feminine), is a crucial part of the process of constructing 'others'. Although the context of Butler's theoretical application of these concepts is different, her work enhances my theorisation of the narrator's strategies. The 'foreigner' women project their 'unwanted' and uninterpretable embodied residues of gendered oppression onto the image of the 'bad whore' South African female other. In this way, they narratively 'get rid' of these negative parts of themselves. They can manage negative emotions through disavowal of these aspects of the self. The narrative function is as follows: *they* as non-South African women are not deviant sexually; *they* are very different to South African women; *they* have greater moral capacity than South African women. The narrators work so they are not 'weighed down' by the presence of these negative residues. Importantly, it is through this narrative strategy that the women negotiate a sense of a positive/untainted sexual self. This narrative strategy happens within the moment of telling within these specific collective spaces. However, this expression is significant. It is an important part of the dynamic process of constructing identity, which as Taylor (2010) reminds us, is a work in progress, part of an ongoing reconstruction of 'who I am'. The narrators are mobilising these residues of gendered oppression. Such narrative strategies may be one of the initial important steps through which women can begin to voice the uninterpretable known. The core narratives of black South African women as faulty feminine subjects form part of a crucial psychological strategy to cope with the emotionally and physically violent context within which they live. We see that women take up these discourses while at the same time moving to resist them. As Davies (2000, p. 72) states in *A Body of Writing 1990–1999*,

> Through taking up as her own the discourses through which femaleness is constituted, each woman becomes at the same time a speaking subject and one who is subjected or determined by those discourses ... women's desires are the result of bodily inscription, and of metaphors and storylines that catch them up in ways of being/desiring from which they have no escape unless they can reinscribe, discover new storylines, invert, invent, and break the bounds of old structures and old discourses.

The narrators whose voices I have chosen to outline in this chapter challenge patriarchal meanings (of female sexuality) by finding strategies and working with dominant discourses in creative ways. They collectively construct positive sexual selves in the face of harmful patriarchal discourses. Such a process of working with a combination of discourses in different ways to construct a sense of self 'beyond' patriarchal restrictions is a core aspect of Davies' (1990, 1991) notion of agency.

In this chapter, I explore the ways in which the women engaged with the social textures of their lives and memories within the research spaces. I critically examine the deep intersections of identities at play, including the powerful effects of my own presence during the tellings. I focus on the ways in which the narrators work with broader patriarchal discourses surrounding the oppression of female sexuality in the process of making sense of themselves as social beings in South Africa. Dominant discourses of xenophobia in South Africa convey negative and damaging meanings about black foreigners from other African countries (Hayem 2013; Sinclair 1998; Strauss 2011). The narrators invert these dominant xenophobic discourses conferring 'strangeness' and deviance onto black female South African citizens. They do this by drawing on culturally situated patriarchal meanings around female sexuality and morality.

The narrative strategy of 'othering' South African women raises critical questions about the notion of *ubuntu* in South Africa. Ubuntu is a concept that denotes a sense of one-ness, a collective concept of interconnectedness, respect and compassion for all humanity. The narratives in this chapter also highlight important challenges for the women's struggle in South Africa. They suggest that these foreigner women may experience themselves as divided from other women in this context. I suggest that their narrative process is intricately linked to issues surrounding belonging and the strong undercurrents of xenophobic attitudes in current post-apartheid South Africa. In the next chapter, I conclude the book drawing together insights related to the narrative landscapes of female sexuality spoken through this collective biography work.

References

Artz, L. (2009). The Weather watchers: Gender, violence and social control. In M. Steyn & M. van Zyl (Eds.), *The Prize and the price: Shaping sexualities in South Africa* (pp. 169–191). Cape Town, South Africa: Human Sciences research Council.

Bennett, J. (2011). Subversion and resistance: Activist initiatives. In S. Tamale (Ed.), *African sexualities* (pp. 77–100). Cape Town, South Africa: Pambazuka Press.

Blackman, L., Cromby, J., Hook, D., Papadopoulos, D., & Walkerdine, W. (2008). Editorial: Creating subjectivities. *Subjectivity, 22*, 1–27.

Boonzaier, F., & de la Rey, C. (2003). "He's a man and I'm a woman": Cultural constructions of masculinity and femininity in South African women's narratives of violence. *Violence Against Women, 9*, 1003–1029.

Butler, J. (1990). *Gender trouble*. London: Routledge.

Chigeza, S., De Wet, A., & Roos, V. (2013). African migrants' experiences of xenophobic violence in South Africa: A relational approach. *Journal of Psychology in Africa, 23*, 501–506.

Davies, B. (1990). The problem of desire. *Social problems, 37*, 801–816.

Davies, B. (1991). The concept of agency. *Social analysis, 30, Postmodern critical theorising*, 42–53.

Davies, B. (2000). *A body of writing 1990–1999*. Walnut Creek: AltaMira Press.

Davies, B., & Gannon, S. (2006). The practices of collective biography. In B. Davies & S. Gannon (Eds.), *Doing collective biography* (pp. 1–15). New York: Open University Press.

Davies, B., Dormer, S., Honan, E., McAllister, N., O'Reilly, R., Rocco, S., & Walker, A. (1997). Ruptures in the skin of silence: A collective biography. *Hecate-A women's Studies Interdisciplinary Journal, 23*, 62–79.

Eisikovits, Z., & Winstok, Z. (2002). Reconstructing intimate violence: The structure and content of recollections of violent events. *Qualitative Health Research, 12*, 685–699.

Enander, V., & Holmberg, C. (2008). Why does she leave? The leaving process(es) of battered women. *Health Care for Women International, 29*, 200–226.

Ferguson, A. (1996). Can I choose who I am? And how would that empower me? Gender, race, identities and the self. In A. Garry & M. Pearsall (Eds.), *Women, knowledge, reality: Explorations in feminist philosophy* (pp. 108–126). New York: Routledge.

Gqola, P. (2015). *Rape: A South African nightmare.* Auckland Park, South Africa: Jacana Media.

Gqola, P. (2017). *Reflecting rogue: inside the mind of a feminist.* Johannesburg: Jacana Media.

Haaken, J., & Reavey, P. (2010). Why memory still matters: Disturbing recollections. In J. Haaken & P. Reavey (Eds.), *Memory matters: Contexts for understanding sexual abuse recollections* (pp. 1–14). New York: Routledge.

Haram, L. (2004). Prostitutes or modern women? Negotiating respectability in Northern Tanzania. In S. Arnfred (Ed.), *Re-thinking sexualities in Africa* (pp. 211–229). Uppsala, Sweden: The Nordic Africa Institute.

Harris, B. (2002). Xenophobia: A new pathology for a new South Africa. In D. Hook & G. Eagle (Eds.), *Psychopathology and social prejudice* (pp. 169–184). Cape Town, South Africa: Cape Town University Press.

Hayem, J. (2013). From May 2008 to 2011: Xenophobic violence and national subjectivity in South Africa. *Journal of Southern Africa Studies, 39*(1), 77–97.

Herman, J. (1992). *Trauma and recovery: From domestic abuse to political terror.* New York: Basic Books.

Hodza, F. (2015). Beyond Heteronormativity: Doing gender and sexuality in university contexts. In S. van Schalkwyk & P. Gobodo-Madikizela (Eds.), *A reflexive inquiry into gender research* (pp. 27–45). Newcastle upon Tyne, UK: Cambridge Scholars Publishing.

Hollway, W. (1984). Gender difference and the production of subjectivity. In J. Henriques, W. Hollway, C. Venn, & V. Walkerdine (Eds.), *Changing the subject* (pp. 227–263). London: Methuen.

Hunter, M. (2002). The materiality of everyday sex: Thinking beyond 'prostitution'. *African Studies, 61*, 99–120.

Kambarami, M. (2006). *Femininity, sexuality and culture: Patriarchy and female subordination in Zimbabwe.* Africa Regional Sexuality Resource Centre, Understanding Human Sexuality Seminar Series, 1–10.

Langellier, K. M., & Peterson, E. E. (1992). Spinstorying: An analysis of women storytelling. In E. C. Fine & J. C. Speer (Eds.), *Performance, culture, and identity* (pp. 157–179). Westport: Praeger Publishers.

Langellier, K. M., & Peterson, E. E. (2004). *Storytelling in daily life*. Philadelphia: Temple University Press.
Macdonald, M. (1995). *Representing women: Myths of femininity in the popular media*. London: Edward Arnold.
Mauthner, N. S., & Doucet, A. (2003). Reflexive accounts and accounts of reflexivity in Qualitative data analysis. *Sociology, 37*, 413–431.
McFadden, P. (2003). Sexual pleasure as feminist choice. *Feminist Africa, 2*, 50–60.
Melucci, A. (1995). The process of collective identity. In H. Johnston & B. Klandermans (Eds.), *Social movements and culture* (pp. 41–63). Minneapolis: University of Minnesota Press.
Moore, E. (2013). Transmission and change in South African motherhood: Black mothers in three-generational Cape Town families. *Journal of Southern African Studies, 39*, 151–170.
Morris, A. (1998). 'Our fellow Africans make our lives hell': The lives of Congolese and Nigerians living in Johannesburg. *Ethnic and Racial Studies, 21*, 1116–1136.
Mupotsa, D. S., & Mhishi, L. (2008). This little rage of poetry/researching gender and sexuality. *Feminist Africa, 11: Researching for Life: Paradigms and Power*, 97–107.
Pereira, C. (2002). *Between knowing and imagining: What space for feminism in scholarship on Africa? Feminist Africa intellectual politics*. Cape Town, South Africa: African Gender Institute.
Reavey, P., & Brown, S. D. (2009). The mediating role of objects in recollections of adult women survivors of child sexual abuse. *Culture & Psychology, 15*(4), 463–484.
Shefer, T., Clowes, L., & Vergnani, T. (2012). Narratives of transactional sex on a university campus. *Culture, Health & Sexuality, 14*, 435–447.
Sinclair, M. R. (1998). Community, identity and gender in migrant societies of Southern Africa: Emerging epistemological challenges. *International Affairs, 74*(2), 339–353.
Squire, C. (2008). Experience-centred and culturally-orientated approaches to narrative. In M. Andrews, C. Squire, & M. Tamboukou (Eds.), *Doing narrative research* (pp. 41–63). London: Sage.
Strauss, H. (2011). Cinema of social recuperation: Xenophobic violence and migrant subjectivity in contemporary South Africa. *Subjectivity: International Journal of Critical Psychology, 4*, 103–120.
Tamale, S. (2011). Introduction. In S. Tamale (Ed.), *African Sexualities*. Cape Town, South Africa: Pambazuka Press.
Tamboukou, M. (2008). A Foucauldian approach to narratives. In M. Andrews, C. Squire, & M. Tamboukou (Eds.), *Doing narrative research* (pp. 102–120). Thousand Oaks, CA: Sage.

Taylor, S. (2010). *Narratives of Identity and Place*. London: Routledge.
The South African Press Association. (2013). Calls to end xenophobic attacks. *News, 24*. Retrieved from http://www.news24.com/SouthAfrica/News/Calls-to-end-xenophobic-attacks-20130315.
Tsanga, S. (2011). Dialoguing culture and sex: Reflections from the field. In S. Tamale (Ed.), *African sexualities* (pp. 57–72). Pambazuka Press: Cape Town, South Africa.

CHAPTER 7

Narrative Landscapes of Female Sexuality in Africa: Concluding Thoughts

Narrative Landscapes of Female Sexuality in Africa documents women's geographic and psychological journeys through various moral landscapes. The collective narratives of the support group speak to broader questions about migrant women's experience of, and resistance to, patriarchal oppression of female sexuality in Africa. To reiterate the questions posed at the beginning of this book: How can women break free from negative internalisations generated by patriarchal oppression of female sexuality and claim a positive sense of self in the world? What are the potentials for studying women's agency within contexts where social resources are scarce and poverty a harsh reality of life? What alternative understandings about the self can women create, and claim, in the face of harmful oppressive discourse, and what would such strategies look like? Through a unique collective methodology which opened space for creative and intuitive engagement, the research has generated rich insights into three specific narrative strategies which emerged as central motifs of the women's collective memory. This research provides important insights into what agency and the process of transformation may look like for women who are situated within violent patriarchal cultures that suppress and shame female sexuality.

The focus is on three central motifs identified in the women's collective narratives traced through their stories of their memories of 'back home' in Africa; travelling through border posts, or physical entry points between African countries; and their current experience living in post-apartheid

S. van Schalkwyk, *Narrative Landscapes of Female Sexuality in Africa*, https://doi.org/10.1007/978-3-319-97825-3_7

South Africa. The first is the *mubobobo* cultural script narrated by Shona women in Zimbabwe who 'look back' engaging in memories of experience in their home country. Next, the women draw on the script of the *foreigner self* in transit, the desperate and damaged self which emerged while travelling through Africa. The final linguistic strategy is women's constructions of black South African women as *faulty feminine subjects*—a narrative strategy which enabled them to voice 'unnarratable' aspects of their gendered subjectivities living in a South Africa rife with xenophobia, racism, and gender violence. These narrative strategies provide rich insights into the women's experience of patriarchal oppression of female sexuality—their sense of themselves in the world and their perceptions of ways in which their bodies are used by men (literally and imaginatively). This work also highlights women's capacity for agency using culturally accepted resources, trauma language, symbolic images, and moral discourse in ways that subvert harmful patriarchal meanings about female sexuality and women's bodies. The women found collective ways to communicate the complexity of their experience while at the same time creating positive selves through their narratives.

In this chapter, I provide an overview of the key findings from the research. I draw together the main themes and link these findings to broader concerns about social change/transformation in South Africa. I then discuss the methodological and practical insights gained from my work and discuss the potentials of the collective biography approach for achieving new knowledge which promotes an African-gender perspective. In the final section of the chapter, I provide suggestions for future research that will enrich African-based knowledge and intellectual activism contributing to what South African feminist scholar Macleod (2006, p. 348) calls 'patchworks' of global patriarchies.

The Oppression of Female Sexuality: A New Language of Trauma and Transition

Postcolonial feminist scholars in Africa have long argued that Westernised frameworks are not useful for exploring the experiences of women in Africa (see Mohanty 1991). Westernised frameworks often convey a normative lens of African women's powerlessness. The result is that African women are constructed as less civilised politically immature subjects (Okin 2000; Sokoloff and Dupont 2005). According to such a narrative, to inhabit a female body is to be reduced to powerless psychically suffering object (Bakare-Yusuf 2013). This book offers a fresh perspective with a focus on women's agency rather than women's static powerlessness. It therefore opens new ways of thinking about women's experience in a patriarchal world. Below I discuss the main findings of the research and comment on the broader implications for social change/transformation in South Africa. I analysed the collective narratives through a feminist post-structuralist and social remembering lens. As such, I was not concerned with any stable 'truth' of the narratives. Rather, I focused on the creative and strategic act of narrating and what this tells us about the women's constructions of identity.

Chapter 4 'Mubobobo: Memories of the Past, Metaphors for the Current Self' provides an in-depth exploration into the ways in which Shona women from Zimbabwe experience, and resist, patriarchal oppression of female sexuality within a South African context where social discourses pervasively and powerfully render women's bodies inferior and create an ever-present sense of vulnerability for women. Gqola (2015) has termed this patriarchal power the 'female fear factory' that works to create a constant sense of vulnerability for women through repetitive theatrics of recognisable signals and cues. Dominant trauma scripts do not offer women language with which to convey the trauma associated with such pervasive and ongoing 'everyday' assaults to the self—what Root (1992) has termed 'insidious trauma'.

Within this context, the women found ways of communicating their complex gendered experiences. A prominent theme which emerged from the collective work was that of mubobobo. The women described this as a practice whereby men obtain a magical muti that enables them to rape women from a distance. A central thread of these narratives was the act of 'looking back' and narrating their childhood experiences in Zimbabwe through the lens of the mubobobo cultural script. Particularly evident and powerful here was that mubobobo seemed to be an intergenerational narrative passed on from older women to younger women as a way of communicating a sense of female vulnerability. Such a feeling of self as vulnerable may be a core element of women's experiences. Often dominant power systems do not provide a language through which women can express the textures of their gendered lives. It seems as if mubobobo is an accepted cultural script through which these women can express these aspects of their experience.

Findings showed that the women also constructed mubobobo perpetrators as socially powerless, 'dirty' and 'disgusting'. I argue that mubobobo served as a metaphor for the women's feelings and intuitions associated with various forms of bodily and psychic disruptions of feminine boundaries. I interpret the psychological function of the mubobobo narratives as follows: their constructions of the social and material bodies of mubobobo perpetrators signify a process whereby the women narratively project 'tainted' parts of themselves—products of patriarchal oppression of female sexuality—onto these men. I interpret mubobobo as a narrative resource/metaphor through which the women communicated previously 'unspeakable' aspects of their experiences of patriarchal oppression of female sexuality.

The findings resonate with other work that has been done on women's sexual agency in Africa. Scholars argue that women are engaging with their sexuality in new ways in response to changing cultures (see Haram 2004; Spronk 2005). Research has found that women find a different language using metaphors and other masked forms to express aspects of their sexualities in oppressive contexts (see Tamale 2013; Thompson 2011; Wekker 1997). Women work with cultural scripts to communicate aspects of their sexual subjectivity in subtle, yet powerful, ways. Often these ways of communicating are 'hidden' and exist as 'women's secrets', to use Tamale's (2013) term. This book has provided a new lens with which to understand these 'different languages' of gendered experience, interpreting the women's voices through a strong theoretical framework (feminist poststructuralism and social remembering) which allows us insight into the psychological processes at play 'beneath the surface'.

These findings have important implications. Western frameworks often interpret culture as a negative force that contributes to women's oppression. However, the narratives outlined in this book suggest that we need to look deeper at how women may work with cultural scripts in ways that are subversive and transformative. Future research needs to acknowledge these complexities and explore what cultural scripts mean for women themselves. This entails moving beyond the obvious to explore powerful psychological work 'behind the scenes'. It is through such work that we can gain a better understanding of what agency looks like in different patriarchal contexts.

In Chap. 5, 'Crossing Borders in Africa: Collectively Narrating the "Foreigner" Within', I provide insights about the textures of migrant women's experiences of patriarchal oppression of female sexuality through an in-depth examination of their collective narratives of travelling through border posts in Africa. The narratives convey rich meaning about their actual and symbolic consideration of these border posts—what these spaces mean for them now. This chapter is framed around a particularly powerful narrative silence about a sexual experience with a man at a border post. The rest of the chapter 'fills in' this silence in powerful ways documenting women's narratives of sex with men at border posts in exchange for money/material goods. Silence is a powerful way of communicating. Silence, as a strategy for constructing identity and managing shame, tells us what the narrator is 'allowed' to say in any given context (Davies and Gannon 2006a). As such, silence provides powerful insights about subjectivity. These linguistic absences suggested that the narrators associated the topic of sex with men with deep shame. Silence was a way of managing their presentation of self. The complex meanings surrounding such shame became evident through the narrative strategy of the *foreigner self* which 'filled in' the gaps of what may have very well been silence about these experiences in transit.

Social trauma scripts offer limited scope of who can be considered 'victim' and under what circumstances (Lamb 1996). Women who display levels of agency (such as choosing to engage in sexual relations with men) are not afforded the status 'victim'. Such women are often blamed and shamed for their actions—especially if this involves female sexuality. Studies have shown that women who travel from town to town in search of better economic opportunities are often shamed and rendered 'bad' sexual subjects because they are challenging patriarchal rules of the nuclear family and women's domestic role. There is a direct link with women's movement/mobility and stigmatisation/shaming of the female body (Haram 2001). Research on women's vulnerability in public spaces has powerfully shown that women expect that they should monitor their behaviour in public spaces or face the threat of being considered culpable if they experience violence (see Dosekun 2007; Gqola 2015). Women who exert agency by leaving their homes and travelling to South Africa to find a new life are already in dangerous territory in the broader field of female sexuality/morality. This is the context within which the women told their stories.

The second central motif of the women's collective stories—the *foreigner self*—had two components. The first was the 'desperate' self and the second was the 'damaged' self. Rather than falling into the trap of interpreting these narrations as evidence of the women's static powerless position in transit or viewing powerlessness as the only feature of women's lives (see Mohanty 1991; Reid and Walker 2005), I looked deeper to explore the psychological significance of such accounts. Both these narrated selves ('desperate' and 'damaged') served a narrative purpose for the women: they were able to manage a sense of their own agency in transit. They conveyed that these selves had no morals and were functioning in terms of a unique pathology brought about by the 'other world' of transit. The women narrated this *foreigner self* as specific to the space of transit—they emphasise that when they arrived in South Africa their 'good' 'true' self emerged. It is important to note, then, that the women did not own this powerless 'victim' position, but rather used it strategically to construct certain kind of identities.

I argue that the *foreigner self* was a narrative strategy through which the women could talk about their complex experiences in transit while at the same time constructing positive selves. Evident was a strong 'cultural pull' towards the position of 'good' female subject and on the other hand the reality of poverty and desperation which 'push' women into engaging in sexual acts regarded as shameful/deviant. The women made sense of these experiences together negotiating identities that are available to them.

Interestingly, the women drew on hegemonic language of trauma (O'Dell 2003) to create their own language for expressing their complex experiences in transit. This 'new' language enabled them to manage blame/shame. They managed the aura of shame that is so intricately linked to female sexuality so that they were not 'weighed down' by this emotion. This was about positioning themselves as 'good' feminine subjects. The women utilised the narrative of *foreigner self* to construct a sense of ambivalence about their agency in transit (a 'desperate' and 'damaged' self that had no agency). Scholars have identified that this notion of ambivalence is central to women's identity project. Reavey and Brown (2007), for example, found that women draw on meanings around space to produce ambivalence in their accounts and manage their sense of agency in the present (I had no agency then, therefore I cannot be blamed). Producing ambivalence is an important part of managing a sense of agency in the present moment of telling (Reavey and Gough 2000; Reavey 2012).

In light of these findings, more research needs to be done on the meanings surrounding 'victim' and 'survivor' and how women may creatively work with such concepts in ways that are subversive and that challenge harmful patriarchal scripts. We need to move beyond dominant Westernised language of trauma toward more contextualised meanings surrounding these concepts. We need to understand what 'victim' and 'trauma' mean for women in different spaces. This necessarily entails exploring the deeper, more subtle meanings of narratives. It is about looking at, not through, the linguistic surface (Weedon 1987).

Often Westernised research focuses on the common oppression of all women without an acknowledgement of other pertinent dimensions of oppression that shape women's experience in third world contexts. It is crucial to examining the multiple and layered intersecting oppressions that women in Africa face in different contexts (Fish 2006; Pereira 2000). The book offers rich insights into these women's experiences living as foreigners in South Africa and the intersections of gender and sexuality, class, race and citizenship, situating the narratives within the wider context of poverty and migration in sub-Saharan Africa. As such, it contributes to the rich body of work on intersectionality (Crenshaw 1991) by expanding the definition of 'intersectionality' to include the complex experience of women within this specific location in South Africa.

Although evident throughout the book, these deep intersections of oppression are seen most powerfully in Chap. 6, 'Psycho-Social Borders and Imagining the South African Female "Other"'. Living in current post-apartheid South Africa has very particular meanings for African foreign nationals. In an era of rife xenophobia, non-South Africans are often rendered 'other' status stripped of a life of worth and a sense of belonging and humanity (Strauss 2011). Blame and shame are projected onto the foreign 'other' who is accused of contaminating South Africa and stunting the success of the post-apartheid democracy (Morris 1998). The context of harmful xenophobic discourse powerfully shapes the ways in which African migrant women experience patriarchal oppression of female sexuality. It also shapes the ways in which they resist harmful discourses surrounding female sexuality.

A powerful effect of patriarchal oppression of female sexuality is what McFadden (2003) calls the 'muting' of female sexual memory and instinct. Importantly, where there is no space and no language with which to express aspects of female sexuality, then negative aspects 'absorbed' from culture and past/ongoing experience result in a build-up of, often unrecognised, shame and guilt (Herman 1992). I call this the residues of gendered oppression. The social responsibility of 'holding' such residues of oppression has a powerful effect on women's subjectivities.

The third central motif identified in the collective narratives was that of black South African women as *faulty feminine subjects*. The narrators constructed black South African women as sexually 'loose', morally incorrect, shameful, 'bad' feminine subjects who cannot control their sexual urges. They also constructed the South African culture as sexually immoral. This was focused around South African women—women who the narrators could identify with in terms of poverty and race. However, an important difference was citizenship. An important feature was their narration of South African men wanting to marry foreigner women because they are suited to be appropriate wives (they are not sexually promiscuous like South African women). Ultimately, these rigid constructions of 'us' (non-South Africans) and 'them' (black South African women) speaks powerfully to these women's experiences in current South Africa.

I argue that the women's co-constructions of South African women as *faulty feminine subjects* served a psychological purpose for the narrators. The image of the South African women 'other' was a symbolic screen onto which they could project negative aspects of their sexuality that have been instilled by patriarchal culture. It is through this narrative strategy that they could give voice to their shame, desire, and 'faulty-ness'—aspects of the self that patriarchy so neatly embeds in the psyche. The narrators were thus able to mobilise these aspects of the self while constructing positive selves and maintaining a sense of belonging.

The narrative strategy of 'othering' South African women raises broader questions about the concept of ubuntu—an African concept connoting shared humanity and interconnectedness. While such 'othering' is a feature of many cultures, it takes on a particular texture in South Africa. There is a sense that these women may experience themselves as divided from other women. How might this affect the project of women's emancipation? What does this mean for the women's struggle in South Africa? How can women heal within a context within which they 'hold' a sense of un-belonging? These are important questions for current post-apartheid South Africa and the ongoing quest for a country striving towards greater dignity for all humans.

The above outlines the ways in which the women in this study disrupted patriarchal scripts of female sexuality by collectively inverting the binaries of dominant narratives. In doing so, they were able to express previously 'unspeakable' aspects of their experience and they managed negative emotions/remnants which have been instilled by patriarchy. The result was the collective construction of positive selves and a sense of belonging. In the next section, I discuss what these findings suggest for transformation in the South African context. I draw on the theoretical insights gained using Davies' (1991) definition of agency as a lens. I then discuss methodological insights situating the collective biography methodology as a uniquely transformative methodological approach.

Transforming Selves: Possibilities for Agency in the South African Context

Theoretical Insights

There is a significant tension present throughout the women's stories documented in this book. Their narratives suggest a strong desire to present themselves in 'appropriate' ways. They worked to position themselves as 'good' moral subjects through the 'strong pull' of patriarchy. Shame, blame and violence are the consequences of presenting oneself in ways that defy the patriarchal scripts of femininity. However, at the same time there was a subtle, yet powerful, undercurrent evident in the collective narratives. This was an energy of mobilising what has been silenced, of speaking the 'unspeakable' albeit in a disguised form. This was about narratively 'getting rid' of negative aspects of their sexual subjectivities that have been socially ingrained by patriarchal culture. It is through the three core narrative strategies that the women were able to mobilise previously concealed emotions and residues of gendered oppression associated with sexuality within a context within which there is no language to express such experience. What do these narratives suggest about the possibilities for transformation? I turn to this question next.

In her book *A Body of Writing 1990–1999*, Bronwyn Davies (2000) provides theoretical understanding about the implications of such work for identity. Collective work, says Davies, comprises of a combination of various 'truths' drawn from a multitude of social discourses. These 'truths' are often narrated through imagined and creative stories. The act of speaking about one's experience in a different way holds powerful potential for the disruption and decentring of patriarchal discourse that one has been bound to. In this way, the speaker is able to slowly 'unstitch' themselves, bit by bit, from the confines of patriarchal meanings. This, according to Davies (2000) constitutes the core of the process of transforming the feminine self.

The women utilised narrative strategies which enabled them to tell their stories in their own way through their own voices and frameworks. This notion of authorship and creative discursive work is central to

Davies' (1991) definition of agency. Within the research space the community of women shared knowledge and cultural resources (like mubobobo). The women utilised the narrative resources—mubobobo; the foreigner self; and South African women as faulty feminine subjects—to tell their complex stories while at the same time constructing positive selves. Davies (1991) states that a core process of agency is the ability to work with multiple discourses in creative ways in order to imagine new ways of being in the world. The women in the study did this in powerful ways. Through their stories they managed shame and positioned themselves as moral agents. They carved out linguistic space to tell their complex stories in a 'safe' way without implicating themselves and without entering the realm of 'bad' feminine subject. The new ways of being that Davies (1991) speaks of is evident through the women's positioning of themselves as authors of their own past. Scholars in the field of trauma and memory consistently argue that telling is an act of agency. The very act of speaking provides women with the opportunity to create something new. Expressing embodied, or silenced, experience is of critical importance. As Culbertson (1995) says, remembering itself 'creates a "me", rather than a disembodied, confused recipient of harm' (p. 184).

The other group members acknowledged their stories and the women were able to claim a sense of being heard—something which is intricately connected to a sense of belonging and worth. Such spaces of support were central in shaping the women's emergent meaning making and their strength to enter the sexual terrain, which is not so easily spoken. Bakare-Yusuf (2013) states that it is critically important for women to hear stories that promote a positive sense of self because these stories shape who we can become. The very act of speaking and re-creating one's past may be an invaluable resource for these migrant women who are situated within the South African context with a severe lack of resources and sources of support for women.

In the moments of the research spaces, the women were able to co-create positive identities in the face of harmful and restrictive discourses. They co-created 'new' selves that were not bound by patriarchal meanings (shame, blame, inferiority). Patriarchal meanings are moulded onto the female body continuously. Many women internalise such meaning—there are limited alternative subject positions available. However, through the three central motifs, or narrative strategies, the women worked to disrupt patriarchally defined subjectivities. In their documentation of collective biography processes, Davies et al. (2006) draw on Barthes' concept of decomposition, a strategy of interrupting regulatory discourses, and describe their own process of 'movement from one configuration to another in the lines of flight that make new realities' (p. 81). This refers to a slow process of 'breaking down' negative aspects of the self which have been imbedded through patriarchal (gendered) socialisation and experience. We see powerful examples of this in the women's collective narratives. Their mobilisation and narrative projection of shame, 'disgust' and symbols of the 'dirty body' through mubobobo; their managing of blame and shame about female sexuality through the co-created script of the foreigner self; and, finally, their projection of 'bad' aspects of their sexuality onto the image of black South African women. This process is about working through negative meanings about female sexuality enforced by patriarchy, forcefully bringing these feelings to light, and negotiating positive selves in the face of it all. The 'cracks', or fissures are evident through moments of disruption through which the women position themselves as sexual subjects and carve positive identities in the face of oppression. Davies (1991) reminds us that agency is always negotiated within systems of power and one must negotiate a sense of self by drawing on the discourses available. The voices documented here are voices of resistance in that the narratives carve alternative meanings and positive identities—which are often closed off in patriarchal culture.

These linguistic constructions of positive selves are not mere theoretical observations. Such narrations of the 'self' shape the ways in which women *experience* the world. Gavey (2005) argues that by resisting certain discourses and by constructing the self in different ways, one shapes the ways in which they experience themselves in relation to others. Breaking gendered silence, even via metaphor and narrative projection, is a crucial step in the complex process of moving towards a position of agency. As women mobilise previously 'hidden' embodied emotions they can begin to engage with these aspects of the self and work towards an integrated self and a position of fuller humanity.

Methodological Insights

Much research on women's agency in South Africa has focused on the individual dimension. However, South African feminist scholar Macleod (2008) reminds us that individualistic stances and modes of healing may not be relevant for the lives of women from Africa. This study is unique in that it explores the collective dimension of agency. The grassroots support group, formed by women from various parts of Africa, stand as a natural site of women's meaning making. It is at such political sites that we can understand more about women's agency. This allows us to mobilise in ways that suit the needs of specific communities and individuals with different life histories.

The collective biography method with its feminist poststructuralist underpinnings, offered an invaluable means to explore both the individual and collective dimensions of the women's experience. Individual experience/memories were interwoven with the memories of other narrators, resulting in a dynamic collective meaning-making process. The stories presented in this book provide insight into the process of 'selving' whereby individual experience is moulded into a collective presentation of the world. The collective biography workshops and focus group discussions where dynamic spaces through which the women connected their experience/memories with the memories of others and were stimulated by points in others' narratives. As women witness real/imaginative stories in the dramas and through visual texts and dialogue something is ignited—masculine structures become visible. As is common of collective biography work, they threaded one experience onto the last and narrated a 'shared understanding' or common perspective about the world (see Davies and Gannon 2006a). They reinvented old discourses and discovered new storylines about their lives (see Davies 1990). The result was rich and textured narrative landscapes of experience. Such depth of expression would not have been possible using a traditional approach to psychological research such as individual interviews.

Davies et al. (2006) have highlighted that collective biography spaces are useful sites through which women can collectively take up, and resist, certain discourses, constituting themselves in concert with one another. In this study the women's narratives no longer created individual identities but rather common collective selves. It is through such collective self-constructions that they managed to transform their past in safe and 'intelligible' ways. Such processes may not be imaginable for isolated individuals. The findings suggest that collective biography work is particularly suited for exploring self in relation—an important concept in many African cultures (Mkhize 2004).

The collective biography methodology was crucial in helping me address the aims of my study and the broader African-centred feminist agenda. These emergent methods challenged everything that I knew about doing research and writing academically. I was forced to move beyond my comfort zone in embracing alternative, creative and intuitive methods. I was prompted to begin to think seriously about my own subjectivity as it emerged throughout the research process. Such meaningful reflexivity is of critical importance for collective processes where the energy of emergence takes on a life of its own. This book outlines my own personal journey and my grappling with how to represent the experience of the 'other'. Through this collective process I had to follow the women into unanticipated places and interrogate my own reactions and emotional processes along the way. The process of revisiting the data was central for gaining deeper insight into the women's voices. Distance gave me the perspective to take on the topic of female sexuality seriously—another example of the ways in which this research challenged patriarchal moulds. The process of documenting how my presence may have influenced the data and the ways in which the data affected me is invaluable in producing a meaningful text about the possibilities of transformation in South Africa—across the multiple vectors of oppression. My insertion of my own positionality adds another reciprocal layer of analysis.

The collective biography methodology served a twofold purpose, moving beyond the limitations of conventional qualitative research. Firstly, the collective spaces (workshops and focus group interviews) provided rich data allowing me to theorise about women's strategies through their shared narratives and the psychological processes at play. The composition of the collective spaces and the long-term nature of the study was critical for producing such data. Secondly, the research facilitated practical spaces of change through which the women could negotiate agency in their lives. These spaces were actual sites of change through which the women voiced aspects of their subjectivities that had, for the most part, never been spoken.

Practical Insights

During my work, I witnessed the practical benefits that such long-term and engaged research had for the women who took part. In their extensive documentation of collective biography methods, Davies and Gannon (2006a, b) suggest that such work has certain therapeutic effects for those who take part. I witnessed throughout my work that these spaces where beneficial for the members of the support group. The spaces were filled with an energy of mobilisation of making new sense about the world and expressing previously 'uninterpretable' and 'unspeakable' aspects of experience. This process was transformative because it allowed space for the women to engage with important aspects of their traumatic past. Such relational spaces offer 'unfolding' and openness to change through 'many small moments of individuation' (Camden-Pratt 2009). These small escapes from the world, or what Camden-Pratt (2009) calls 'lines of flight' are movements towards the not yet known of becoming, of different ways of thinking, feeling and experiencing the self as subject. For the women this was about the possibilities of redefining a self not determined by patriarchal scripts.

It is through the collective biography spaces that the women co-created their own language to express the 'unspeakable' and unnameable violence of patriarchal oppression of female sexuality. This kind of storytelling may function to 'repair' gaps in their life narratives. Such construction of 'new' life narratives signifies changes in women's self-understandings. Importantly, this process was also political in the broadest sense of the word. It allowed the women to speak their truth among others, rupturing patriarchal silencing of women's experience. It also allowed the women to insert their knowledge into wider academic discourse in the form of this book.

Suggestions for Future Research

The narrative expression of 'unspeakable' aspects of the experience of patriarchal oppression of female sexuality may be one of the first steps towards transforming the self. However, this is necessarily a long and complex journey. It requires sustained and committed work. It requires careful consideration of the dynamics and impact of collaboration with the people who we study. Researchers and activists interested in promoting actual change need to develop connections 'on the ground' with sensitivity and care about what is needed for such collective work to be done. This book has shown that it is counterproductive to assume meanings of 'trauma', 'victim' and 'abuse' at face value. We need to be prepared to engage in deeper, more difficult work.

Further research needs to be done on the potentials for disrupting dominant patriarchal scripts. Such work should explore the 'cracks' in women's neatly constructed narratives—the underlying and subtle meanings through which women express the 'unspeakable'. This work needs to pay fine-tuned attention to the ways in which women utilise various cultural resources at their disposal. Thompson (2011) suggests that we need to explore ways in which discourses of resistance can be sustained beyond the narrated moment or isolated conversations. This is of critical importance within a South African context where there is a severe lack of resources for women. More work needs to be done in communities in

South Africa to contribute understanding of the different ways in which patriarchal oppression manifests in different contexts. This will provide insights about the best ways to work towards collective engagement for transformation. This is a mammoth task, but one that is powerful and significant for the people who take part. Our role as researchers and activists is to privilege women's narratives and their unique ways of knowing. Our role is to acknowledge the quest for creating alternative discourses which stand in opposition to the discourses prescribed by patriarchy.

An important thread throughout this book was the migrant women's position of 'other' in South Africa and the ways in which this position significantly shaped their experiences of patriarchal oppression of female sexuality and the kinds of strategies that they used to resist this oppression. This was most powerfully evident through their co-constructed images of black South African women as 'bad', loose, morally incorrect sexual subjects. Such processes of othering, although a common feature of many cultures, takes on a very particular texture in the post-apartheid South African context. Further research should explore this 'us'/ 'them' divide within the context of violence against women and gender healing.

Conclusion

The story I have chosen to tell through this book, one of many possible stories, is one about female sexual subjectivity. This book documents women's powerful experiences of patriarchal oppression of female sexuality. It explores the psychological texture associated with such experience and, of course, the strategies which these women use to resist oppression. I explore the complex terrain through which women must travel in the process of re-claiming the self and a sense of humanness. It is a moral terrain where one is always in danger of slipping into positions which are judged and shamed. It is a search for language through which one can express what has been silenced by the patriarchal system.

This collective work is of critical importance for a feminist project that strives towards generating new knowledge for Africa. In the face of Western feminist discourses which produce normativity based on the experiences of women in North America and Europe, an 'exclusion through inclusion' (Macleod 2008, p. 348) is powerfully at play which ignores the unique experience of African women in specific contexts. This book brings the complexity of women's lives in Africa into the foreground, challenging hegemonic perspectives about women's existence. The women's narratives paint an eloquent picture through which you, the reader can begin to engage in new ways of understanding agency and women's strength. This book puts forward a new chapter for gender research that is serious about the goals for developing a comprehensive African-gender perspective. Most importantly, such work has powerful potentials for social change. It is about creating a world where women can claim a life of fuller, uninhibited humanity.

References

Bakare-Yusuf, B. (2013). Thinking with pleasure: Gender, sexuality and agency. In S. Jolly, A. Cornwall, & K. Hawkins (Eds.), *Women, sexuality and the political power of pleasure* (pp. 28–41). London: Zed Books.

Camden-Pratt, C. (2009). Relationality and the art of becoming. In B. Davies & S. Gannon (Eds.), *Pedagogical encounters* (pp. 52–68). New York: Peter Lang Publishers.

Crenshaw, K. (1991). Mapping the Margins: Intersectionality, identity politics, and violence against women of color. *Stanford Law Review, 43*(*6*), 1241–1299.

Culbertson, R. (1995). Embodied memory, transcendence, and telling: Recounting trauma, re-establishing the self. *New Literary History, 26*(*1*), 169–195.

Davies, B. (1990). The problem of desire. *Social Problems, 37*(4), 801–816.

Davies, B. (1991). The concept of agency. *Social analysis, 30, Postmodern critical theorising,* 42–53.

Davies, B. (2000). *A body of writing 1990–1999.* Walnut Creek: AltaMira Press.

Davies, B., & Gannon, S. (2006a). The practices of collective biography. In B. Davies & S. Gannon (Eds.), *Doing collective biography* (pp. 1–15). New York: Open University Press.

Davies, B., & Gannon, S. (2006b). A conversation about the struggles of collaborative writing. In B. Davies & S. Gannon (Eds.), *Doing collective biography* (pp. 114–144). New York: Open University Press.

Davies, B., Browne, J., Gannon, S., Honan, E., & Somerville, M. (2006). 'Truly wild things': Interuptions to the disciplinary regimes of neo-liberalism in (female) academic work. In B. Davies & S. Gannon (Eds.), *Doing collective biography* (pp. 79–87). New York: Open University Press.

Dosekun, S. (2007). Don't be sexy, don't be there. Discourses of space, danger, and women's sexuality in South Africa. In *Sexuality in Africa magazine* (pp. 7–9). Lagos, Nigeria: Africa Regional Sexuality Resource Centre.

Fish, J. (2006). *Domestic democracy: At home in South Africa.* New York: Taylor & Francis Group.

Gavey, N. (2005). *Just sex? The cultural scaffolding of rape.* New York: Routledge.

Gqola, P. (2015). *Rape: A South African nightmare.* Johannesburg, South Africa: Jacana Media.

Haram, L. (2001). 'In sexual life women are hunters': AIDS and women who drain men's bodies. The case of the Meru of northern Tanzania. *Society in Transition, 31*(1), 47–55.

Haram, L. (2004). 'Prostitutes' or modern women? Negotiating respectability in Northern Tanzania. In S. Arnfred (Ed.), *Re-thinking sexualities in Africa* (pp. 211–229). Uppsala, Sweden: The Nordic Africa Institute.

Herman, J. (1992). *Trauma and Recovery: From domestic abuse to political terror*. New York: Basic Books.

Lamb, S. (1996). *The trouble with blame: Victims, perpetrators and responsibility*. Massachusetts, MA: President and Fellows of Harvard College.

Macleod, C. (2006). Radical plural feminisms and emancipatory practice in post-apartheid South Africa. *Theory & Psychology, 16*, 367–389.

Macleod, C. (2008). 'Who? What?: An unindicted view of towards a new psychology of women from post-apartheid South Africa. *Feminism & Psychology, 18*, 347–357.

McFadden, P. (2003). Sexual pleasure as a feminist choice. *Feminist Africa 2: Changing Cultures*, 50–60.

Mkhize, N. (2004). Psychology: An African perspective. In D. Hook (Ed.), *Critical psychology* (pp. 24–52). Lansdowne, Cape Town: University of Cape Town Press.

Mohanty, C. T. (1991). Under western eyes: Feminist scholarship and colonial discourses. In C. T. Mohanty, A. Russo, & L. Torres (Eds.), *Third world women and the politics of feminism* (pp. 51–80). Indianapolis: Indiana University Press.

Morris, A. (1998). "Our fellow Africans make our lives hell": The lives of Congolese and Nigerians living in Johannesburg. *Ethnic and Racial Studies, 21*(6), 1116–1136.

O'Dell, L. (2003). The "harm" story in childhood sexual abuse: contested understandings, disputed knowledges. In P. Reavey & S. Warner (Eds.), *New feminist stories of child sexual abuse: Sexual scripts and dangerous dialogues*. London: Routledge.

Okin, S. M. (2000). Feminism, women's human rights, and cultural differences. In U. Narayan & S. Harding (Eds.), *Decentering the centre: Philosophy for a multicultural, postcolonial, and feminist world* (pp. 26–46). Bloomington: Indiana University Press.

Pereira, C. (2000). Feminist knowledge. *African Transitions, 490*, 77–85.

Reavey, P. (2012). The spaces of memory. In J. Haaken & P. Reavey (Eds.), *Memory matters: Contexts for understanding sexual abuse recollections* (pp. 131–141). New York: Routledge.

Reavey, P., & Brown, D. (2007). Rethinking agency in memory: Space and embodiment in memories of child sexual abuse. *Journal of Social Work Practice, 21*(1), 5–21.

Reavey, P., & Gough, B. (2000). Dis/locating blame: Survivors' constructions of self and sexual abuse. *Sexualities, 3*(*3*), 325–346.

Reid, G., & Walker, L. (2005). African sexualities: Editorial introduction. *Culture, Health and Sexuality Journal, 7*(3), 185–194.
Root, M. P. P. (1992). Reconstructing the impact of trauma on personality. In L. S. Browne & M. Ballou (Eds.), *Personality and psychopathology* (pp. 229–265). New York: Guilford Press.
Sokoloff, N. J., & Dupont, I. (2005). Domestic violence at the intersections of race, class, and gender: Challenges and contributions to understanding violence against marginalised women in diverse communities. *Violence Against Women, 11*, 38–64.
Spronk. (2005). Female sexuality in Nairobi: Flawed or favoured? *Culture, Health & Sexuality, 7*(3), 267–277.
Strauss, H. (2011). Cinema of social recuperation: Xenophobic violence and migrant subjectivity in contemporary South Africa. *Subjectivity: International Journal of Critical Psychology, 4*(2), 103–120.
Tamale, S. (2013). Eroticism, sensuality and 'Women's secrets' among the Baganda. In S. Jolly, A. Cornwall, & K. Hawkins (Eds.), *Women, sexuality and the political power of pleasure* (pp. 265–285). London: Zed Books.
Thompson, K. D. (2011). Zanbari women's discursive and sexual agency: violating gendered speech prohibitions through talk about supernatural sex. *Discourse & Society, 22*, 3–20.
Weedon, C. (1987). *Feminist practice and poststructuralist theory*. New York: Basil Blackwell Ltd.
Wekker, G. (1997). One finger does not drink Okra soup: Afro-Surinamese women and critical agency. In M. J. Alexander & C. T. Mohanty (Eds.), *Feminist genealogies, colonial legacies, democratic futures* (pp. 330–352). London: Routledge.

Index[1]

[1] Note: Page numbers followed by 'n' refer to notes.

S. van Schalkwyk, *Narrative Landscapes of Female Sexuality in Africa*, https://doi.org/10.1007/978-3-319-97825-3